the grid
BLUE COMPENDIUM

© Scripture Union 2018

First published 2018

ISBN 978 1 78506 742 6

Scripture Union, Trinity House, Opal Court, Opal Drive, Fox Milne, Milton Keynes, MK15 0DF, UK

Email: info@scriptureunion.org.uk

Website: www.scriptureunion.org.uk

Unless other stated, Scripture quotations are taken from *The Youth Bible*, New Century Version (Anglicised Edition) © 1993 by Thomas Nelson www.thomasnelson.com

British Library Cataloguing-in-Publication Data. A catalogue record of this book is available from the British Library.

Printed and bound in India by Thomson Press

Cover design: Kevin Wade

Internal design: Martin Lore and Sandra Taylor

Photography: Chris Brown

Please note that this content has been updated from previously published material.

🍂 Scripture Union is an international Christian charity working with churches in more than 130 countries.

Thank you for purchasing this book. Any profits from this book support SU in England and Wales to bring the good news of Jesus Christ to children, young people and families and to enable them to meet God through the Bible and prayer.

Find out more about our work and how you can get involved at:

www.scriptureunion.org.uk (England and Wales)

www.suscotland.org.uk (Scotland)

www.suni.co.uk (Northern Ireland)

www.scriptureunion.org (USA)

www.su.org.au (Australia)

CONTENTS

INTRODUCTION

Welcome to the *Grid Blue Compendium*! We're so pleased you've chosen this book to help you in your work with 11- to 14-year-olds.

It is our prayer that the materials contained within these pages will equip and inspire you whilst engaging and empowering the young people you work with.

The material in this book has been compiled from the wealth of *Grid* content that Scripture Union has produced over the years – and with 52 sessions included, there should be plenty to choose from over the course of a year.

The *Grid Blue Compendium* is part of the *Light* range of materials, which are designed to enable children, young people and adults to develop a personal relationship with Jesus, to understand the Bible and the Christian faith, and to live for God as light in a dark world.

- *Light* is about... discovering who God is, what he is like, what he does and how we can get involved in that. The Bible is 'light to live by', so it is the centre of every session for every age group in the *Light* range of resources. Everyone will be able to follow the story of salvation that runs through the Bible, with its focus clearly on Jesus.

- *Light* recognises that children and young people can know and respond to God and does not expect too little or too much from them.

- *Light* celebrates every step taken towards and with God, letting the Bible shape our thinking about human nature and relationships with children and young people, and the way in which we minister with and to them.

- *Light* values exploration and discovery, fun, feelings and creativity and uses these approaches to inspire children, young people and adults to meet God through the Bible.

We hope you enjoy this resource, and we pray that God will bless you and those you work with as you use it.

The Scripture Union Mission Innovation Team

HOW TO USE THIS BOOK...

This book provides 52 sessions of activities, and extra photocopiable resources, designed for your *Grid* group of young people aged 11 to 14. Choose sessions from this *Blue Compendium* in any order to suit you and your group.

You will also find that some sessions have further additional online resources which you will be able to download for free in a zip folder from the Scripture Union website, via the resource centre.

Leading up to Christmas time, you may wish to choose from the Christmas-themed sessions (numbers 45 to 49). Around Easter time, you will find there are Easter-themed sessions (numbers 50 to 52), to choose from. These 'seasonal' sessions are grouped together at the back of this book.

If you would like to work through a number of sessions on a similar theme with your *Grid* group, look out for the **More on this theme** boxes as you consider your session choice. Here you will find a list of other sessions on a related theme to the session you are looking at.

On page 7, you will find a helpful guide that explains **How to plan your session**. This section will help you to choose activities from within the sessions, including a selection of *Grid* activities to suit you and your group, enabling you to achieve the Learning aim for the session. Here you will also find a **Basic kit** list of essential items to keep handy for all your *Grid* group sessions.

Each session in this *Grid BlueCompendium* is based on a Bible passage. You will find an **Index of Bible passages** on page 320 listed in the order they appear in the Bible.

The most important thing about this book is to enjoy using it to help you and your *Grid* group engage with the Bible and meet with Jesus, through a mixture of play, creativity, music, quiet reflection, noisy exuberance, and friendship!

> Download the zip folder to find many answers to frequently asked questions about the *Light Compendiums*, and help to choose your session order.

HOW TO PLAN YOUR SESSION

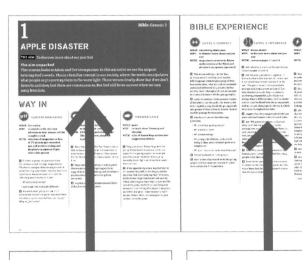
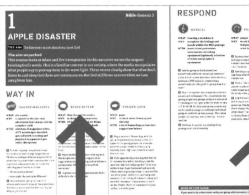

1

Read the Bible passage.

Think about your own group and situation: the individuals, the leaders, your equipment and facilities. Pray about your group and the individuals within it, and for God to guide you and help you as you prepare and lead the session.

Begin by reading the Bible passage. Then read **The aim** and **The aim unpacked** to find out how the Bible passage can relate to young people.

Sart choosing which activities you will do. The activities you use will be dependent on what kind of group you have. Different activities are tailored towards different groups, large or small, Sunday or mid-week, churched or non-churched.

2

Choose one of the Bible experience activities first. This is the heart of your session, as you help the young people explore the Bible and respond to God's message.

Level 1 Connect is the first level of Bible interaction, ideal for a group that is at the lower end of Bible literacy and interest.

Level 2 Interface is suitable for a group who are committed and want to learn more.

Level 3 Switch on is a more demanding, in-depth Bible study for committed young people who want to grow in their faith.

3

Choose one or more Way in activities to introduce the session's theme.

Scene setters introduce a link between the world of the young people and the aim of the session.

Themed games or activities act as an introduction to the session aim for larger or more 'open' groups and are suitable to use with non-churched young people.

grid One of these activities will usually use a magazine resource page.

4

Choose one or more Respond activities to help the young people relate what they have learned in the session to their lives, to help them live for God.

Musical uses music and sound as a response to God's Word.

Practical is an ongoing activity that the young people can take part in, reflecting the aim in their everyday lives.

Creative uses creative and imaginative skills to respond to God's Word.

Most sessions include **photocopiable resource pages** for you to copy and use with your group. All the resources are also available in a zip folder to download from **www.scriptureunion.org.uk**.

Basic kit

To run your session, you will need these items:
Bibles (*The Youth Bible*, New Century Version, works best with *theGRID*), pencils, felt-tip pens, pencil sharpener, paper, glue sticks, sticky tape, scissors, sticky tack, sticky notes and erasers

1

APPLE DISASTER

THE AIM: To discover more about our just God

The aim unpacked

This session looks at Adam and Eve's temptation. In this narrative we see the serpent twisting God's words. This is a familiar concept in our society, where the media manipulates what people say to portray them in the worst light. These verses clearly show that if we don't listen to and obey God there are consequences. But God still loves us even when we turn away from him.

WAY IN

 theGRID MAGAZINE

WHAT: discussion
WHY: to introduce the idea that advertisers don't always tell the complete truth
WITH: selection of magazines or lots of TV adverts (pre-recorded; you will need recording and playback equipment if you select this option)

1 Divide the group into pairs or threes. Invite them to look through magazines or TV adverts and spot different ways in which advertisers try to sell their products. Ask them to pick out a few adverts and consider the following questions for each one:

• What does it promise?

• How might the reality be different?

2 Ask each small group to show their adverts and answer the questions about them. Are there any answers that keep coming up? Why might that be?

 SCENE SETTER

WHAT: film clip and discussion
WHY: to think about temptation
WITH: DVD of *The Lord of the Rings: The Two Towers*, playback equipment

1 Show the clip from *The Two Towers* where Gollum has an argument with himself about whether he should kill Frodo and Sam (scene 22, 1 hr 10 mins into the cinema version of the film).

2 Point out that Gollum was wrestling with this temptation. Ask the young people to suggest what was motivating each of Gollum's personalities. Which one do they think overcame?

3 Say that we all face temptation and find it difficult to obey God at times.

 THEMED GAME

WHAT: game
WHY: to think about listening and obeying
WITH: a list of Simon Says actions (see suggestions below)

1 Play a version of Simon Says with the group. Use some more unusual actions to appeal to the young people – for example, pose like a supermodel; act like a dying housefly; have a light-sabre battle; squawk like a vulture.

2 If the opportunity arises, say that later in the session they will be thinking about the question: 'Did God really say that?' Of course, unlike Simon Says, God doesn't ask us to do ridiculous things or try to trip us up so we'll be 'out of the game'. God loves us and only asks us not to do something if he knows it may hurt us or if it's not what he wants us to do. But if we don't listen, there are consequences, just as there are in the game.

BIBLE EXPERIENCE

 LEVEL 1: CONNECT

WHAT: advertising discussion
WHY: to discover more about our just God
WITH: magazines and adverts, Bibles, audio version of the Bible and playback equipment (optional)

1 This works well if you do the *Way in 'theGRID magazine'* activity first from the previous page. Remind your group of their discussion about what each advert promised and what it delivered. (If you didn't do this activity, read it through and have an example to show and discuss with the young people.)

2 Listen to Genesis 3 from an audio version of the Bible or use the audio *The Word on the Street* by Rob Lacey. Divide the young people into groups of three or four and invite them to read the passage for themselves.

3 Ask them to answer the following questions:

- What did that apple promise?
- What did it deliver?
- What went wrong?
- What might be different in the world today if Adam and Eve hadn't given in to temptation?
- Why is it important to do what God says?

4 Gather feedback from the groups.

5 Have a time of quiet and invite the young people to think about times when they have been tempted in their own lives.

 LEVEL 2: INTERFACE

WHAT: drama sketch
WHY: to discover more about our just God
WITH: resource pages 11 and 12

1 Ask volunteers to act out the sketch from resource pages 11 and 12.

2 Ask the young people to suggest what blame is. After Adam ate the fruit, he blamed his disobedience on both God and Eve. He said, 'You gave this woman to me and she gave me fruit from the tree, so I ate it!' Eve then blames the snake. Say that blame is attributing responsibility for a fault or a wrong. What is different about God's attitude? Ask for some feedback from the young people. God is just and always speaks the truth, which we can see throughout the Bible.

3 Suggest that the young people divide into pairs and read Genesis 3 aloud to each other.

4 Ask: 'Why should we listen to God and obey him?' Ask the pairs to find, in the passage, one reason why we should listen to and obey God. (Because he is God, he is the One, not us; because he loves justice; because otherwise someone somewhere gets hurt; because it's a good way of showing how much we love and respect him.)

5 Ask: 'What are the consequences of not listening to or obeying God?' Ask the young people to list their answers.

6 Remind the young people that we are all to blame for the wrong things we do, but that when Jesus died, he took the blame for us so that we can be forgiven.

 LEVEL 3: SWITCH ON

WHAT: Bible study and discussion
WHY: to discover more about our just God
WITH: Bibles, copies of resource page 13, audio version of the Bible and playback equipment (optional)

1 Read Genesis 3 to the group, or listen to an audio recording, and explain that Adam and Eve were ejected from the garden for not doing what God said.

2 Divide the young people into small groups (if possible, have four groups or multiples of four). Give each group a Bible study from resource page 13. Ask them to investigate the questions and prepare a presentation of their findings to the rest of the group.

3 Allow them about 15 minutes to prepare this. Group one should present information about Lucifer or Satan. He is a fallen angel, liar, accuser, tempter, murderer, and can appear in the guise of a righteous angel. Group two should present information about temptation and conclude that we are enticed to sin by our own desires. Group three should talk about how we can resist temptation with God's Word. Group four should talk about why we should do what God says.

4 Invite the groups to present their findings in turn.

5 In conclusion, explain that not doing what God says is rejecting him, and because God is just, there are consequences to this. If we reject him (and everyone does), the only way back is through Jesus. Encourage the group to think about the following in silence:

- Do I need to say sorry for rejecting God?

RESPOND

 MUSICAL

WHAT: creating a soundtrack
WHY: to explore the feelings and moods within the Bible passage
WITH: musical and percussion instruments, recording equipment (optional), selection of music and playback equipment

1 Ask the group to think about how soundtracks add to the mood and passion of a film. Ask if anyone has seen a documentary (perhaps a DVD extra) on constructing soundtracks. Can they tell the group how it is done?

2 Say that together you are going to create a soundtrack to Genesis 3. You could divide the young people into groups and give a section of the passage to each group (for example, verses 1–7, 8–19, 20, 21–24), work as one large group on the whole passage or challenge each small group to tackle the whole passage. The young people can use any instruments you have or use CDs.

3 Perform the pieces to a reading of the passage as an act of worship.

 PRACTICAL

WHAT: prayer
WHY: to ask God not to lead us into temptation and to help us do what he says

1 Explain that being tempted not to do what God says is something that we all face. Being tempted does not mean we are a bad person, or not a Christian.

2 Ask the group to look up Matthew 6:9–13. Ask them what the prayer tells us to do about temptation.

3 Have a time of quiet and invite the young people to talk to God about this, asking him not to 'cause us to be tempted' and to help them when they are tempted.

4 Say that temptations are all around us so it's important to pray this prayer as often as we can. Challenge the young people to think of ways that they could remind each other about this. They should do this in pairs or threes. Some ideas are by text message, postcards, email, online.

 CREATIVE

WHAT: produce a commercial
WHY: to show why we should do what God says
WITH: painting materials

1 Explain to the group that TV commercials are designed to make us want their products.

2 Divide the group into pairs or threes and ask each group to write, produce and act out a TV commercial to say why we need to do what God says.

3 Give the group time to write the scripts, create props and practise their commercials. Then bring the groups together to watch each other's commercials. Have a time of quiet after each one for the young people to respond to God if they would like to.

4 If you have access to a video camera or a mobile phone with video function, you could record the commercials and play them back.

MORE ON THIS THEME:

If you want to do a short series with your group, other sessions that work well with this one are:

2	*Fugitive from justice?*	*Genesis 4:1–16; 6:1–8*
3	*Saving grace*	*Genesis 6:9 – 8:19*
4	*Gracious promise*	*Genesis 8:20 – 9:17*

BIBLE EXPERIENCE

 LEVEL 1: CONNECT

WHAT: courtroom drama
WHY: to discover more about our just God
WITH: area set up to look like a courtroom, resource pages 18 and 19

1 Tell the young people that they are the members of the jury in a court case. Invite three people to act out the drama on resource page 18. (You could ask them to rehearse this before the session.)

2 Ask the 'jury' to reach a decision as to whether they believe Cain is guilty and invite them to present this to the court to conclude the case. Ask the jury what made them come to their conclusion and what evidence they used.

3 Say that the story behind the drama comes from the Bible. Challenge the young people to find out whether they were right in their verdict by reading Genesis 4:1–12.

4 Ask them to think about that murder again and then to discuss, in pairs, what the cause of the murder was.

5 Encourage them to feed back their answers to the whole group. If it hasn't been said, explain that the problem was Cain's anger. Instead of saying sorry to God, Cain allowed his feelings of anger and frustration to build up inside him and this motivated him to kill his brother. Here, almost at the beginning of the Bible, we learn just how dangerous anger and other emotions can be if we don't keep them under control.

 LEVEL 2: INTERFACE

WHAT: murder mystery
WHY: to discover more about our just God
WITH: dummy or large doll to represent the deceased Abel

1 Ask a leader to play the part of Cain, and to read up on their character from the Bible account before the session. Tell them that if they are asked a question that is outside their knowledge of the character they should try to avoid it rather than make something up.

2 Ask another leader to take the group out of the meeting room briefly while you arrange the dummy victim on the floor.

3 Bring the group back in and explain that the young people must investigate the murder and find out who the dead man is by interviewing the only witness: Cain.

4 'Cain' should introduce himself and briefly tell the young people about his family. He should deny the murder but be as truthful about his actions as possible.

5 After the questioning, give the young people time to work out the solution to the mystery. Ask:

- Who is the witness?
- Who has been murdered?
- Who committed the murder?
- Why?

6 Explain that the incident is from the Bible. Ask a volunteer to read Genesis 4:1–16. Ask:

- Were your conclusions correct?
- Did the suspect say anything that doesn't fit with what you have read?

Say that Cain simply needed to recognise that he had done wrong, apologise to God and make another offering – this time with the right attitude. Instead he allowed his feelings to fester until he killed his own brother. The consequence of his action was that he was cut off from his family and friends.

7 Ask the young people to think about times when they have let their anger motivate them and have endured the consequences. Suggest that they spend a few moments saying sorry to God for these times.

 LEVEL 3: SWITCH ON

WHAT: Bible study
WHY: to discover more about our just God
WITH: dramatised Bible, resource page 20

1 Divide the young people into small groups of between two and four and give each group a copy of resource page 20 and a dramatised version of Genesis 4.

2 Encourage them and help them to do the Bible study, then bring the group together to discuss their findings.

3 In the first part, listen to their suggestions about why God rejected Cain's offering. What did they discover from verse 4? What does Hebrews 11:4 say about Abel's offering? What would Cain have had to do to put things right after God was unhappy about the offering? How could Cain have put things right after Genesis 4:7–12? He had murdered Abel and there was no way he could bring him back.

4 Talk with the young people about what this means for us, and how individual acts of disobedience can escalate into serious consequences. What do they suggest we do? We need to give God our best; we should control our emotions and not let them rule our behaviour.

5 As a group, have a look at Genesis 6:1–8. This is a confusing passage, but the main thing to draw out is that human beings gradually became so disobedient to God that he was sorry he had made them (v 6). This led to drastic consequences, as we shall find out in the next session.

RESPOND

 MUSICAL

WHAT: singing with music
WHY: to ask God for help to deal with our anger and other strong emotions
WITH: chill-out music, CD or MP3 of 'Speak Life' by Toby Mac or 'Live the Life' by Michael W Smith from the album *Live the Life*, playback equipment

1 Divide the young people into pairs and ask them to think about two or three strong feelings or emotions they have experienced in the past day or week. Can they think of songs to go with each of the emotions, as a kind of soundtrack of their feelings?

2 Suggest that they talk through their feelings with their partner and reflect on how their feelings affected their behaviour. Then encourage them to ask God for help with their emotions and to pray for each other. Play some chill-out music to encourage a prayerful atmosphere.

3 Play 'Speak Life' by Toby Mac or 'Live the Life' by Michael W Smith. Invite the young people to listen to the words and respond to God silently.

 PRACTICAL

WHAT: apology
WHY: to acknowledge how our emotions have got the better of us in the past and to seek to make amends
WITH: gentle instrumental music, cross (made from wood or paper)

1 Put the cross in the centre of the group and give each young person a sheet of paper and a pen.

2 Remind the group how Cain let his anger get the better of him. If he had said sorry at the beginning, the situation might not have got worse. For us, our anger can turn into grudges that we hold against others, and these can get in the way of our relationships with one another and with God. Ask the young people to think of anyone that they need to forgive. Suggest they spend a couple of minutes thinking over their relationships and asking God to highlight anything that needs to be put right.

3 Invite them to write or draw something to represent these things on their sheets of paper. When they have finished, encourage them to place their sheets of paper at the foot of the cross and say, 'I'm sorry. Help me to forgive as you do.'

4 Pray, 'Lord God, thank you that you forgive us for the times when we let our emotions control our behaviour and when we hold grudges against each other. Give us the courage to say sorry for those grudges. Amen.' Encourage the young people to do what they can to put the relationships right at the first suitable opportunity.

 CREATIVE

WHAT: paper chain
WHY: to recognise the danger of letting our emotions build up
WITH: newspaper, marker pens

1 Remind the young people of how Cain allowed his anger to build up until it got the better of him and caused him to murder his brother. Say that we too can have strong emotions. As one large group, have a brief look at the contents of a newspaper. Ask the young people to identify any situations where someone has let strong emotions control their behaviour.

2 Divide the young people into pairs and give out sheets of newspaper. Ask them to think about what emotions can control behaviour and what behaviour it might invoke. For example, envy can lead to stealing. Ask them to tear off strips of newspaper (roughly 20 cm by 4 cm) and write the name of a strong emotion, a bad behaviour or a specific situation on it.

3 Invite the young people to glue or tape the strips together to make a chain.

4 Ask for a volunteer and wrap the chain around them. Explain that our emotions can control us and prevent us from being the person God wants us to be – if we let them. Read out Psalm 116:16–19, which speaks about God setting us free from chains. As a demonstration of their resolve not to let their emotions control them, ask the group to break the chain and free the volunteer.

MORE ON THIS THEME:

If you want to do a short series with your group, other sessions that work well with this one are:

1	Apple disaster	Genesis 3
3	Saving grace	Genesis 6:9 – 8:19
4	Gracious promise	Genesis 8:20 – 9:17

THAT MAKES ME SOOOOO... MAD!

How annoyed would you be in these situations? Draw an arrow from each one of these situations to the place on the thermometer that shows how angry that situation would make you (the higher the mark, the angrier you'd get!).

5 Your parents have finally given in and let you have a TV in your bedroom – they've always said that you were too young yet they give your brother one at the same time, and he's four years younger than you!

1 Your dad's been on at you about your hair, saying you need to have it cut. You come home and discover that he's had his hair done like Justin Bieber.

6 A boy in the year below you pushes in front of you in the lunch queue.

2 You've just bought a cone from the ice cream van when your neighbour's dog bounds up to say 'hello' and knocks it out of your hand!

7 Your best friend is upset about embarrassing herself in front of her crush. You tell her an embarrassing story from your past to cheer her up but ask her to keep it secret. The next day, it seems like everyone at school knows and is having a good laugh about it!

3 You slogged your guts out all week to do a piece of homework and were given an average mark. Your teacher makes a point of congratulating your friend for his 'excellent work' – you know he only spent an hour on it and copied from a book!

8 You're watching a really exciting film when your older brother comes in and tells you how it ends!

9 Write here any other situations that regularly annoy you. How angry do you get?!

4 A school computer has been damaged. You were there at the time but know nothing about it. As no one will own up, the head is going to keep you all in until someone confesses!

Members of the jury

Scene: a courtroom

Cast: Cain, the Judge, the Prosecuting Barrister

Judge: Cain, you have been charged with the murder of your brother, Abel. How do you plead?

Cain: Not guilty, Your Honour.

Judge: Barrister, he's all yours.

Barrister: Thank you, Your Honour. Cain, can you tell me what you were doing on the day of your brother's murder?

Cain: Well, I was gathering in my harvest, which was a real good one – lots of it, and quality stuff. So I thought, I know what I'll do. I'll bung God a few spuds and other veg, just to say cheers for sorting the weather for my crops to grow.

Barrister: I see. And how did God respond?

Cain: Well, he wasn't too impressed.

Barrister: Really?

Cain: Yeah, it seems Abel (he was a shepherd, see) had the same idea. He offered a lamb to God. And God was really pleased with it. I was really gutted and I told God so.

Barrister: I see. So God is not a vegetarian then?

Cain: Oh, no! It's nothing to do with his eating habits. Apparently Abel had given him the very best, firstborn lamb of his flock, and God thought my stuff didn't make the grade.

Barrister: So how did you respond to that?

Cain: Well, I was furious, wasn't I?! After all, the veg might have been a little bit past its sell-by date but it was fine. Peel it, cut out the grotty bits, throw it in a pot with Abel's lamb and you would have a lovely stew. But, oh no! God gets all high and mighty and tells me that I ought not to be angry. I should just take a leaf out of Abel's book and do better in future.

Barrister: So what did you do then?

Cain: Well, I needed some chill-out time so I went for a walk in one of my fields.

Barrister: On your own?

Cain: Well, no. I asked Abel to come with me.

Barrister: And that's when you murdered him?

Cain: No! We split up. He went one way and I went another, and then I heard God asking me where Abel was. I told him I didn't know. I can't keep an eye on him all the time, can I, just because he's my little brother?

Barrister: So you didn't kill him?

Cain: No.

Barrister: Even though there was no one else around who could have done it?

Cain: No.

Barrister: Looks a bit suspicious, doesn't it? You're angry, you invite your brother for a walk, you split up, so you say, and next minute he's dead.

Cain: Look, I didn't kill him!

Barrister: No more questions, Your Honour.

Judge: Thank you. (*Turning to the jury*) Well, members of the jury, you have heard the evidence and now you must decide: is Cain guilty, or not guilty, of Abel's murder? Did he have a motive, and could he have done it?

Read Genesis 4:1–12 to find out what happened next!

1 Read Genesis 4:1–5 in your group, either reading a verse each or from a dramatised version.

Why was God pleased with Abel's offering but not with Cain's?

Write down any reasons you can think of.

HINT: Is there a difference in the way the Bible describes what Abel gave and what Cain gave (vs 3,4)?

Check out Hebrews 11:4. What do you think now?

What would Cain have had to do to put things right? Did he do it?

2 Read Genesis 4:6–12, either reading a verse each or from the dramatised version.

How could Cain have put things right now?

How does this relate to us?

Is there anything we can learn from Cain?

SAVING GRACE

THE AIM: To discover more about God's grace

The aim unpacked

Our society urges us to be tolerant of different attitudes, beliefs and behaviour, and advocates that everything is permissible as long as it doesn't hurt anyone else. The Bible has a slightly different take on things. In this session we explore the story of Noah and learn that if we do wrong there are consequences. God does not tolerate any kind of sin, even if it may appear that no one is getting hurt.

WAY IN

 **theGRID MAGAZINE**

WHAT: questionnaire
WHY: to introduce the idea that we all do wrong things
WITH: magazine page 24

1 Give out copies of the questionnaire 'Have you ever…?' from page 24. Challenge the young people to get a signature in each box from a person who can answer 'yes' to that question. If everyone has told the truth, no one should be able to sign the last box.

2 Ask what the young people found out from the questions. Did they find someone to sign every box? Say that no one can sign the last box because we all do things wrong, all the time! No one is or ever has been perfect – except Jesus.

 **SCENE SETTER**

WHAT: consequences
WHY: to introduce the idea that actions have consequences

1 Play a few rounds of consequences. This game works best with about ten young people but will work with four or five.

2 Give each young person a sheet of paper and a pen. Ask them to write a boy's name at the top of the paper and fold it over to hide the name. Suggest that they use famous people, to make the game more amusing. Ask everyone to pass their paper to the player on their left. Next, ask them to write a girl's name, fold the paper over and pass it on again. Then they should write where they met, what he said to her, what she said to him, folding and passing the paper each time. Lastly, write down what the consequence was.

3 Put all the folded papers in the middle. Invite each young to person pick one and read it out.

4 Ask the young people to share about times when something they have done has had a direct consequence, good or bad. Alternatively, think of some examples from films or TV shows. Pick up on this idea of 'consequences' through this session.

 **THEMED GAME**

WHAT: to explore the idea that when rules are broken, everyone suffers
WITH: equipment for a game (for example football, volleyball, rounders, Monopoly, Pictionary)

1 Before you play the game, tell a couple of players, privately, to cheat as much as they like. Play a game, either an active running game or a board game.

2 After the game, explain that you gave some people permission to cheat, and point out that when one or two people break the rules, everybody suffers. Ask for some suggestions as to how it affected the group. (Perhaps there was no game left to play; it wasn't fun any more; people lost their temper; it made it very frustrating…) Would any young people say it doesn't matter?

3 Say that when we break the rules, somebody gets hurt and relationships can be damaged. Although today's example ruined the game, it probably won't have any long-lasting effect, but what about real life? Today we'll check out the extremes of what happened once when almost everyone on earth 'broke the rules'.

BIBLE EXPERIENCE

 LEVEL 1: CONNECT

WHAT: demonstration
WHY: to discover more about God's grace
WITH: plastic globe or map of the world covered with plastic laminate, water-soluble marker pen, water, cloth, *The Lord of the Rings: The Two Towers* DVD, playback equipment

1 Invite the young people to suggest actions that are really bad. For each one, invite someone to draw a blot on the globe or map with the water-soluble marker pen.

2 Ask the group to suggest how to clean it again. They should suggest using water! As you prepare, explain that this is a popular story to tell children because it has lots of animals in it and a nice boat. But actually, it's a horrific story, showing us how much it matters to God when we do wrong stuff.

3 Tell the story of the flood, using the following key points (from Genesis 6:9 – 8:19):

- People were doing terrible things that made God wish he'd never created them. He decided to clean up the earth.

- Because he is a God of grace, he found one good person, Noah, and saved the human race through him. God told Noah to build a boat and bring on board his family and two of every kind of animal to give the whole of creation a second chance.

- God sent a great flood that wiped out every living thing, except what was on the boat. (Wipe the blots off the map.)

- Things were so bad on earth that only a really drastic solution would do.

4 Show the scene from near the end of *The Two Towers* where the Ents march on Saruman's tower and 'cleanse' the filth by flooding the area (scene 49 on the cinema version of the DVD, 2 hrs 33 mins in).

5 Invite the young people to read Genesis 6:9 – 8:19 together in pairs. Ask them to think about how the episode from *The Two Towers* is similar to the Noah story. How is it different? Bring the group back together to share feedback.

 LEVEL 2: INTERFACE

WHAT: drama and discussion
WHY: to discover more about God's grace
WITH: magazine page 25, flip chart or whiteboard, Bibles, audio Bible and playback equipment (optional)

1 Before the session, invite some young people to practise the drama 'Chain of pain' on page 25, and to perform it in the session as an introduction.

2 Divide the young people into pairs and ask them if there is any crime that doesn't hurt anyone. What do they come up with? Ask them to feed back their ideas and write them on the flip chart or whiteboard.

3 Say that someone is hurt as a consequence of every crime. Read Genesis 6:5,6 to the group and ask them who else gets hurt when human beings do wrong. The Bible shows us that our wrong actions hurt God. Ask the group what they think God did next, and then summarise the story of Noah as in *Bible experience* 'Level 1 Connect', or listen to Genesis 6:9 – 8:19 from an audio Bible.

4 Ask the young people to think about the following questions in pairs or threes, before coming back together for discussion and feedback:

- Did the punishment fit the crime?

- Do you think God overreacted? Why? Why not?

- What does this story tell us about how seriously God takes sin?

- Why doesn't God flood our world on a regular basis?

- What has God done to take the punishment for us?

 LEVEL 3: SWITCH ON

WHAT: visual Bible study
WHY: to discover more about God's grace
WITH: eight squares of card, toy boat, Moses basket, bowl of water, cross, globe, magazine page 26, Bibles, audio Bible, playback equipment (optional)

1 Put the globe, boat, basket and cross each on a square of card in a square shape. Everyone should be able to see them and, ideally, reach them. These represent creation, the flood, Moses and Jesus' crucifixion. Place the water in the middle.

2 Ask the group to guess which stories might be represented by these symbols. Briefly remind them of the stories of creation (especially the waters of chaos before creation) and Moses (especially the basket which carried Moses to safety). Touch the toy boat. Say that you're going to hear a familiar story and the young people should look at the symbols for the other three stories and think about whether the flood story has any links with them.

3 Read aloud (or listen to from an audio Bible) Genesis 6:19 – 8:19. Then ask if the young people thought of any links between the stories.

4 Look at page 26 and use the table for some more ideas. Challenge them to fill in the blank line with another story where people mess up and God deals with it.

5 Put out three more squares of card and ask the young people to draw or suggest symbols that could represent other stories that might be linked to the water in the centre.

6 Put out the last square of card and ask, 'Is there any way your life could be said to be part of this pattern? Are there any new links you would want to make between the stories now?'

7 Conclude by saying that the Bible gives many accounts of how God feels when people mess up and about his ways of dealing with the messes. Because of his grace, he is ready to rescue us from our sin and forgive us.

RESPOND

 MUSICAL

WHAT: sound effects composition
WHY: to try to express feelings through music
WITH: musical instruments and anything else that makes sound

1 Challenge the group to try to describe the stages of the flood story using only sounds. Can they get across the feelings of:

- people hurting each other
- God's pain
- the isolated goodness of one man – Noah
- the power of the flood
- seeing the rainbow?

2 This could be a random selection of sounds, or perhaps the group would like to present it as a sort of symphony. If appropriate, you could ask the young people to take this one step further by adding a one-line prayer after each section.

 PRACTICAL

WHAT: practical service
WHY: to show in a practical way that members of the group want to be part of the solution, not part of the problem
WITH: appropriate cleaning equipment

1 Ask the young people if they would rather be part of the problem of sin in the world, or part of the solution to it. (Actually, we are all part of both!)

2 Challenge them to clean something as a demonstration of being part of the solution. What can they do that involves water and cleaning? For example, they could wash the cars of church members (with permission!) or clean the kitchen or bathroom at home.

3 When they carry out their cleaning task, ask them to remember that they are doing it to symbolise how we can be a part of God's solution to sin in the world. Perhaps you could all report back next session.

 CREATIVE

WHAT: creative confession
WHY: to take sin seriously in our own lives
WITH: water, soap, paper towels, coal or paint, ambient music and playback equipment, images of crime, poverty, pollution and suffering (from newspapers or magazines), cross

1 Play some music to set a quiet atmosphere.

2 Invite the group to look at the pictures and think about what responsibility they have for what is wrong in the world or in their own lives. Invite them to be honest before God who knows everything and who is longing for us to be honest with him so that he can forgive us.

3 As a sign of our guilt or responsibility, invite the young people to hold a piece of coal or to paint their hands while they look at the pictures and pray quietly. You might like to have a large sheet of white paper that group members could put their dirty handprints on.

4 As a sign that they want to be forgiven, ask them to wash their hands and sit quietly in front of the cross. You could end with a quiet song like 'Spirit of the Living God, Fall Afresh on Me'.

MORE ON THIS THEME:

If you want to do a short series with your group, other sessions that work well with this one are:

HAVE YOU EVER...?

Bible bit
Genesis 6:9 – 8:19

Zero tolerance. How many times have you heard that phrase used? God has zero tolerance to sin – the bad stuff we do. God hates it! There is always a consequence to our sin; it always leads to someone – mostly ourselves – getting hurt. But the great thing is that God offers a way back. Jesus took the penalty for that sin so we can be forgiven! How great is that?!

Ask some of your friends to sign their names in the boxes where they can answer 'yes' to the question.

1 STOLEN A BISCUIT

2 TOLD A FIB SO YOU WOULDN'T GET INTO TROUBLE

3 FELT JEALOUS OF SOMEONE AT SCHOOL

4 SHOWN OFF ABOUT PASSING AN EXAM

5 FELT SO ANGRY WITH SOMEONE YOU'VE FELT LIKE HURTING THEM

6 HURT SOMEONE ON PURPOSE

7 CHEATED IN A MATHS TEST

8 SPENT A WHOLE DAY WITHOUT DOING ANYTHING WRONG

CAN ANYONE HONESTLY SAY 'YES' TO THAT FINAL QUESTION...?

ALF BOB CAZ DEZ

CHAIN OF PAIN

Perform this sketch with some friends in a very stylised, over-the top, in-yer-face, tongue-in-cheek sort of way.

Characters: Alf, Bob, Caz, Dez
Scene: the characters are standing in a line

Alf: Ha! I shall nick Bob's wallet when he's not looking! *(Does so.)*

Bob: Here! Someone's nicked my wallet! I'll nick Caz's wallet. *(Nicks Caz's wallet.)*

Caz: Oy! Someone's nicked my wallet! I'll nick Dez's wallet! *(Nicks Dez's wallet.)*

Dez: Hey! Someone's nicked my wallet! I'll nick Alf's wallet! *(Nicks Alf's wallet.)*

Alf: Pah! Someone's nicked my wallet! I'll have to get my own back. *(Thumps Bob.)*

Bob: Here! Someone thumped me! I'll have to get my own back. *(Thumps Caz.)*

Caz: Oy! Someone thumped me! I'll have to get my own back. *(Thumps Dez.)*

Dez: Hey! Someone thumped me! I'll have to get my own back. *(Thumps Alf.)*

Alf: Pah! I'll sort this! *(Stabs Bob.)*

Bob: *(Staggering.)* Here! I'll sort this! *(Stabs Caz and dies.)*

Caz: *(Staggering.)* Oy! I'll sort this! *(Stabs Dez and dies.)*

Dez: *(Staggering.)* Hey! I'll sort this! *(Stabs Alf and dies.)*

Alf: *(Staggering.)* Ummm. Sorted? *(Dies.)*

Photocopiable resource © Scripture Union 2018

25

GOD'S BIG PLAN

Check out the Bible passages below and see if you can fill in the table by working out the problems, God's view and how he rescued the people.

	THE MESS PEOPLE ARE IN	HOW GOD FEELS	HOW PEOPLE'S MESS AFFECTS THE WORLD AROUND THEM	HOW GOD SHOWS HIS POWER	GOD'S RESCUE PLAN
CREATION GENESIS 1:1 – 2:3; 2:4–25					
THE FLOOD GENESIS 6:9 – 8:22					
MOSES EXODUS 3,11,12					
THE CROSS ROMANS 3:21–26					

Can you think of another story that follows the same pattern? Perhaps your own? Where do you fit in God's rescue plan?

YOUR STORY					

4

GRACIOUS PROMISE

THE AIM: To discover more about God's grace

The aim unpacked

Today's Bible passage revolves around Noah's sacrificial offering and God's promise to humanity. It takes into account that we are fallen beings with a propensity to sin. However, God is a God of grace, forgiveness and second chances. He tells Noah to get on with things, to populate the earth, and to live life to the max. The promise that God makes is completed in the work of Jesus.

WAY IN

 **theGRID MAGAZINE**

WHAT: promise vote
WHY: to introduce the concept of keeping promises
WITH: magazine page 30, flip chart or whiteboard, marker pen

1 Invite the group to look at the list of promises on page 30. The young people have to give each promise a rank out of 10 as to how important it is to keep that promise, putting them in order from 1, the most important, to 10, the least important.

2 Feed back the results and record them on a flip chart or whiteboard to find out which promises the young people think are the most important.

3 Discuss with the group whether they would find it easy or hard to keep those promises. Why?

 **SCENE SETTER**

WHAT: group discussion
WHY: to understand what a promise is
WITH: two lengths of wallpaper with 'Keeping promises' and 'Breaking promises' written on them respectively, marker pens, meditative background music

1 Divide the young people into pairs and ask them to talk about what a promise is, and whether they think promises are important or not.

2 Invite the pairs to feed back to the whole group what they have discussed.

3 Ask the young people to gather around the 'Keeping promises' sheet of paper and think about the reasons why we make promises, the kinds of promises we make, why it's important to keep them, and any wider issues. They should write these on the paper. Then they should move over to the 'Breaking promises' sheet and write down their suggestions as to why we sometimes break promises, the consequences to ourselves and others of doing so, and any wider issues.

4 Read out some of the comments on the two sheets. Discuss together, sensitively, the importance of promises, the young people's understanding of why we make them and the consequences of breaking them. Emphasise that a promise is a bond of trust and love that should never be broken.

 **THEMED GAME**

WHAT: balloon race
WHY: to show that it isn't easy to go through life carrying our sin around with us
WITH: inflated balloons, markers such as traffic cones

1 Divide the young people into teams of four or five. Set one marker in front of each team and another at least 10 metres away.

2 Give each team a balloon and explain that this represents sin – all the bad stuff we do. Each team member must put the balloon between their knees, run to the marker and back, and then pass the balloon to the next runner without touching it with their hands.

3 Ask the young people to suggest what hindered them in the race. Say that just as the balloon stopped the young people from running fast, our sin stops us from living our lives the way God wants us to.

BIBLE EXPERIENCE

 LEVEL 1: CONNECT

WHAT: improvisation
WHY: to discover more about God's grace
WITH: flip chart or whiteboard, marker pen

1 Divide the young people into pairs and challenge them to prepare a short improvised drama around the following scenario: A head teacher is interviewing a new pupil for entry into their school. The pupil has been excluded from their last school for … (each pair should make up a reason). The pupil should show how bad they are, with loads of attitude. The head teacher should be shocked at the pupil's behaviour and show that they don't want the pupil in their school. (They could perform these improvisations to the whole group if you have time.)

2 Read Genesis 8:20 – 9:17 to the group and invite the young people to listen out for the promises that God makes. You could use the following questions to help:

- What promises did you hear?
- What does God think of people?
- What does God say about the future?

3 Ask for feedback and collate the answers on the flip chart or whiteboard. Explain to the group that God, because he is a God of grace, has promised us a great life and future even though people will continue to do wrong. Now we can live life to the full and have the best life possible because of what Jesus has done for us. We can have a great relationship with God and a great future, despite the things we have done wrong.

4 In their pairs, invite the young people to improvise the school situation again. This time, whatever the pupil has done, however bad they have been, the head teacher is willing to give them a new start. What kind of future does the head teacher now talk about for the pupil?

 LEVEL 2: INTERFACE

WHAT: discussion
WHY: to discover more about God's grace
WITH: magazine page 31, resource page 32 (optional), flip chart or whiteboard, marker pen (optional)

1 Divide the young people into pairs or threes and ask them to look at the sets of partnerships and relationships on page 31. Ask them to think and then talk about the different stresses and strains that each of these relationships might be under.

2 Next, ask them to talk about how they think the partnerships and relationships handle these strains. How are they coping? Have the relationships continued or have they stopped? How can broken relationships be mended?

3 Invite them to read Genesis 8:20 – 9:17, verse by verse, in their pairs.

4 Ask them to answer the following questions (copy these onto a flip chart or whiteboard or use resource page 32):

- What was the problem with the relationship between God and humanity? (You may need to refer the group to the beginning of the flood story.)
- Did flooding the world solve the problem? (Genesis 8:21)
- What did God promise that he wouldn't do again?

5 Ask the young people to think, on their own, about the stresses and strains that their relationship with God may be under. Is there anything they could do to make the relationship better? What promises about the future has God made to those who love and trust Jesus? Don't pressurise the young people into answering aloud, but do make it clear that you and other leaders are available to listen to anything they want to share. Say that God, because of his grace, was prepared to give humanity a fresh start even though they had messed up so badly.

 LEVEL 3: SWITCH ON

WHAT: Bible study
WHY: to discover more about God's grace
WITH: Bibles or copies of the passage, copies of resource page 33

1 Divide the young people into small groups of three or four and hand out copies of resource page 33. Invite them to read Genesis 6–8 and then Genesis 8:20 – 9:17 around the group, reading a verse each. Then they should go through the questions on resource page 34, discussing the answers in their small groups.

2 Ask the groups to feed back their answers. Discuss as a whole group any issues they have raised. From Genesis 6–8:

- Why do you think God caused the flood? (Genesis 6:11)
- Why do you think God allowed Noah and his family to survive the flood? (Genesis 7:1)

From Genesis 8:20 – 9:17:

- What did Noah do when he left the ark?
- What did God actually promise?

3 Ask the young people to think about the story of Noah, what happened, and the promise God made. Then discuss these questions as a whole group:

- What does God promise us through Jesus, even though we continue to do wrong? (A future, life, forgiveness, hope.)
- What do you think God asks of us in return? Say that God, because of his grace, was prepared to give humanity a fresh start even though they had messed up so badly.

RESPOND

 MUSICAL

WHAT: meditative prayer
WHY: to respond to God's offer of a full relationship with him, despite our sin
WITH: instrumental music suitable for meditation, playback equipment

1 Ask the young people to get into pairs or threes. Make sure no one is left out. Invite them to share together about how and when they pray. What do they do to help them focus on God?

2 Say that we are going to think about the promises God gave to Noah and work out how we should respond to them. Invite the young people to get into a position where they can focus on God. This could be sitting quietly, walking around or lying down. Say that there are pens and paper available to write down any thoughts, words or pictures the young people may receive.

3 Play the music and read God's promises from Genesis 8:20 – 9:17 to the young people. Suggest that they keep whatever they have written or drawn and use it to stimulate prayer.

 PRACTICAL

WHAT: making a covenant
WHY: to enjoy a life that, despite our sin, can be a full relationship with God

1 Explain to the young people that in order to keep a promise, we often need to remind ourselves what that promise entails.

2 Invite them to write down the things in their lives that they want to commit to God as a covenant to him. If the young people would say that they are Christians, they should write down what they have already promised or committed to God. Suggest that they commit everything, and then name a few specific areas or issues that they find really hard to give over to God. If they are not Christians, or aren't sure, they should write down what they want to say to God about what he has promised through Jesus.

3 Challenge the Christian group members to read their covenant to God daily over the coming week, and suggest that they can pray about other things at the same time. Challenge those who aren't yet Christians to talk to God about what they have written.

4 Next time you meet, ask the group how it felt to tell God regularly what they have committed to him. Remind them that, even though we forget what we have committed to him and often break our commitment, the promises from God of everlasting life, unconditional love and forgiveness are never broken.

 CREATIVE

WHAT: rainbow of commitment
WHY: to enjoy a life that, despite our sin, can be a full relationship with God
WITH: large sheet of paper, paint, credit-card-sized pieces of card

1 Invite the young people to paint a rainbow on the large sheet of paper.

2 Ask them to think about what commitments they might make to God. If they would say they are Christians, perhaps there are areas of their lives, situations or issues that they find hard to give God control of, or perhaps there is something about their relationship with God that they find difficult, such as reading the Bible and praying regularly. Give them a small piece of card on which to write any commitment they'd like to make. Suggest that they decorate their cards. If they would say they're not Christians, they can make similar cards but without the same level of personal commitment behind them – that's OK.

3 When the rainbow is dry, invite the young people to stick their cards onto the rainbow. (Be sensitive to those young people who may have written something personal and might not want to display it.)

4 Explain that regular prayer helps keep our relationship with God going. The commitments and thoughts that the young people have written down are not just for today but are ongoing.

MORE ON THIS THEME:

If you want to do a short series with your group, other sessions that work well with this one are:

1	Apple disaster	Genesis 3
2	Fugitive from justice?	Genesis 4:1–16; 6:1–8
3	Saving grace	Genesis 6:9 – 8:19

I PROMISE

How important is it to keep each one of these promises? Rank each promise in order from 1, the most important, to 10, the least important.

Bible bit
Genesis 8:20 – 9:17

After Noah gave thanks to God for keeping him and his family safe in the ark, God told Noah to get on with things, to populate the earth and, to use a popular idiom, to live life to the max. God is a God of grace, forgiveness and second chances. He also wants us to live the life he's given us to the full!

I PROMISE...

1 TO CLEAN MY TEETH EVERY MORNING AND NIGHT.

2 TO WASH THE DISHES FOR A WEEK.

3 NOT TO TELL ANYONE ABOUT MY FRIEND'S SECRET CRUSH.

4 TO GET HOME BY 9PM.

5 TO RESPECT MY PARENTS OR GUARDIANS.

6 NOT TO CHEAT ON MY BOYFRIEND/GIRLFRIEND.

7 TO TELL THE TRUTH.

8 NOT TO GO AND SEE THE NEW BLOCKBUSTER MOVIE WITHOUT MY BEST MATE.

9 TO WALK THE DOG EVERY MORNING.

10 TO PRAY AND READ THE BIBLE MORE.

Promises

Check out these other promises that God has made to us.

Philippians 4:19
God has promised to give us everything we need.

2 Corinthians 12:9
God promises that he will give us strength.

Isaiah 54:10
God promises to always love us.

1 John 5:14
God promises to hear our prayers.

1 Corinthians 15:3,4
God has promised us new life with him through the death and resurrection of Jesus.

Mark 16:16; Acts 2:38
God has promised that if we believe in Jesus we will be saved.

John 10:27,28
God has promised us eternal life.

Hebrews 13:5
God promises to never leave us.

IN PARTNERSHIP?

What pressures, stresses and strains do you think these partnerships each have to face?

How do they, or don't they, cope with them?

What stresses and strains affect your relationship with God?

How do you and God cope with them and restore your relationship?

THE DUKE AND DUCHESS OF CAMBRIDGE (WILLIAM AND KATE)
ANNA AND ELSA
SHERLOCK AND WATSON
HARRY POTTER, RON WEASLEY AND HERMIONE GRANGER
VENUS AND SERENA WILLIAMS
BEYONCÉ AND JAY Z
WOODY AND BUZZ
GOD AND YOU?

Genesis 6:1–8 reminds us about the problem with the relationship between God and humanity. The flood story tells us something about one way God tried to deal with it.

DID FLOODING THE WORLD SOLVE THE PROBLEM? (GENESIS 8:21)
WHAT DID GOD PROMISE THAT HE WOULDN'T DO AGAIN?
HOW ELSE HAS GOD TRIED TO RESTORE THE RELATIONSHIP BETWEEN HIM AND HUMANITY?

Bible study on Genesis 8:20 – 9:17

With a partner, read Genesis 8:20 – 9:17 and think about these questions.

• What was the problem with the relationship between God and people?
  (Look at the beginning of the flood story.)

• Did flooding the world solve the problem?
  (Check out Genesis 8:21.)

• What did God promise that he wouldn't do again?

• Think about your relationship with God. What strain might that be under?

• Is there anything you could do to make it better?

Recap

Read Genesis 6–8.
- Why do you think God caused the flood? (Genesis 6:11)

- Why do you think God allowed Noah and his family to survive the flood? (Genesis 7:1)

Read Genesis 8:20 – 9:17.
- What did Noah do when he left the ark?

- What did God actually promise?

Personal application

Read the info box about covenants. Think about the story of Noah, what happened, and the promise of God, and discuss these questions with your group:

- What does God promise us through Jesus?

- What do you think God asks of us in return?

INFORMATION: Covenant

Another term for a promise that God makes is a 'covenant'. A 'covenant' is a special promise between the 'holy' God and 'sinful' people. There are several covenants between God and the people in the Bible – for example, Abraham (Genesis 15,17) and David (2 Samuel 7). Another example of covenant is seen in the old covenant with Moses (Exodus 19, 20 and 24) and the new covenant through the work of Jesus (Jeremiah 31:31–34; 2 Corinthians 3:6–17). Biblical covenants were confirmed in rituals which involved the slaying of an animal; the spilling of the blood was of significance. This is also seen in the sacrificial spilling of Jesus' blood as the sign of the new covenant.

5

JACOB'S LADDER

THE AIM: To be encouraged that God is always with us

The aim unpacked

Jacob's life was far from straightforward, but God was always with him, working in him and through him and continuing to keep his promises. In this session, we'll follow Jacob running away from his brother, Esau. We'll see a scared and lonely Jacob being reassured by God in a dream, God reaffirming the promises he had made to Jacob's grandad, Abraham, and assuring Jacob that he'd always be with him.

WAY IN

 theGRID MAGAZINE

WHAT: discussion
WHY: to consider who you would want with you in difficult situations
WITH: magazine page 37

1 Make sure everyone has a copy of the 'Help, I need somebody…' activity on page 37. Give them a few minutes, on their own, to decide who they would most like with them in each of the situations.

2 Encourage the young people to chat, in twos or threes, about why they chose the people they did.

3 Explain that we are beginning a series where we'll discover that God was always with Jacob – through the good times and the bad. We'll also learn that God promises to always be with us. You may like to ask the young people how they feel about God's promise to always be with us.

 SCENE SETTER

WHAT: memory game
WHY: to remind us that Jacob was on a journey and God would provide for him

1 Ask the young people to sit in a circle. Explain that you are about to begin a series about Jacob. Tell them that Jacob was on a journey and had to trust God to provide for him.

2 Give the young people a few moments to think, individually, about some of the things they would want God to provide for them if they were preparing to go on a long journey.

3 Ask one person to begin the game by saying, 'On my journey I would need…' and then to say something they would want to have on their journey (for example, a water bottle).

4 The person sitting on their left then has to repeat what's just been said and then add their own item. For example, 'On my journey I would need a water bottle and a pair of trainers.'

5 Why not play two rounds of this game? The first round could be for a present-day journey; then for the second round you could encourage the young people to think about what Jacob would have needed.

 **THEMED GAME**

WHAT: partner tag
WHY: to introduce the idea of not being alone
WITH: large, safe space

1 Before you play this game, make sure you have a space that is safe and big enough for the young people to run around in.

2 Ask the young people to stand around the room and appoint one person as the 'tagger'. Explain that as soon as the tagger touches someone, that person must stand still. The game ends once everyone has been caught by the tagger.

3 Play the game again. Appoint one person as the tagger and divide the rest of the young people into pairs – a leader will need to step in if there is an odd number. Explain that this time, when you're tagged, you still have to stand still, but when your partner touches you, you're back in the game. Again, the game finishes when the tagger has managed to stop everyone from moving, but this time it should last a little longer.

4 Introduce the session by explaining that we'll discover that God was always with Jacob – through the good times and the bad.

BIBLE EXPERIENCE

 LEVEL 1: CONNECT

WHAT: drama
WHY: to be encouraged that God is always with us
WITH: Bibles

1 Recap with the group what happened previously between Jacob and Esau. Explain that Jacob is on the run, scared that if Esau catches up with him, he'll be a dead man. Divide the young people into groups of three or four and ask them to read together Genesis 28:10–22.

2 Reread verses 13 and 15 and ask the groups to chat about how they think Jacob would have felt about these promises.

3 Explain to the young people that the most frequent promise we read in the Bible is not God saying he will forgive us or will give us eternal life (although he does promise us those things). The most common promise God makes in the Bible is, 'I will always be with you.'

4 Ask a volunteer to read Matthew 28:20 and ask the young people how they feel about Jesus' promise to always be with us.

5 In their groups, encourage the young people to prepare two short drama sketches. The first should be a re-enactment of Jacob's encounter with God, and the second should be a modern-day example of God being with someone when they're in a difficult situation.

6 When the groups have finished preparing their dramas, invite them to perform their sketches in front of everyone.

 LEVEL 2: INTERFACE

WHAT: discussion
WHY: to be encouraged that God is always with us
WITH: Bibles, chilled music, magazine page 38

1 Recap with the group what happened previously between Jacob and Esau. Explain that Jacob is on the run, scared that if Esau catches up with him, he'll be a dead man. Then ask a couple of volunteers to read aloud Genesis 28:10–22.

2 Remind the young people that Jacob was on a journey, and in this passage we read that God promises to be with him every step of the way. God promises many different things in the Bible, but the most frequent promise we read is his promise to always be with his people. That includes us! Ask, 'How does that make you feel?'

3 Encourage the group to discuss in what ways life is similar to a journey. You may want to suggest that they compare life to a long car journey or a walk up to the top of a mountain.

4 Then put on some chilled music and invite everyone to find their own space in the room. Ask everyone to look at page 38 and to complete the 'My journey' activity.

5 Gather the group together and, either all together or in small groups, encourage the young people to talk about their 'journey' and times when they have really felt that God was with them. Don't pressurise anyone to share if they would prefer not to, and make sure there are leaders on hand to chat and pray with young people for whom this activity might stir up painful memories.

 LEVEL 3: SWITCH ON

WHAT: Bible search
WHY: to be encouraged that God is always with us
WITH: Bibles, concordances or internet access, whiteboard or flip chart, marker pens

1 Ask the young people what they can remember of the story of Abraham, Isaac, Jacob and Esau so far. If necessary, fill in any significant gaps.

2 Divide the young people into small groups and ask them to read Genesis 28:10–22. Encourage them to discuss how they think this event would have made Jacob feel – especially given his situation at the time (read Genesis 27:41–43 if they need a reminder).

3 Give each group a Bible concordance or access to the internet (whichever is easier) and give them up to ten minutes to look for other passages in the Bible where God promises to be with people (for example, Joshua 1:5,9 and Matthew 28:20).

4 Gather the group together and compare notes. Explain that the Bible contains many promises that God makes to his people, but the most frequent promise he makes is, 'I will always be with you.'

5 Ask the young people to chat about how it makes them feel that God has promised to always be with his people – and that includes us!

6 Encourage the young people to choose one of the verses they came across during their Bible search and memorise it.

RESPOND

 MUSICAL

WHAT: monuments
WHY: to praise God for his faithfulness
WITH: 'How Great Is Our God' by Chris Tomlin, playback equipment, stones

1 Explain to the group that in the Old Testament, when someone had a significant encounter with God, they often created an altar or monument to God. It was a reminder and acknowledgement of what God had said or done. In this session, we've read about Jacob doing this.

2 Give everyone a stone and invite them to reflect on a time when they really knew that God was with them. Listen to the song 'How Great is Our God' by Chris Tomlin. Encourage the young people, as and when they feel ready, to place their stones in the middle of the room, together building a 'monument' that reminds them that God has been with them during some difficult times.

3 Ask someone to pray, thanking God that he's always with you and praying for those who don't feel that God is close at the moment.

 PRACTICAL

WHAT: standing with people
WHY: to discover that we're meant to be representing Jesus
WITH: flip chart or whiteboard, marker pens

1 Talk to the group about how, in this session, we've thought about God's promise to always be with his people. Once, God was physically with us here on earth, in the person of Jesus. Then, when Jesus returned to heaven, the Holy Spirit was sent to be with us. But God also wants to be with people and reveals himself through the church. In the Bible, the church is called 'the body of Christ' (1 Corinthians 12:27). Jesus has asked us to be his representatives, to help people, to care for people and to do whatever we can to reveal God's love.

2 Ask the young people for suggestions of people who might feel that God is not with them, people who are having a difficult time at the moment. Make a list on a flip chart or whiteboard. The list could contain general groups of people (for instance, people who are bullied at school) or specific names (for instance, Sarah, whose grandma died last week).

3 Chat about how you could show these people that God is with them in their difficult situations.

4 Encourage each young person to choose one person or group of people from the list that they will reveal Jesus to over the next week. Then pray for one another in small groups, asking God to help with this.

CREATIVE

WHAT: bookmarks
WHY: to remind the young people that God is always with us
WITH: card, art materials

1 In advance, cut out bookmark-sized or credit-card-sized pieces of card for everyone in your group, plus a few spares.

2 Invite the young people to decorate these cards as a reminder that God is always with them. Suggest that on one side they write Genesis 28:15 and focus on Jacob's story, then on the other side ask them to write Matthew 28:20 and think about how God promises to always be with us.

3 Encourage the young people to keep their bookmarks or cards with them at all times.

MORE ON THIS THEME:

If you want to do a short series with your group, other sessions that work well with this one are:

6	Chat-show Jacob	Genesis 29–31
7	Brothers reunited	Genesis 32,33
8	Jacob's timeout	Genesis 35:1–15
9	Forgiven and forgotten	Genesis 45:1–15

HELP, I NEED SOMEBODY...

...NOT JUST ANYBODY! THAT'S HOW THE LYRICS OF THE FAMOUS SONG BY THE BEATLES GOES.

THE QUESTION IS, WHO WOULD YOU WANT WITH YOU IN THE FOLLOWING SITUATIONS?

AFTER YOU'VE HAD A HORRIBLE NIGHTMARE

TRAPPED IN A BURNING BUILDING

FOUND OUT YOUR PET HAS JUST DIED

LOST IN THE MIDDLE OF THE JUNGLE

JUST BEEN DUMPED BY YOUR BOY/GIRLFRIEND

SOMEONE ASKS YOU A DIFFICULT QUESTION ABOUT GOD

MY JOURNEY

Life is a journey and, in the same way as God promised to be with Jacob on his journey, God promises to be with us on our journey through life.

Start by writing your birth date in the cake.

Then, on the footprints, mark out some of the 'big steps' – the significant moments of your life. They might be big changes (such as moving house or changing school), high moments (such as when your football team won the cup final), or low moments (such as when your pet died).

Think about how God has helped you on your 'journey'. Read Genesis 28:10–22 to see how God promised to be with Jacob on his journey.

Finish by writing in the 'dream cloud' where you'd like to be on your journey with God in five years' time.

CHAT-SHOW JACOB

THE AIM: To be encouraged that God is with us in the complexities of life

The aim unpacked

Previously, Jacob had an encouraging encounter in which God told him that the promises he had first made to Abraham would be fulfilled and that he would always be with him. However, things didn't suddenly become easier for Jacob; his life was still full of difficulties. Despite this, God was busy fulfilling the promises he had made and was certainly always with Jacob.

WAY IN

 theGRID MAGAZINE

WHAT: dingbats
WHY: to illustrate that God sees the solution even if we can't
WITH: magazine page 42

1 Make sure everyone has a copy of page 42. In pairs, challenge them to see how many of the dingbats they can figure out.

2 Gather the group together and go through the answers.

3 Talk about how dingbats can sometimes be quite difficult; however, when someone tells you the solution, it's often really obvious. When we're faced with a difficult situation, it can sometimes seem too much for us and often we can barely cope, let alone find a solution. However, in such times we need to remember that God is with us, and he knows the solution! He knows how the situation is going to end.

 SCENE SETTER

WHAT: support map
WHY: to think about our relationships during hard times
WITH: pens in various colours and thicknesses

1 Give everyone a sheet of paper and a pen. Ask them to write their name in the middle of the paper and then around it write significant people in their life (for example, parents, school friends and teachers, church friends, other family, God). Explain that they can either write down the names of groups (for example, school friends), or specific names (for example, Sarah, Emily and Kate).

2 Then ask them to draw lines between them and the people written down. They could draw thicker lines for the stronger relationships.

3 Ask everyone to imagine that they are going through a really tough time at the moment. Now, in a different colour, ask them to draw lines to the people they would turn to and to indicate which relationships would be the most significant in helping them through this tough time.

4 Say a short prayer, thanking God that we have people to help us when life gets tough. Explain that in this session, we'll be thinking about how God was with Jacob when his life became very complicated.

 THEMED GAME

WHAT: human knot
WHY: to illustrate that God helps us out of complicated situations

1 Ask the young people to stand in a circle, shoulder to shoulder, and to place a hand in the middle of the circle. Instruct them to grasp the hand of someone else.

2 Now tell the young people to put their other hand in the middle and grasp a different person's hand.

3 Explain that they now have to untangle themselves (and end up in a circle) without letting go of hands.

4 Not all attempts will be successful, so have a few goes at this, depending on how much time you have. Explain that in this session you'll be looking at how God helped Jacob when he and his family got into a bit of a knot.

BIBLE EXPERIENCE

LEVEL 1: CONNECT

WHAT: discussion and name quiz
WHY: to be encouraged that God is with us in the complexities of life
WITH: magazine page 43

1 Ask a few volunteers to read aloud Genesis 29:15 – 30:24. Before they read it, warn them that it's quite long and contains lots of things that they may find quite strange. As the passage is being read, pause every now and then and ask the young people to chat about:

- anything that surprises or confuses them
- what they think Jacob might have been thinking
- what he might have learned about God

2 Explain that the culture Jacob lived in was very different from the one we live in today. God engages with us within our culture. That doesn't mean he's happy with everything that goes on within it, just like he didn't agree with everything that went on in Jacob's culture, but it does go to show that we don't have to be perfect for God to relate to us!

3 Invite the young people to look at page 43 and complete the 'What's in a name?' activity in pairs.

4 Conclude by reading Genesis 28:14 to the group and explaining that, despite the complexities of Jacob's family life, he would have been encouraged to see that God was keeping the promises he had made to him, his dad and his grandad.

LEVEL 2: INTERFACE

WHAT: music exploration
WHY: to be encouraged that God is with us in the complexities of life
WITH: music tracks, playback equipment, Bibles, coloured pencils

1 Choose a selection of songs that speak about some of life's difficulties. Here are a few possibilities, but you might like to use some different ones:

- 'Hurt' by Johnny Cash
- 'Trouble' by Coldplay
- 'Because of You' by Kelly Clarkson

Have copies of the lyrics available so the young people can read them as well as listen to them.

2 Depending on the size of your group, venue and the number of MP3 or CD players you have, either keep everyone together and listen to the songs all together, or divide the young people into small groups and designate one song to each group.

3 Ask the young people to make a note of, or draw a picture to illustrate, the difficult situation the song speaks about. Then encourage them to discuss how God could help during those tough times.

4 If this activity is done in small groups, play a clip of each song before inviting each group to share what they have been discussing.

5 In small groups, ask the young people to browse through Genesis 29–31 and make a note of the key events that took place. Then ask each group to compose a song or a poem that sums up how Jacob would have felt as he went through all these complex situations.

6 Explain to the young people that during his life Jacob experienced many difficulties; however, God was always with him, helping him in whatever situation he found himself.

LEVEL 3: SWITCH ON

WHAT: drama
WHY: to be encouraged that God is with us in the complexities of life
WITH: flip chart or large sheet of paper, Bibles, resource pages 44–46

1 Divide the young people into four groups and allocate one of these passages to each group:

- Genesis 29:1–30
- Genesis 29:31 – 30:24
- Genesis 30:25 – 31:24
- Genesis 31:25–55

2 There are some complicated issues in each of these passages, so it would be well worth having a leader with each group to help them get to grips with the complex issues. Resource pages 44–46 will also help. If you don't have enough leaders for one per group, make sure the leaders you do have spend some time with each group.

3 Ask each group to read their passage and then prepare a 'chat-show style' sketch that explores the difficulties Jacob faced and how he felt God's presence with him in these situations.

4 Give the groups time to prepare their sketches. Then gather the young people together and watch each of the sketches.

5 Conclude by explaining that our lives are extremely different from Jacob's. However, that doesn't mean we can't learn from his story and be encouraged. Spend a few minutes chatting about what we have learned about God in this session and consider how we should approach difficult situations in the light of this.

RESPOND

 MUSICAL

WHAT: shout it out
WHY: to remind us that God is with us in difficult situations
WITH: drum (optional)

1 Gather the group together and sit together in a circle. Then, either by using a drum or by encouraging the young people to pat their legs or clap their hands, start a simple rhythm.

2 Then invite someone to mention a difficult situation that someone may experience in life – for example, 'When I have to change school', or, 'When I feel alone'. Then everyone has to say together, in time with the rhythm, 'God is with you.' Then the next person says something and the group responds, and so on.

3 As you work your way around the circle, encourage the response 'God is with you' to increase in volume.

 PRACTICAL

WHAT: encouraging verses
WHY: to find Bible verses to encourage one another
WITH: Bibles

1 Give everyone a piece of paper and ask them to write down a difficult situation they are currently facing or might face in the near future. Tell the young people that what they write will be seen by other people, so it's up to them whether they add their name.

2 Collect in the pieces of paper and hand them out again, ensuring that everyone has a piece of paper that's not their own. Discourage them from trying to work out who wrote what.

3 Challenge everyone to find a Bible verse to encourage the person in the situation they received, and to write the verse on the piece of paper. Pin all the pieces of paper to a notice board or to the wall, so everyone can read them.

4 If the young people struggle to find appropriate Bible verses, you could provide them with a selection of verses to choose from, or use Bibles that have topical indexes in them, such as the Gideon Bible or *The Youth Bible*.

 CREATIVE

WHAT: thank-you cards
WHY: to thank God for being with us in difficult situations
WITH: card, art supplies

1 Give everyone a sheet of card and a selection of art supplies (for example, felt-tip pens, colouring pencils, paints and coloured card). Encourage the young people to make thank-you cards to God, to thank him for a time when he's been with them in a difficult situation.

2 After everyone has made their cards, encourage (but don't pressurise) them to tell the group about the situation where they felt God was with them. Then ask a few people to say short prayers to thank God for being with us in difficult situations.

MORE ON THIS THEME:

If you want to do a short series with your group, other sessions that work well with this one are:

DINGBATS

Can you work out what phrases these dingbats represent? We've done the first one for you.

HOT HANDLE
HOT HANDLE

Too hot to handle

ROUND ROUND

OCEAN

M CE
M CE
M CE

NEPAINCK

STRUGGLE

DAY THE

EI IG EI
T GH HT
T

GROUND LONDON

RASINGINGIN

**Bible bit
Genesis 29–31**

God had spoken to Jacob and assured him that the promises he had made to Abraham would come true. He'd also told Jacob that he would always be with him. However, that didn't mean things were going to suddenly become easier for Jacob! His life was certainly still full of difficulties, but God was busy fulfilling the promises he had made and was definitely always with Jacob.

Be encouraged! There might be many times in life when you're confused and not too sure about what's going on. But keep trusting in God, because he knows the big picture; he knows what's going to happen next, and we need to be confident that God will keep his promise to always be with us.

Dingbats can be quite difficult; however, when someone tells you the solution, it's often really obvious. When we're faced with a difficult situation, it can sometimes seem too much for us and often we can barely cope, let alone find a solution. However, in times like these, we need to remember that God is with us, and he knows the solution! He knows how the situation is going to end.

Answers on page 318

7

BROTHERS REUNITED

THE AIM: To be encouraged that God is with us in difficult relationships

The aim unpacked

Having left his Uncle Laban, Jacob may have been hoping for an easier life. However, in this session, we'll see how he had to confront yet another difficult situation when he was reunited with his brother, Esau. For Jacob and Esau, time really did seem to heal the wounds. At the emotional reunion it appears that there was no desire for revenge; instead, they only seemed to want the best for one another.

WAY IN

 **theGRID MAGAZINE**

WHAT: famous siblings quiz
WHY: to think about our relationships with our siblings
WITH: magazine page 50

1 Make sure everyone has a copy of page 50. Encourage them to have a go at the 'Famous siblings' quiz, in pairs.

2 Gather the group back together and go through the answers.

3 Ask the young people to think about the relationships they have with their brothers and sisters (or if they don't have any, with other members of their family). Ask them to imagine being separated from their siblings for the next five years. Would they consider this to be a good or a bad thing? What would they miss the most?

4 Explain to the group that, in this session, you're going to be seeing what happens when Jacob was reunited with his brother, Esau. If necessary, invite them to have a quick look at Genesis 27 to remind them why they had gone their separate ways.

 **SCENE SETTER**

WHAT: game
WHY: to introduce the idea that we should be after win–win solutions, not win–lose
WITH: game such as Top Trumps

1 Play a game where the 'winner takes all' and the losers get nothing – for example, Top Trumps or Snap. Either divide the young people into small groups to play the game, or adapt it to suit the size of your group.

2 Discuss together whether the young people often want to win; and if that means, therefore, that they want other people to lose. Point out that this can sometimes cause problems, especially when it comes to resolving conflicts. Instead of thinking how we can win and make sure the other person loses, we should be thinking how we can both win! In this session, we'll discover how Jacob and Esau resolved their conflict in a very positive way.

 **THEMED GAME**

WHAT: water fight
WHY: to introduce the idea of conflict
WITH: two water pistols, tissues, sticky tape

1 Work out whether it's possible to take your group outside, and find out in advance whether it's OK for your young people to get wet! If yes, this activity might be quite good fun. If not, don't use this activity!

2 Divide the young people into twos and challenge each pair in turn to have a 'duel'. Do this by taping a piece of tissue to each of their chests and giving them both a water pistol. Tell them to stand back to back and then take five paces forward. Then, on the count of three, they should turn around and 'shoot' each other. After five seconds stop them. The person whose piece of tissue is the wettest is the loser.

3 Do this until everyone has had at least one turn.

4 Introduce the session by explaining that a duel is probably not the best way for two people to resolve a conflict. Explain that in this session you'll be looking at what happened when Jacob and Esau met each other. Ask the group to vote on what they think happened. Did they fight or did they make up?

BIBLE EXPERIENCE

 LEVEL 1: CONNECT

WHAT: drama
WHY: to be encouraged that God is with us in difficult relationships
WITH: Bibles

1 Divide the young people into small groups and challenge them to prepare a short sketch about a conflict between siblings and the consequences of it. For example, a younger sister 'borrows' an item of clothing from her older sister and rips it by accident, then the older sister refuses to talk to her.

2 Gather the young people together and encourage the groups to perform their sketches to everyone else.

3 Ask the young people if they can remember why there was conflict between Jacob and his brother Esau. (If necessary, read or summarise Genesis 27.)

4 Explain that Jacob is preparing to meet his brother Esau for the first time since these events. Understandably, he is extremely scared. Then ask a volunteer to read Genesis 32:22–31.

5 Ask the young people to think about how this bizarre encounter with God would have encouraged Jacob and prepared him to meet Esau.

6 Back in their small groups, challenge them to prepare another short sketch to show how the conflict situation in their first sketch might be resolved. Once everyone has prepared their sketches, invite them to perform them to everyone else, as before.

7 Ask a few volunteers to read Genesis 33. Then chat about the attitudes with which both Jacob and Esau approached this encounter. What can we learn from this? Would the young people's sketches have finished differently if the characters involved had shown the same attitudes as Jacob and Esau?

 LEVEL 2: INTERFACE

WHAT: discussion
WHY: to be encouraged that God is with us in difficult relationships
WITH: large sheets of paper, pens, Bible, magazine pages 51 and 52

1 In pairs, encourage the young people to complete the 'You're so annoying!' activity on page 51.

2 Gather everyone together and discuss the activity. Then recap as a group why there was conflict between Jacob and his brother Esau. (If necessary, read or summarise Genesis 27.)

3 Divide the young people into two groups. Give each group a large sheet of paper and ask them to divide it into three columns. In the first column, ask one group to write down Esau's thoughts and the other group to write down Jacob's thoughts after the events of Genesis 27.

4 Invite the groups to feed back, and then explain that Jacob and Esau are about to meet up for the first time since these events. Ask the groups to jot down in the second column how they think their character might be feeling before this encounter.

5 Feed back again, then read Genesis 32:22–32 together. Discuss how Jacob may have been feeling about meeting Esau after this bizarre encounter with God. Change the list that the 'Jacob' group made in their second column accordingly.

6 Invite each group to read Genesis 33 and to make a note, in the third column, of how they think their character might have felt after meeting his brother. Also make a note of the attitudes shown by their character.

7 Feed back, and then chat about what we can learn from Jacob and Esau about how we should approach people we have wronged or who have wronged us. Conclude by asking everyone, individually or in pairs, to complete the 'Let's be friends' activity on page 52.

 LEVEL 3: SWITCH ON

WHAT: Bible study
WHY: to be encouraged that God is with us in difficult relationships
WITH: Bibles, copies of resource page 53

1 Ask the young people if they remember why there was conflict between Jacob and his brother, Esau. (If necessary, read or summarise Genesis 27.)

2 Divide the young people into twos or threes and make sure each group has a Bible, a copy of resource page 53 and a pen. Ask them to read Genesis 32 and 33 and discuss the questions on the resource page.

3 Gather everyone together and chat about what they've been reading. Spend some time discussing any questions that they may have.

RESPOND

 MUSICAL

WHAT: song
WHY: to thank God for restoring our relationship with him
WITH: words and music for 'How Deep the Father's Love for Us' by Stuart Townend, playback equipment or musical accompaniment

1 Talk to the group about how during this session we've thought about how Jacob and Esau were reunited and restored their relationship. God is very much into restoring relationships. In fact, the whole Bible is about him restoring the relationship between the people he made and himself, their Creator.

2 Encourage the young people to spend some time reflecting on how amazing it is that God has made it possible for our relationship with him to be restored. Do this by either listening to or singing the song 'How Deep the Father's Love for Us' by Stuart Townend.

3 You may like to use a different song or additional songs. Conclude by encouraging the young people to say short prayers thanking God for making it possible for us to have a relationship with him.

 PRACTICAL

WHAT: card making
WHY: to take the first step towards reconciliation
WITH: card, art supplies

1 Remind the group that, as we read Genesis 33, we discover that both Jacob and Esau seemed to approach their meeting with a positive attitude.

2 Encourage everyone to think of someone they have a difficult relationship with at the moment – maybe someone they need to say 'sorry' to – perhaps a brother or sister?

3 With the materials available, ask everyone to make a 'sorry' card for the person they are thinking of. Ask them to think carefully about the message they write inside it and encourage them to actually give it to the person, if appropriate.

4 Ask a leader to conclude by praying for the group. Pray that we would have attitudes like Jacob and Esau when it comes to resolving conflict, and thank God that he is with us in whatever difficult situations we face.

 CREATIVE

WHAT: seed planting
WHY: to let go of past conflicts and learn forgiveness
WITH: plastic cups, potting soil, sunflower seeds, plastic sheets

1 Before you start, make sure you cover with plastic sheets any surfaces that need protecting!

2 Give everyone a plastic cup and invite them to three-quarters fill it with potting soil.

3 Next, instruct them to make a little hole in the soil a centimetre or so deep.

4 Encourage the young people to think of someone, maybe a brother or a sister, with whom they are in conflict at the moment. Perhaps they are holding a grudge against someone and they know they need to let go of it.

5 After they have had the opportunity to think of a situation, give everyone a sunflower seed. Tell them that the seed represents the conflict, and then invite them to place the seed in the hole.

6 As they cover the seed with soil, encourage them to spend some time talking to God about the conflict. They may like to pray that God would help them move on from the situation, to offer forgiveness to the person involved and rebuild the relationship.

7 Encourage the young people to take good care of their sunflowers and, as they grow, to remember that they have 'buried' their past conflict and should be trying to rebuild and strengthen their relationship with the other person.

MORE ON THIS THEME:

If you want to do a short series with your group, other sessions that work well with this one are:

Can you match up these pictures of famous siblings? For a bonus point, do you know who the older sibling in each family is?

FAMOUS SIBLINGS

1  WILLIAM

A  VENUS

Bible bit
Genesis 32,33

Having left his Uncle Laban, Jacob may have been hoping for an easier life. However, there were yet more obstacles in his way. It was now time for him to be reunited with his brother Esau. It's understandable that Jacob was a little nervous about this: after all, the reason for Jacob's sudden departure all those years ago was the fact that Esau wanted to kill him!

2  KEVIN

B  CASEY

However, it seems that time really did heal Jacob's and Esau's wounds, because at their emotional reunion it appears that there was no desire for revenge; instead they only seemed to want the best for one another.

3  BEN

C  MAGGIE

This story not only shows us how God is with us in difficult relationships, but we'll also be able to learn how we can handle conflict situations wisely, especially with our brothers and sisters!

4  KYLIE

D  HARRY

5  JAKE

E  DANNII

6  SERENA

F  JOANNE

Answers on page 318

YOU'RE SO ANNOYING!

Have you got a brother or sister who occasionally annoys you? Whether you have or haven't, which of the following situations would annoy you the most?

1 Your dad asks you both to do the washing up but your brother refuses to help. You do the washing up on your own while he watches TV.

2 You share a room with your sister. She's really messy and you always have to wade through her dirty clothes to get to your bed.

3 Your brother borrows your new hoody and spills a drink down it.

4 Whenever there's a mess in the house, your parents blame you rather than your little brother.

5 Your older sister always borrows your stuff, but she never lets you borrow any of hers.

6 Your sister uses your mobile phone without your permission.

LET'S BE FRIENDS

What advice would you give the following people to deal with their family feuds?

Clare can't find her favourite jumper. She's convinced that her sister, Elli, has borrowed it. However, when Clare asked her if she knew where it was, Elli said she didn't. So yesterday Clare went looking for her jumper in Elli's room. The problem is, Elli caught her and, well, things erupted! They haven't spoken to each other since (and the jumper still has not been found).

_____
_____
_____
_____
_____
_____

Chris is fed up that his brother Paul never helps out around the house. Their parents are really busy and Chris does his best to help out, but whenever he asks Paul to help, Paul says he's busy and then locks himself in his room and plays on his Xbox. Chris is angry with Paul for not helping and he's angry with his parents for not making Paul help him.

_____
_____
_____
_____
_____

Yesterday, Kate found out that her brother Tom not only went into her bedroom but also found her diary and read it! But that's not all he did; he then posted some of what he read on his Facebook page. What he wrote was about Kate's best friend Sarah, and now Sarah's not speaking to her. Kate is so upset that she just doesn't know what to do.

_____
_____
_____
_____
_____

Read Genesis 32:1–12. Jacob is worried about meeting up with his brother after so many years and so much conflict between them (read Genesis 27 to remember why!). What would you advise him to do?

_____
_____
_____
_____
_____
_____

Read Genesis 32:13–21 to find out what he actually did!

Do you think it will work? — YES / NO

Check out Genesis 33 to find out whether it worked or not!

Brothers reunited

In your groups, discuss these questions as you read Genesis 32 and 33.

Genesis 32:1–8
• If you were Esau, what would you be planning to do to Jacob after all these years? Kill him? Punch him? Hug him? Or would you be planning something else?

Genesis 32:9–12
• Sensibly, Jacob turned to God. When was the last time you turned to God when you faced a difficult situation? What did you say to God? What happened?

Genesis 32:13–21
• Jacob prepared a gift for Esau; what do you think we can learn about Jacob's attitude from this? How do you think Esau is going to respond to the gift?

Genesis 32:22–32
• Have you ever laid awake in bed, knowing you have something difficult to face the next day? Imagine how Jacob must have felt before and after this bizarre encounter with God. How do you think it changed how he was thinking about meeting his brother?

Genesis 33
• Esau and Jacob both seemed to approach this situation very positively. How do you think the situation might have turned out if one or both of them had approached it with an 'I'm still mad at you' attitude? What do you think we should learn from this?

8

JACOB'S TIMEOUT

THE AIM: To be encouraged to frequently pause and reflect on life and our relationship with God

The aim unpacked

After an epic journey full of lots of adventures, in this session we see Jacob 'pausing' and spending some time with God. As he did so, he acknowledged that God had been with him, he dealt with the things that were getting in the way, between his family and God, and God reaffirmed his promises to him once more.

WAY IN

 **theGRID MAGAZINE**

WHAT: word search
WHY: to introduce the idea of taking time out
WITH: magazine page 57, prize (optional)

1 In pairs, ask everyone to attempt the word search on page 57. If they need help finding the ten words, tell them that the words they are looking for are: adjournment, halftime, holiday, interlude, intermission, interval, pause, recess, timeout, vacation.

2 Then give each pair a sheet of paper and challenge them to write down as many things as they can think of that people might do during the half-time of a football match. Give them a minute to write down as many things as possible. They get two points for things they write down that no other group writes down and one point for things that other groups also write down.

3 Repeat this activity as time allows with other scenarios. For example, why might you press 'pause' while watching a film?

4 Award a prize to the team that scores the most points.

 **SCENE SETTER**

WHAT: eating slowly
WHY: to think about how we miss things if we rush through life
WITH: selection of snack foods and drinks

1 Have a selection of common snack foods and drinks available for your group to try.

2 Ask each young person to take something to eat or drink and hold it in their hands. Encourage them to look at it for a few moments and then to eat and drink it really slowly. Encourage them to really think about what it tastes like, to savour the texture, and to really enjoy the experience of eating or drinking.

3 Allow them to sample all the different foods and drinks.

4 Then, in small groups, ask them to think about some of the things we might 'miss' because we rush too much. For example, the amazing scenery we walk past on the way to school each day.

5 Explain that in this session we'll be thinking about how it's important that we frequently take time to pause and reflect on life and our relationship with God.

 **THEMED GAME**

WHAT: musical statues
WHY: to introduce the idea of 'pausing'
WITH: large, safe space, music, playback equipment

1 Make sure you have a large, safe space in which the young people can move around.

2 Invite everyone to stand up, and then explain that when the music is playing, they must move around. As soon as the music stops, they must freeze. The last person to freeze, and any people who move when the music isn't playing, are out.

3 Start playing the game, and keep starting and pausing the music until there is only one person left in the game.

4 Introduce the session by saying that today you're going to be thinking about the importance of 'pausing'.

BIBLE EXPERIENCE

 LEVEL 1: CONNECT

WHAT: discussion
WHY: to be encouraged to frequently pause and reflect on life and our relationship with God
WITH: Bibles

1 Read together Genesis 35:1–15 by going around the group asking each person to read one verse at a time.

2 Explain to the young people that Jacob certainly had some adventures during his life, and now we see him pausing and spending some time with God. This involved getting his family to get rid of their 'foreign gods'. As his family had lived among people who didn't worship God, they had started to worship the various gods that these people worshipped. That didn't necessarily mean they rejected God; it meant they worshipped him alongside other gods. That, as we discover throughout the Bible, is not something that God wants. He is the only God, and he wants us to worship him alone. These 'foreign gods' would probably have been represented by statues (idols).

3 Invite the young people to reflect on what 'idols' they might worship alongside God.

4 Then, in pairs, ask them to make a note of what a person's life might look like if they were to worship that particular 'idol' above anything else. Conclude by discussing this activity as a whole group.

 LEVEL 2: INTERFACE

WHAT: Bible study
WHY: to be encouraged to frequently pause and reflect on life and our relationship with God
WITH: Bibles, reflective music (optional)

1 Read together Genesis 35:1–15 and chat about any questions the young people have about the passage.

2 In small groups, ask the young people to divide a sheet of paper into three columns, titled 'Past', 'Present' and 'Future'.

3 Explain that Jacob seems to be pausing and spending some quality time with God. Ask the groups to reread Genesis 35:1–15 and make a note of the following:

- Past: What did Jacob say about what had happened (v 3)? How might he have felt towards God?

- Present: What did Jacob ask his family to do (v 2)? Why did he want them to do this?

- Future: What did Jacob learn about his future (vs 10–12)? How would this have encouraged him?

4 Gather together and obtain feedback. Chat about Jacob's time with God and, if necessary, summarise by saying that he acknowledged that God had been with him (and probably thanked him for this), he dealt with the things that were getting in the way, between his family and God, and God reaffirmed his promises.

5 Ask the young people to divide another sheet of paper into three sections, titled 'Past', 'Present' and 'Future', and to find some space in the room where they can spend some time with God alone. You may like to put on some quiet, reflective music.

6 Ask them to think about the following:

- Past: How have things been with God lately? What have you got to thank him for? What questions would you like to ask him?

- Present: Are there things in your life that you need to deal with? What are they? What are you going to do to sort them out?

- Future: What are your prayers for the future? What are you looking forward to? What are your dreams? And your concerns?

 LEVEL 3: SWITCH ON

WHAT: spiritual check-up
WHY: to be encouraged to frequently pause and reflect on life and our relationship with God
WITH: Bibles

1 Ask the group to recap Jacob's story so far, and then invite a couple of volunteers to read Genesis 35:1–15.

2 Use some of the ideas from 'Level 2 Interface' to help the young people delve into the time Jacob spent with God, reflecting on his life and relationship with God.

3 Either all together or in small groups, discuss why it's important that we frequently pause to spend time with God.

4 Explain that cars have to have an annual MOT to check they are in good working order, and it's recommended that we all have annual check-ups at the dentist to check our teeth are healthy. In the same way, it's important that we frequently give ourselves a 'spiritual check-up' to ensure our life and relationship with God are healthy.

5 Divide the young people into twos and threes and encourage them to devise a 'spiritual health check'. Encourage them to be creative, but suggest that the check-up could be based around a series of ten questions.

RESPOND

 MUSICAL

WHAT: time with God
WHY: to encourage young people to spend time with God
WITH: quiet worship music, playback equipment

1 Encourage the young people to spend some time alone with God, thinking about their life and their relationship with him. Suggest they find some space in the room where they won't be disturbed by anyone else. Put on some quiet worship music that will help them focus on God. Have Bibles, paper and pens around the room that the young people can use if they would like to.

2 If the young people created a 'spiritual health check' during the *Bible experience* section, perhaps they could use it here.

3 Afterwards, encourage the young people to chat in small groups about how they found this activity. What were they thinking about? Do they think God said anything to them?

4 You may like to conclude by singing a song together. 'Be Thou My Vision' or 'In the Secret' (Andy Park) are two possibilities.

 PRACTICAL

WHAT: prayer feet
WHY: to encourage young people to think about the future
WITH: cards, scissors

1 Give everyone three sheets of card and ask them to draw around their foot three times and to cut out the foot shapes.

2 Chat together about what you've learned about Jacob over the past few sessions. Emphasise that God was always with Jacob (Genesis 35:3) and that, during Jacob's 'timeout', God encouraged him regarding the future (Genesis 35:10–13).

3 Ask the young people to think about their future and about how they want to develop their relationship with God. On one of their 'feet', encourage them to write what they want their life and relationship with God to be like over the next month. On another 'foot', encourage them to write what they want it to be like in three years' time, and on the final 'foot', encourage them to write what they want it to be like in ten years' time.

4 Invite them to lay their 'feet' on the floor, and then ask a few people to pray for the group.

 CREATIVE

WHAT: prayer hands
WHY: to help the young people develop their prayer lives
WITH: card, scissors

1 Explain to the group that taking a 'timeout' each day to pray is a good idea. Spend a few minutes chatting with the group about their experiences of prayer. When do they usually pray? What do they find difficult?

2 Give each person a sheet of card and ask them to draw round their hand and then cut out the shape.

3 Encourage the young people to write a Bible verse on the thumb. This could be their favourite verse, a verse from this session or perhaps a verse about prayer (for example, Philippians 4:6).

4 Now invite them to write the words 'Adore', 'Confess', 'Thank' and 'Supplicate' on the four fingers.

5 Explain that it can sometimes be difficult to know what to include in our prayers. Suggest that using the acronym 'ACTS' might be helpful. Explain what each of the words mean:

- Adore: Praise God for who he is.
- Confess: Say sorry for the things you know you've done wrong.
- Thank: Thank God for the good things he has done.
- Supplicate: Ask God for things. Speak to him about the things that are on your mind; pray for yourself, your friends, your family and the world.

6 In small groups, encourage the young people to pray using this as their model. Then encourage them to spend a few minutes each day in prayer, using this as the model.

MORE ON THIS THEME:

If you want to do a short series with your group, other sessions that work well with this one are:

HAVE A BREAK

Can you find ten different words you might use for 'taking a break' in the word search? If you need help there is a list of the words on page 318.

Bible bit
Genesis 35:1–15

After an epic journey full of lots of adventures, in this session we see Jacob 'pausing' and spending some time with God. As he does so, he acknowledges that God has been with him, he deals with the things that were getting in the way between his family and God, and God reaffirms his promises to him once more.

It's so important that we frequently pause and reflect on life and our relationship with God, and this story provides us with a great model. 1) Thank God for being with us in the past. 2) Deal with anything in the present that is getting in the way of our relationship with God. And 3) spend some time chatting to God about the future.

D	H	W	A	Q	Y	U	S	I	O	M	B	N	C	R	X
A	S	H	Q	H	W	P	T	F	J	K	L	I	H	E	W
B	Z	A	D	J	O	U	R	N	M	E	N	T	X	C	Q
S	U	L	O	I	Y	L	G	H	L	K	E	A	C	E	E
A	S	F	T	R	U	F	I	W	A	F	J	H	L	S	B
V	B	T	X	Z	S	J	I	D	U	Y	W	U	T	S	O
P	N	I	M	V	C	E	N	E	A	G	U	Q	D	K	L
R	U	M	Y	I	K	D	J	L	G	Y	D	Z	V	C	X
B	M	E	N	R	E	U	Y	U	O	I	P	J	R	I	N
W	F	D	V	H	R	L	A	V	R	E	T	N	I	J	O
M	J	T	P	T	R	R	E	W	Q	F	D	S	J	K	I
M	M	N	A	R	J	E	S	H	J	C	K	L	R	Y	T
Q	W	B	U	D	S	T	L	Y	I	J	O	T	E	R	A
T	T	O	S	E	N	N	N	V	M	X	U	Z	S	O	C
I	N	T	E	R	M	I	S	S	I	O	N	W	R	G	A
J	H	S	Y	O	P	Q	R	S	E	H	G	D	J	Y	V
U	E	W	T	Y	I	O	P	M	T	E	G	S	R	N	B
A	S	C	C	V	B	M	I	F	S	D	Y	I	J	K	L
E	S	T	U	W	R	T	S	D	C	H	K	A	X	O	R

9
FORGIVEN AND FORGOTTEN

Bible: Genesis 45:1–15

THE AIM: To be secure in God's faithfulness when we need to forgive and move on

The aim unpacked

We 'grow up' when we forgive and move on; we are 'diminished' when we seek revenge. Joseph found he could forgive his brothers at the same time as he told them clearly about his place in God's whole scheme of things (Genesis 45:7,8). His awareness of God's love and faithfulness seemed to make forgiveness for such a terrible wrong possible.

WAY IN

 **theGRID MAGAZINE**

WHAT: diary
WHY: to think about the shape of our own lives
WITH: magazine page 61

1 Give out pens and copies of page 61.

2 Invite everyone to look at 'Diary'. This is an individual and private activity. Encourage the young people to fill in the blank spaces for the previous week, leaving the 'To do' section to complete later.

3 If you have the kind of group that easily shares news and is generally supportive of one another, invite anyone to share their news with the rest of the group, if they would like to.

 **SCENE SETTER**

WHAT: photo album
WHY: to map the story of your life so far
WITH: PowerPoint of photos of your life and family from birth to present day

1 Chat your way through your life so far, illustrated by the photos you have collected. Make sure you include as many funny incidents as possible, to keep things light and moving along. Tell the story in such a way that you trace God at work in the events (if you can), leading you to the present moment, through hardships (what did you learn that you need now?); skills, qualifications and training (what did you gain that you use now?); and the good times (how do you now see them as God's gracious provision?). How aware are you of God leading you through your life to this point?

2 Invite questions about your life. It's OK for you to refuse to answer if it all gets too personal!

 **THEMED GAME**

WHAT: standing still game
WHY: to see that God's plans and timing may not be the same as ours
WITH: small prize

1 Don't tell the group exactly what you're about to do, but encourage them to take part.

2 Ask everyone to stand still with their eyes closed. This will be a good test of how much they trust you! Don't say anything else, but let the time go on and on. How do the young people react? Open their eyes? Fidget? Shuffle about? Give up and sit down? Ask, 'What are we doing this for?'

3 See who is the last person left doing what you originally asked them to do, and reward them with a small prize. Alternatively, stop the activity after about five minutes before it all falls apart!

4 Sometimes God's planning and timing don't match with the way we want things to be. Things may seem to take longer than we thought they would, and we can't always see God's purpose behind the events of our lives. Explain that, after many years, Joseph was able to see clearly what was in God's mind for his stay in Egypt.

BIBLE EXPERIENCE

LEVEL 1: CONNECT

WHAT: film critics
WHY: to be secure in God's faithfulness when we need to forgive and move on
WITH: film about Joseph, playback equipment, large sheets of paper or flip chart, marker pens

1 Find the part of your chosen Joseph film that shows the events of Genesis 42–45, from the first visit of Joseph's brothers to Egypt through to their reconciliation with him and to the whole family settling in Egypt. This will fill in the broad sweep of the rest of the story since this session only really focuses on Genesis 45:1–15. Cue the film so that it is ready to show.

2 Explain that you want the group to listen carefully to the way the Bible describes the key moment when Joseph reveals who he is to his brothers when they arrive in Egypt to obtain food.

3 Read Genesis 45:1–15 aloud. Ask:

- How does Joseph react to his brothers?

- How do they react to Joseph's reaction to them?

- From the way Joseph talks, what do you think has helped him to respond in this way?

4 Ask the three questions one after the other, asking a group member to write the young people's answers to each question on a separate large sheet of paper. The key things to cover are that Joseph loved and forgave his brothers, helped by his memory of how faithful God had been.

5 Now set up the film by challenging the group to see how well the director has communicated what they themselves have discovered from the Bible. Show the film, then encourage the young people to critique it according to what they have written on the three sheets. Was the film a good portrayal of the Bible verses?

6 When we're aware of God's purposes and faithfulness, as Joseph was, we'll overflow with love and forgiveness for everyone, whatever they have done in the past, and we'll be able to move on.

LEVEL 2: INTERFACE

WHAT: blog
WHY: to be secure in God's faithfulness when we need to forgive and move on
WITH: magazine page 62, Bibles

1 Distribute a copy of page 62 to each group member and ask everyone to turn to 'Jo's Blog.com'. Invite someone to read the next episode of Joseph's life.

2 Ask, 'What do you think made Joseph able to forgive his brothers?'

3 Now invite everyone to listen to Genesis 45:1–15 as you read it aloud. Challenge the young people to count how many times God gets a mention and what Joseph says about him.

4 Obtain answers from the group. (It's five times.) Joseph doesn't blame his brothers (v 8), but instead speaks of God sending him to Egypt to save lives (v 5) and to make sure his family has some descendants (v 7), and of God putting him in his position of authority (vs 8,9). Maybe his assurance of God at work through everything made it easier to forgive his brothers and to move on.

LEVEL 3: SWITCH ON

WHAT: Bible overview
WHY: to be secure in God's faithfulness when we need to forgive and move on
WITH: resource pages 63 and 64 cut into cards and strips, Bibles

1 Shuffle the cards, keeping them separate from the Bible reference strips. Give out the cards – at least one each. You may need to give more than one card to each person if you have a smaller group, or make more complete sets (on different-coloured paper) for a larger group.

2 Challenge the group to lay out their cards in the right order (and colour), to show the whole Bible story. (They are in the correct order on the resource page, reading down each column.) Each person must place the card(s) they hold, though do prompt them if they get stuck.

3 Make sure that the young people recognise that this is all God's Big Plan, with Jesus right at the centre. Because Jesus died, everyone (not just the people of Israel) can be forgiven and become God's people.

4 Divide the group into pairs or threes and give them one or more of the Bible reference strips. Encourage them to read the Bible passage(s) and write down what the verses tell us about God at work in Joseph's life. Then invite them to place each slip on God's Big Plan to show where Joseph gets a mention. So, for instance, the Acts Bible reference will be placed against 'The spread of the good news of Jesus'.

5 Obtain feedback from the Bible reference strip(s) about Joseph's life. God allowed his people to become slaves in Egypt until the Promised Land was ready for them. Joseph played a major role in helping his family to survive and moving them to Egypt. Joseph knew that God was being faithful to him and to his Big Plan (Genesis 45:7,8). Because he was aware of God's faithfulness, Joseph could forgive his brothers – there was something much bigger and better going on than family rows!

RESPOND

 MUSICAL

WHAT: worship wander
WHY: to encourage the young people to commit their whole lives to God for him to take and use
WITH: contemporary instrumental worship music, playback equipment

1 Explain the activity carefully before you start, so you don't need to interrupt with further explanation during it.

2 As you play the first track, encourage the young people to wander around the room and, as they walk, to reflect on the way God has brought them this far in their lives. What are their most vivid memories? What has been the good news? And the not-so-good? Have they been aware of God at work in and through the things that have happened? They should have a natural, silent conversation with God about it all. Fade the first track. Everyone stops wandering.

3 Fade in the second track and invite the young people to wander around again, this time committing their future to God. What has he given them? What skills do they have? What might they do? Where might they go? Who might hurt them? Who will they need to forgive? Encourage them to express their lifelong commitment to our God, who will always be faithful.

4 At the end, sing to God using songs on the theme of God who is faithful.

 PRACTICAL

WHAT: diary prayer
WHY: to be ready to forgive and forget, because of God's faithfulness
WITH: magazine page 61, ambient music, playback equipment, yellow wool

1 Make sure everyone has a copy of page 61 and a pen.

2 If you didn't do the first part of the 'Diary' activity, invite everyone to do it now, individually.

3 Now encourage them to think carefully through the events they have noted in their 'diary' to see if there is any action they need to take. They should make a note of anything in the 'To do' column for each day again, individually and secretly.

4 As you play some ambient music softly in the background, encourage the young people to pray silently about what they have written, asking God to help them actually do something about it soon.

5 Pray for each person by name, if possible, asking God to make them so sure of his love and faithfulness that it will be easier for them to do what they have noted in the 'diary'.

6 Invite everyone who has written something in their 'To do' column to take a length of wool and tie it round their wrist to remind them of what they need to do. Only when they have done the things in the 'To do' column can they remove the wool!

 CREATIVE

WHAT: beads
WHY: to pray for each other to be committed to God for life
WITH: small beads of assorted shapes and colours, string or leather laces cut to size for bracelets or necklaces

1 Draw the group into a circle to pray, or into several smaller circles if you have a large group. Give each group a selection of beads and string or laces.

2 Explain that you would like them to pray for each other to stay committed to God all their life and to be people whose lives are remarkable for the amount of forgiveness in them.

3 One person chooses a length of string or leather lace and ties a knot in the end so the beads won't fall off. This will become their bracelet or necklace. Everyone else selects a bead of their choice. The person who chose the lace passes it around the circle. When each person receives it, he or she should thread their bead on to it and then pray silently or out loud for the person who chose the lace. Then the lace is passed to the next person round, and so on. When the bracelet or necklace arrives back at the original person, it's theirs to keep – to wear or to hang in their room as a reminder of the prayers of their friends.

4 Repeat until everyone in the circle has a beaded lace.

MORE ON THIS THEME:

If you want to do a short series with your group, other sessions that work well with this one are:

5	Jacob's ladder	Genesis 28:10–22
6	Chat-show Jacob	Genesis 29–31
7	Brothers reunited	Genesis 32,33
8	Jacob's timeout	Genesis 35:1–15

10

BE BIG

THE AIM: To grow more confident in God

The aim unpacked

For Joshua, to follow in the footsteps of Moses took a lot of courage, and a lot of faith and reliance on God. For our young people, making a stand for Jesus can be equally daunting. In a world where 'self-help' and 'self-confidence' are thrust upon us from the media, it can be difficult to rely on God and to step out with the confidence that he gives.

WAY IN

 theGRID MAGAZINE

WHAT: reflection on comfort zones
WHY: to introduce the idea that we all have a comfort zone we would like to stay safe in
WITH: magazine page 68

1 Talk about what a 'comfort zone' is. Give an example from your own life, perhaps by demonstrating a time when you have been out of your comfort zone and why.

2 Hand out page 69 and invite the young people to reflect on the limits to their own personal comfort zones. Which of the scenarios would they find the hardest to do?

3 Ask if any of the young people have examples they would like to share of the experiences on the page, or of other times when they have had to step out of their comfort zone. Encourage them to explain how they felt about it, why they did it and whether they were glad they did afterwards.

4 Encourage them to chat further in twos or threes. If appropriate, explain that in this session they'll be looking at how a character from the Bible stepped out of his comfort zone, with God's help.

 SCENE SETTER

WHAT: discussion game
WHY: to introduce the idea of risk
WITH: three copies of resource pages 70 and 71

1 Talk about the biggest risk you've ever taken yourself and how you felt before, during and afterwards. Ask the group what the biggest risk is that they have ever taken and how that felt.

2 Designate two leaders to be Victor the Vile and Villainous, and Trisha the True and Trustworthy. Give them a copy of the script from resource pages 70 and 71. Read it through, encouraging Victor and Trisha to give their advice each time. The young people should move to sit with the person whose advice they would follow. Then read out the consequences each time. Encourage Victor and Trisha to ham it up as much as possible.

3 Point out that we are much happier to take a risk if we trust the person asking us to take it. This activity showed that one person was more trustworthy than the other. Explain that in this session, they'll be thinking about someone who had to take a huge risk.

 THEMED GAME

WHAT: tag game
WHY: to illustrate the idea of taking risks to win
WITH: five trophies (paper cups or similar), large space

1 Divide the young people into teams of five. Designate two safe bases at either end of the room. Place five trophies in the centre of the room.

2 The aim of the game is for the team to move the five trophies into the safety of base two at the far end of the room within the set time limit. The team starts by standing in base one. Another person is 'It' and tries to stop them by tagging them – no one can be tagged in the bases. If 'It' tags them, they must return to base one; if they are carrying a trophy, they must put it back in the middle. When they have safely carried a trophy to base two, they must stay there and cheer on the others. For the first round, set the time limit to two minutes. You may want to shorten it in subsequent rounds.

3 Make the point that if you don't venture out, you won't ever win the trophies, even though there are risks involved. Get feedback on their thoughts.

BIBLE EXPERIENCE

 LEVEL 1: CONNECT

WHAT: role play
WHY: to grow more confident in God
WITH: each verse of Joshua 1:2–9 printed on a separate card and numbered, resource page 72

1 Invite a volunteer to sit on a chair in front of the others. Introduce him as Joshua, using the script from resource page 72.

2 Divide the group into two teams. Tell one team that they must try to persuade Joshua to wimp out. The other team must persuade Joshua to cross the raging river and take hold of the Promised Land. Give the teams one minute to prepare and jot down a few ideas.

3 In turn, each team has one minute to try to convince Joshua they have the best idea. At the end of the time, the young person playing Joshua should choose which advice to follow. Say that this was a decision the real Joshua had to face. But he didn't have mixed advice – God gave him a pep talk that would see him through the tough times ahead.

4 Give out the verses on numbered cards and ask the young people to read them out in order. Say that this was God's pep talk to Joshua. Ask the young people to choose which piece of encouragement they think Joshua would find most useful. Say that when we face challenging times – even when the people we rely on let us down or disappear – we can have courage and be confident in God, just as Joshua did.

5 Ask the young people to think of a difficult change that they're facing at the moment, or will be facing soon – new things at school, a new activity, a house move or a change in their family or group of close friends. Encourage them to picture that situation and, in their minds, to give it to God, asking God to be with them as he was with Joshua.

 LEVEL 2: INTERFACE

WHAT: encouraging messages
WHY: to grow more confident in God
WITH: Bibles, magazine page 69, flip chart or whiteboard, mobile phones (optional)

1 Explain that Joshua is at a turning point. He could go forwards or backwards. God wants Joshua to lead the Israelites forward into the Promised Land. Will God be with him? Can they trust him?

2 Divide everyone into pairs and make sure each pair has a Bible. Assign one of the characters from 'Help!' on page 69 to each pair. Invite them to see what God says to Joshua in Joshua 1 that might give their character confidence too. Should they go forwards in faith or backwards into familiar safety?

3 Invite each pair to feed back what they have discovered. Write up the key verses on a flip chart or whiteboard. Ask, 'If you had to pick one verse to help you be confident in the future, which would you choose? Which verse would you choose as a challenge?'

4 Back in pairs, challenge the young people to put God's message to Joshua in text form in no more than 160 characters (including spaces). If they have their mobiles with them, suggest they send their version to someone they would like to encourage; otherwise, they can write it down on paper and give it to someone. Be sensitive to anyone who may not have a mobile phone, and also be aware of how distracting they could be for the rest of the session!

5 Explain that God's encouragement was for Joshua going into the Promised Land. There are other encouragements in the Bible that are directly for us – check out Matthew 28:20 to see that we are not alone. Challenge the young people in the next few days to text a friend who needs some encouragement to have confidence in God.

 LEVEL 3: SWITCH ON

WHAT: Bible study
WHY: to grow more confident in God
WITH: teen magazines, Bibles and concordances, resource page 73

1 Provide some teen lifestyle magazines and ask the young people to find examples of things that are supposed to give young people confidence, such as perfect make-up or great biceps.

2 Share their ideas. Discuss:

- Which of these really makes you feel more confident deep down?
- What would happen if they were taken away from you?
- Would you have any confidence left if you had no nice clothes, money, and so on?
- What can you think of that would give you confidence that outlasts all these temporary things?

(Make it clear that it's not wrong to have any of these things, but that God wants us to build our lives on something longer lasting.)

3 Explain that Joshua faced a crunch situation and had to decide whether to step out in faith or not. The Israelites were on the edge of the Promised Land, with the River Jordan to cross and a whole new land to conquer. Joshua was now the leader. What would give him the confidence to move forward instead of holding back?

4 In pairs, ask everyone to read Joshua 1:1–9 and discuss the questions on resource page 73.

5 Again, in pairs, invite everyone to read Joshua 1:10–18. Ask them how Joshua responded to his call and how the people reacted to him. Encourage the young people to share with their partner any issues they are facing that will require them to have the same confidence as Joshua.

6 Explain that the promises God made to Joshua in this passage were for a specific task. Can the young people find any verses in the Bible that are promises to us, which can give us confidence today? Some suggestions are Matthew 28:20 and Philippians 4:19.

RESPOND

 MUSICAL

WHAT: composing
WHY: to compose your own song
WITH: musical instruments (optional),
recording equipment (optional)

1 If members of your group play musical instruments, you might like to encourage them in advance to bring their instruments along to this session.

2 In groups of four or five, invite everyone to look again at Joshua 1:1–9 and pick out the verse or phrase they would most like to commit to memory.

3 Ask each group to make up a song based on the verse they have chosen. Suggest some different styles of music: a worship song, a rap, a children's song with actions, a Taizé-style repeated chant, or a tune they already know to which they can write new words. This will take some time. If one group finishes before the rest, they might like to record their song or make up a dance to accompany it. The songs could be used as part of a worship service with the rest of the church.

4 If the group isn't musical, they could make up a poem or 'song' without music and create actions to either a spoken version or a rap.

5 Alternatively, spend some time listening to and reflecting on one of these songs:

- 'Though I Feel Afraid' by Ian White
- 'Here We Are, Lord' by Noel and Tricia Richards and Gerald Coates
- 'I Walk by Faith' by Chris Falson
- 'We Shall Stand' by Graham Kendrick

 PRACTICAL

WHAT: prayer walking
WHY: to have faith in God and commit to him
WITH: pebbles, permanent markers, grapes, strip of blue cloth or big bowl of water

1 Arrange the objects to represent a ground plan of Joshua's situation. Put the pebbles on the side of the room where the group is, the cloth or bowl representing water in the centre, and the grapes on the far side.

2 Ask everyone to think of a situation they are nervous about at the moment, where they feel they're being asked to step out of their 'comfort zone'. Invite them to take a pebble, representing the desert where Joshua faced his big decision. They should write a word or symbol on their pebble to represent their situation.

3 Encourage them to walk to the water, praying silently or out loud that God will be with them in this situation. Invite them to place the pebble into the water as a sign that they're leaving all the anxiety and doubt behind them.

4 Invite everyone then to walk over to the grapes. Invite them each to eat one as a sign that they trust that God's plans for their future are good ones. For Joshua, it was to enter a land where the grapes were so massive that it took two men to carry a bunch on a pole!

5 You might want to finish with a rounding up prayer, such as, 'Lord God, thank you for promising to be with Joshua. Thank you that he grew in confidence in you. Please be with us as we face our challenges, and help us grow in confidence, trusting in you. Amen.'

 CREATIVE

WHAT: putting yourself in Joshua's shoes
WHY: to pray imaginatively
WITH: large sheets of paper, Bible, Bible atlas (optional)

1 Give each young person a large sheet of paper and ask them to draw a map of where Joshua was at this point: a desert with the Hebrews' camp, the River Jordan, and the Promised Land across the river. (Consult a Bible atlas – the river runs roughly north to south and the people crossed from east to west.) The Promised Land is a wonderful place, with huge grapevines, beehives, cornfields, olive trees and other fruit. The desert is, of course, bleak and inhospitable, but it's familiar! Explain that the river is in full flood and looks impossible to cross.

2 The young people should draw a stick figure on the map by the edge of the river, on the desert side. Encourage them to imagine they're Joshua looking across the river and to write what they can see in all directions, and any words describing how they feel.

3 Read Joshua 1:2–9. Ask, 'If you were Joshua, how would that make you feel?' Encourage everyone to write or draw their feelings now.

4 Ask, 'What situation are you in that feels like this?' Suggest that they draw symbols of this situation on their map. Now read God's words again. How do they feel now?

5 Encourage everyone to share their pictures and reactions in pairs or threes.

6 Finish with a prayer, thanking God that he is with us always, in every new situation, as he was with Joshua. Pray specifically for any new situations facing your young people.

MORE ON THIS THEME:

If you want to do a short series with your group, other sessions that work well with this one are:

11	*Help for the spies*	*Joshua 2*
12	*Making a mark*	*Joshua 3:1 – 4:9*
13	*The bigger they are…*	*Joshua 6:1–20*

COMFORT ZONES

Bible bit
Joshua 1

Moses led the people of Israel out of slavery in Egypt into the desert, where they have now been for 40 years. But Moses, the well-respected and great leader, is dead. Joshua is now the guy in charge of the Israelites. They're about to cross into the land that God has promised them. So God gives Joshua a bit of a pep talk. He tells him to be big and brave, for God is with him. It's going to be a challenge, but with God on Joshua's side, his confidence grows.

WHAT'S YOUR COMFORT ZONE? YOU KNOW – THE LITTLE CIRCLE OF SAFETY WHERE YOU DON'T HAVE TO DO ANYTHING YOU DON'T WANT TO DO, OR CROSS ANY SCARY LINES INTO NEW AND UNKNOWN TERRITORY... FOR WHICH OF THESE SCENARIOS WOULD YOU FIND IT HARDEST TO STEP OUT OF YOUR COMFORT ZONE AND RISE TO THE CHALLENGE?

Would you **go to a dangerous country as a volunteer?**

Would you **hand out flyers on the high street for a youth outreach event?**

Would you **go and talk to someone who doesn't have any friends?**

Would you **join a new club or team even though you don't know anyone there?**

Would you **sing or play in the worship band at church?**

Would you **try a new flavour of crisps?**

Would you **get up on stage at school to do a speech?**

BIBLE EXPERIENCE

 LEVEL 1: CONNECT

WHAT: Bible exploration with maps
WHY: to encounter the power of God at work
WITH: magazine page 78

1 Chat together about spies. Who do the young people think the best spies in films or on TV are? Which are the worst?! Discuss what spies do and why they do it.

2 Read Joshua 2 to the group and ask them to listen out for what the spies are doing and how they go about it.

3 Give out copies of magazine page 78. Explore the story once again, using the maps and plans to plot what's going on, where the spies travel from and to, where Rahab's house is, etc.

4 This story is full of danger and intrigue, as well as promises made and promises to be kept, but where is God? Ask the group where they think God is at work. Why do the group think Joshua needs to use spies and traitors (Rahab betrays her own people in favour of joining God's people) and armies?

5 Wonder together what you would have done if you had been in Rahab's place. Would the young people have sheltered the spies and asked for their protection? Or would they have turned them in? Would they have trusted in the solid walls of the city and in its king? Or in the invading army and their God?

 LEVEL 2: INTERFACE

WHAT: storyboarding
WHY: to encounter the power of God at work
WITH: art materials

1 Read, or ask a confident reader to read, Joshua 2. Ask the group to try to imagine what's going on in the story as they listen.

2 Ask, 'What is God doing in this story?' Give out pens and paper and ask them to fold their sheet of paper into three. In one third, challenge them to write or draw what God is doing through the spies. In the next third, what God is doing through Rahab; and in the final third, what God is doing through the Israelites at Acacia. Once everyone has finished, share together your thoughts on what God is doing.

3 Give out some more paper and share out your art materials. Challenge the group to pick out the three most important events in the story and illustrate those in three panels of a storyboard. If you have some young people who aren't keen on drawing, pair them up with a more enthusiastic artist to work together.

4 Once everyone has finished, display the artwork and chat about the choices the young people made. Is there a big difference? Or did they choose similar events?

5 Finally, wonder together about what is happening in this story. What is God doing? What does that mean for us? You might get some questions about the threat God seems to pose to the people of Jericho – don't brush these away, but consider them together.

 LEVEL 3: SWITCH ON

WHAT: hot seating
WHY: to encounter the power of God at work
WITH: flip chart or whiteboard, marker pen, Bibles, study Bibles and/or access to the internet, chair

1 Ask the young people what they can recall about the story of Moses and the Exodus. Write all the suggestions on a flip chart or whiteboard. Help them to piece together the story of God's people in the desert.

2 Give out Bibles and turn together to Joshua 2. Read the chapter together and then split into three groups. Assign one group the character of Rahab, one the spies and the other one the city guards. Ask the groups to reread the story and concentrate on the thoughts, actions and words of their character(s). Challenge them to wonder how they felt, why they acted the way they did and what they thought of these events. They can make notes, and use the study Bibles or internet to get extra background on their characters.

3 After about five minutes, draw the group back together and ask for a volunteer from each of the three groups to pretend to be their character. In turn, invite them to sit on a chair in the middle of the group. Encourage all the other young people to ask that person questions. The volunteer should try to answer these questions as if they were their character. If they get stuck, someone from their group can help them to answer.

4 Once you have interviewed your characters, ask the group what they have discovered about the story, the characters and their motivations. What stands out the most? Ask what this story says about God. How was he with Rahab? And the spies? You might start talking about betrayal, destruction and fairness – let the group talk about these honestly and openly. If you still have unanswered questions at the end of your session, invite your church leader to come to the next session to continue the discussion.

RESPOND

 MUSICAL

WHAT: poem writing
WHY: to reflect on the power of God
WITH: guitars and pianos (optional)

1 Challenge the young people to create poems about God's power, referring particularly to the story of the spies and Rahab. When was God with the spies? And when was God with Rahab? The young people can write any kind of poem they like: rhyming or not, acrostic, haiku, limerick... They can write them in pairs or on their own.

2 Depending on the amount of time you have, invite anyone who would like to read out their poems to do so. If you have enough time, encourage the young people to set their poems to music. (If you know you're going to do this from the start, then pair keen writers with keen musicians to form creative teams.)

3 If any of the songs are finished by the end of your time, invite the creators to perform them.

 PRACTICAL

WHAT: praying for others
WHY: to pray for people in difficult situations
WITH: red wool

1 Give out lengths of red wool to the young people and ask them to think about what it represents. It was the spies' promise to Rahab that she would be kept safe.

2 Think together about the people in our lives who are also in dangerous situations. How might they be kept safe, just as Rahab was? Chat about the fact that we might not be able to do anything practical, but we can pray for them. Encourage the young people to choose two or three people they would like to pray for, and to take a length of red wool for each person. Invite them to hold these in their hands and to ask God to show his power and make a difference in those situations.

3 Challenge the group to take the lengths of wool home with them to act as a prompt for them to pray through the coming week for the people they have chosen.

(Note: if there is anything practical you can do to help, which won't put the young people at risk, then explore together what you might be able to do.)

 CREATIVE

WHAT: model making
WHY: to reflect on the power of God
WITH: large sheet of paper or whiteboard, marker pen, modelling clay

1 The story of Joshua, Rahab, the spies and Jericho is one of many in the Old Testament where God shows his power. See if the young people can come up with some of those other stories and write them all down on a large sheet of paper or whiteboard. You could briefly retell (or ask the young people to retell) the stories so that everyone knows what happens in each one. You could talk about the Exodus, Elijah and Elisha, Daniel and his friends, among others.

2 Give out pieces of clay and encourage the young people to make a model of today's story or one of the ones that you have just talked about. Their model should reflect in some way the power of God.

3 As the young people work, chat with them about what they have discovered today about God's power. Be available for any questions they might have. If you can't answer them, be honest, and say that you'll try to find out an answer for the next time you meet.

4 Once everyone is done, if anyone wants to, give time for them to share what they have created and why.

MORE ON THIS THEME:

If you want to do a short series with your group, other sessions that work well with this one are:

10	Be big	Joshua 1
12	Making a mark	Joshua 3:1 – 4:9
13	The bigger they are...	Joshua 6:1–20

WHAT WOULD YOU DO?

Read these dilemmas and decide what you would do if you were the person involved.

1
Jamie is being bullied. Every morning he has to walk past a group of lads who pick on him on his way to school.
What would you do?

2
Ruth is studying to play the piano and is going to be taking her grade 5 exam.
What would you do?

3
Benjamin lives in the bush in Malawi. He has to walk across a dangerous river every day to get to school.
What would you do?

4
Harriet wants to be an actor. She is going to an audition at a stage school. If she gets in, she'll get lots of opportunities to be on stage.
What would you do?

5
Matt is going to see his mum. His mum left his dad when he was small and he only sees her every few months. The past few visits have not gone well.
What would you do?

6
Grace has been suffering from a bad illness. It's had a huge impact on her life, and she's going to see the consultant to see how much she's got better... or worse.
What would you do?

DO YOU THINK GOD IS IN ANY OF THESE SITUATIONS? WHY? WHY NOT?

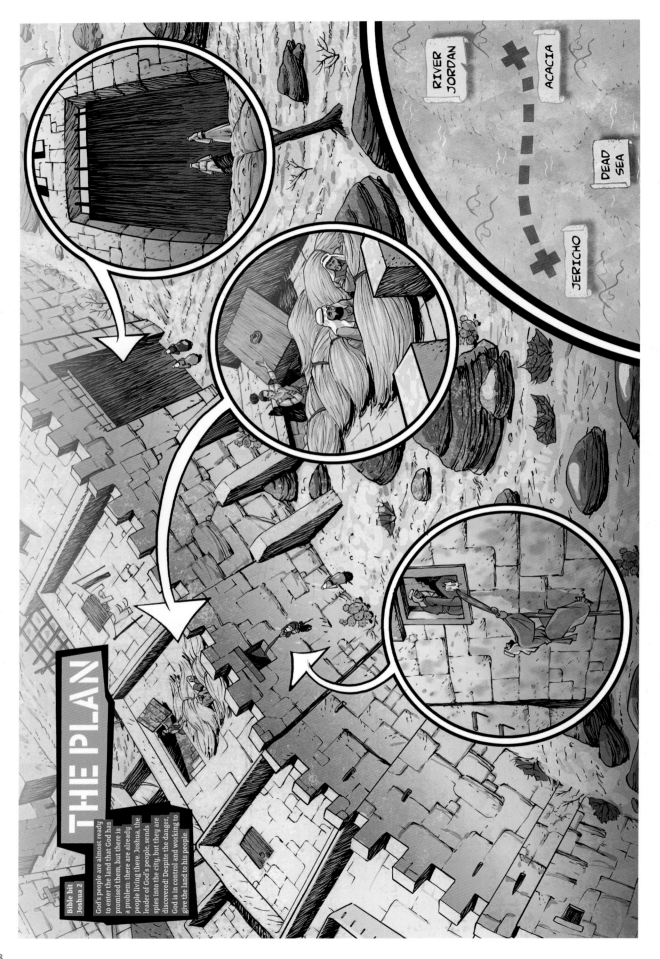

THE PLAN

Bible bit
Joshua 2
God's people are almost ready to enter the land that God has promised them, but there is a problem: there are already people living there. Joshua, the leader of God's people, sends spies into the city, but they are discovered! Despite the danger, God is in control and working to give the land to his people.

RIVER JORDAN

ACACIA

DEAD SEA

JERICHO

MAKING A MARK

THE AIM: To learn to step out in faith because of what God has done

The aim unpacked

The Israelites have a new leader in Joshua, and now it is time to become God's people, stepping out in faith. Our young people face many obstacles as they grow and develop. Moving into adulthood is as alien an experience for them as it was for the Israelites to move into the Promised Land. However, God is with us every step of the way, and that is the faith we need.

WAY IN

 **theGRID MAGAZINE**

WHAT: magazine quiz
WHY: to see how we can overcome obstacles
WITH: magazine page 82

1 On their own, invite the young people to do the 'Choosing the way forward' quiz from page 82. Explain that they should choose a problem to tackle in each situation, and then come up with a solution before moving on.

2 Once they have done this, bring the group together and discuss what solutions they came up with. (This is a light-hearted activity, so don't be too harsh on some of their responses if they are not exactly ethical.)

3 Explain that in today's session, they'll see how a guy called Joshua overcame a huge physical barrier in order to move forward.

 **SCENE SETTER**

WHAT: making your mark
WHY: to look at one way in which we make a mark
WITH: felt-tip or marker pens

1 Explain that graffiti artists often have a stylised way to write their name – 'a tag'. Your group may be able to tell you about some of the local 'tags'.

2 Hand out paper and pens and encourage the young people to create their own individual 'tags'. Explain that their tag should say something about them in its style, and perhaps even represent an event in their lives.

3 Invite the young people to show their tags to the group and explain why they have designed them in that way.

4 Explain that later they'll see how a guy called Joshua made a mark to remember a great event in his and Israel's life. If you choose to go on to *Bible experience* 'Level 1 Connect', they won't hear this part of the story, so you might like to give an explanation at the end about Joshua's response in Joshua 4:1–9 and link it back to this activity.

 **THEMED GAME**

WHAT: game
WHY: to see that many people are known by who they are with
WITH: sticky notes

1 Before the session, prepare some sticky notes by writing the names of famous pairs of people on them – one half of the pair on each sticky note. Make enough for the young people to have one each.

2 Ask everyone to stand in a circle facing inwards. Move round the outside of the circle and put a name on the back of each player.

3 Now challenge the young people to discover who they are and to find their partner. They can only ask questions that can be answered 'Yes' or 'No' – for example, 'Am I female?', 'Am I alive?', 'Am I a singer?', 'Am I one of the Spice Girls?', 'Am I married to David Beckham?' If all the answers were 'Yes', the person would be Victoria Beckham.

4 If appropriate, explain that Joshua was a great man in the Bible, a respected leader of the nation of Israel. He was great and respected because of who he partnered with.

BIBLE EXPERIENCE

 LEVEL 1: CONNECT

WHAT: active learning
WHY: to learn to step out in faith because of what God has done
WITH: list of questions from resource page 84, Bible

1 Invite the young people to stand next to each other in a straight line across one side of the room. Explain that sometimes we need help in life, as God's people did.

2 Ask the questions from resource page 84. If the answer is that they decide without help, they can move one step forward; if they have help from a friend, two steps forward; if they have help from an adult, three steps forward. The 'winner' is the first one to cross the gap (you determine how wide it is beforehand).

3 Talk all together about times when we need help from someone more powerful than us, perhaps sharing a personal example.

4 Read Joshua 3 to the group, preferably from a modern version. Encourage the young people to try to imagine themselves standing at the side of the river as they listen.

5 Explain that the Israelites often needed God's help, and that crossing the River Jordan into the Promised Land was one of those times. Ask the young people to think silently about how often they ask for help.

6 Line the group up across the room again and tell them they are Joshua and the Israelites. This time the gap across the room is the raging River Jordan. Doing things by themselves (taking one step), by letting their friends help (taking two steps), and even letting their parents help (taking three steps), won't help them get across. Explain that it is only by trusting, or having faith, in God that they are able to cross the 'river'. Invite them to cross the 'river'.

7 Explain that sometimes we can't do things on our own. Sometimes the only way to get through something is to have faith in God.

 LEVEL 2: INTERFACE

WHAT: discussion
WHY: to learn to step out in faith because of what God has done
WITH: magazine page 83, Bibles

1 Invite the young people to look at the 'Do you dare?' article on page 83. Challenge them to link up the 'action' with the person who did it – either on their own, or suggest that they work in pairs if they are finding it difficult. After a while, go through the answers.

2 Ask the group which of the actions they would be prepared to do and in what situations. Give them some time to discuss this in pairs and then feed back to the rest of the group. Draw attention to 'Step into a raging river'. Explain that this is what they'll be thinking more about in this session.

3 In their pairs, invite them to read Joshua 3:1 – 4:9. Ask them to identify why the Israelites decided to go through the river. Why were they able to go through the river while it was in full flood?

4 Invite feedback from the whole group. If necessary, explain that the answer is not just that they saw that God stopped the river – it could have started flooding again at any moment. They needed faith in God in order to get to the other side.

5 Explain that the people in 'Do you dare?' had faith: not always in God, but in the fact that what they were doing was right. It enabled them to step out and take a risk. Joshua had faith in God and was able to lead the Israelites into the Promised Land. Ask, 'If we have faith in God, what could we end up doing?'

 LEVEL 3: SWITCH ON

WHAT: Bible study
WHY: to learn to step out in faith because of what God has done
WITH: Bibles, resource page 85 (optional)

1 If you have a large group, split into four smaller groups. If not, decide which of the four viewpoints (from the resource page or step 3) you will look at.

2 Encourage each group to read Joshua 3:1 – 4:9.

3 Give each group one of the sets of questions from resource page 85, or use the ones below. Answer them from the viewpoint of Joshua, the Levitical priests, the people or the men who carried the stones.

- What are the risks for you?
- What are you afraid of?
- What does God ask you to do?
- How does he help you?
- How do you feel after the event?

4 Invite each group to share their answers, and notice any differences in the answers from the different points of view.

5 Remind the young people that this is similar to the start of the Israelites' journey when God's people crossed the Red Sea (Exodus 13:17 – 14:31). Invite the groups to read these verses quickly to recap the story and discuss what the major differences are between that account and this.

6 Invite each group to feed back. Try to draw out that this time the people were not being chased, and that they were going into the Promised Land, not into an inhospitable desert. Explain that God had been with the Israelites for their whole journey and was now giving them the land he had promised. God is with us too, and with faith we, too, can step out into what he has promised us.

7 Finish by reading Hebrews 11:1 to the group.

RESPOND

 MUSICAL

WHAT: listening to music
WHY: to encourage response of mind and heart to God
WITH: appropriate music, playback equipment

1 With the group together, encourage them to get comfortable, ready to listen to some music. Play a melancholic, isolationist song about being alone – such as the Jamie O'Neal version of 'All By Myself' (from the *Bridget Jones's Diary* soundtrack), or 'Eleanor Rigby' by The Beatles. Ask the group to think about how the song makes them feel.

2 Then play and listen to a more upbeat song about interdependence, such as 'Help!' or 'With a Little Help from My Friends' by The Beatles, 'You've Got a Friend' by Carole King, or 'You've Got a Friend in Me' by Randy Newman (from the *Toy Story* soundtrack).

3 After reading today's Bible verses, ask the group to think about which song gives a better picture of what the Christian life should be like. Explain that we can rely on and trust in God, who is our Friend.

4 Spend some time in prayer and invite the young people to talk silently to God about his role in their lives. Encourage them to ask God to give them confidence in their faith, and to take a step forward in trusting him – but don't pressure them. You could play some quiet music while this is happening.

 PRACTICAL

WHAT: challenge
WHY: to remind us to step out in faith because of what God has done
WITH: cross, small stones, Bibles (optional)

1 Invite the young people to sit in a semicircle around the cross. Arrange the stones in a pile around the base of the cross. Explain that because Joshua and the Israelites trusted in God and stepped out in faith, they were able to enter the Promised Land. A pile of stones was arranged as a visual reminder of the crossing of the river. (Recap Joshua 4:1–9 if you wish.)

2 In a time of quiet, ask the young people to think about parts of their lives where they feel challenged, or are struggling. Encourage them to pray silently, asking God to help them.

3 Explain that the best way to cross our 'rivers' is to have faith in God. Remind the group that because of Jesus' death and resurrection we can have a close relationship with God.

4 Invite the young people to take a stone each. Suggest that they put it in their pocket, purse or wallet, or in a place where they will see it regularly. This will be a reminder of what God has done for them, which should encourage them to step out in faith.

5 Close with a prayer such as, 'Lord God, thank you for being with us every day. Please help us to have the faith to step out boldly and do your will, just like Joshua and the people of Israel. Amen.'

 CREATIVE

WHAT: breaking chains
WHY: to break free of anything that is holding back our faith
WITH: strips of paper, Bibles

1 This activity is best done with young people who are already following Jesus. However, it has pointers for those who have not yet taken this step of faith.

2 Remind the group that by Jesus' death and resurrection we are free from everything that has kept us away from God. Symbolically, the 'chains' have been broken.

3 Say that we often hold on to things that God has forgiven us for. This can stop us deepening our relationship with God, because we find it hard to really believe that God would forgive us. Ask everyone to think of anything they feel guilty about and to write these things on strips of paper.

4 Invite the young people to glue the strips together to make one paper chain.

5 Ask everyone to stand in a circle, facing outwards, holding the paper chain. Encourage them to talk to Jesus silently about the things on the strips.

6 Explain that you are going to pray, and when you say 'break', they should 'break out' of the paper chain. Say, 'Dear Jesus, thank you that you came to break(!) the power of sin and guilt in our lives.'

7 Explain that this is a symbol of complete forgiveness and a new start with God. You will need to be aware of where your young people are in their journey with God. For some this will be a renewing of their faith; for others it could be the first time that they are taking this step.

MORE ON THIS THEME:

If you want to do a short series with your group, other sessions that work well with this one are:

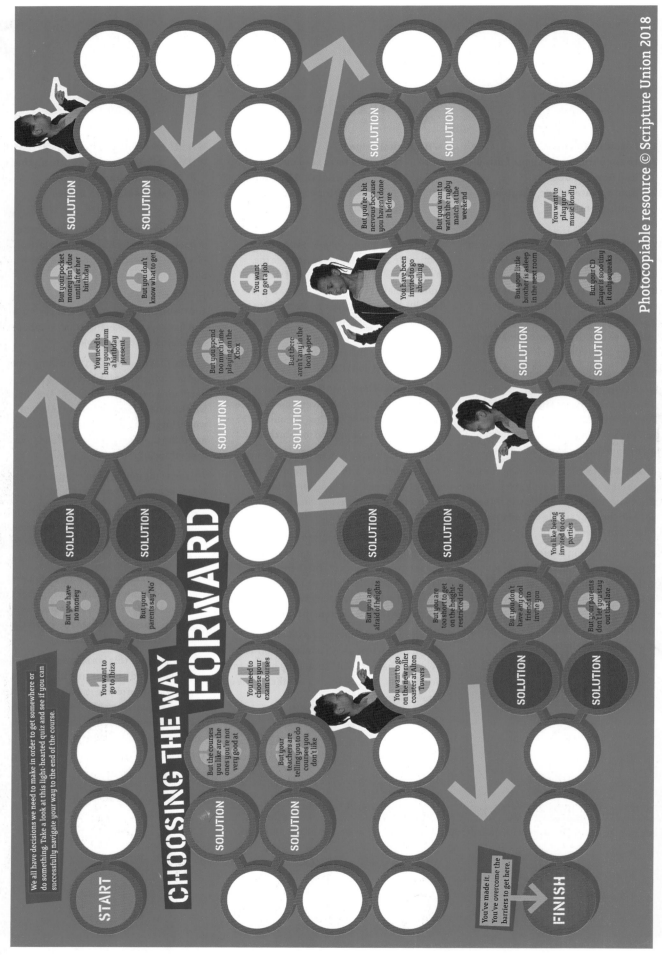

CHOOSING THE WAY FORWARD

We all have decisions we need to make in order to get somewhere or do something. Take a look at this light-hearted quiz and see if you can successfully navigate your way to the end of the course.

START

FINISH

You've made it. You've overcome the barriers to get here.

SOLUTION

You want to go to Ibiza
But you have no money
But your parents say No

You need to choose your exam courses
But the courses you like are the ones you're not very good at
But your teachers are telling you to do courses you don't like

You want to go on the new roller coaster at Alton Towers
But you are afraid of heights
But you are too short to get on the height-restricted ride

You like being invited to cool parties
But you don't have any cool friends to invite you
But your parents don't let you stay out that late

You need to buy your mum a birthday present
But your pocket money isn't due until after her birthday
But you don't know what to get

You want to get a job
But you spend too much time playing on the Xbox
But there aren't any in the local paper

You have been invited to go abseiling
But you're a bit nervous because you haven't done it before
But you want to watch the rugby match at the weekend

You want to play your music loudly
But your little brother is asleep in the next room
But your CD player is so tinny it only squeaks

DO YOU DARE?

Take a look at these things that individuals or groups have done in the past. Which of them would you do? Can you link the event with the person or people who actually did it?

Answers on page 318

Bible bit
Joshua 3:1 – 4:9

Joshua and God's people, Israel, now had to move forward. They stood at the River Jordan, a 'physical' barrier that they needed to overcome. Joshua had faith in God. He had seen all the great things God had done when Moses was leader and now he had faith that God would again do great things.

Paul Rusesabagina

Grace Darling

Step into a raging river?

Volunteer to die in someone's place?

Hide a spy?

Hide hundreds of your enemies?

Go to a country where you can't speak the language?

Fight a giant?

Cycle 80 km for charity?

Row a boat to save sailors?

David

Father Maximilian Kolbe

Israelites in Joshua 3

Rahab

Gladys Aylward

Hundreds of people every year

You can find out more about these people by either looking in the Bible or searching for their names on the web – their stories are fascinating.

Choices

Who helps you choose the following?

- Move one step if you make the decision yourself.
- Move two steps if a friend helps you.
- Move three steps if an adult helps you.

Choosing which socks to wear today.

Choosing which school to go to after Year 6.

Choosing which GCSE options to take.

Choosing which band is your favourite.

Choosing what to eat at dinner.

Choosing when to obey your teachers.

Choosing who to hang around with.

Choosing what to believe.

Choosing a Saturday job.

Choosing what to watch on TV.

Choosing where to go on holiday.

Choosing whether to get a piercing.

Read Joshua 3:1 – 4:9. Answer these questions from the viewpoint of one of or one group of the characters.

Viewpoint: Joshua
- What are the risks for you?
- What are you afraid of?
- What does God ask you to do?
- How does he help you?
- How do you feel after the event?

Viewpoint: Levitical priests
- What are the risks for you?
- What are you afraid of?
- What does God ask you to do?
- How does he help you?
- How do you feel after the event?

Viewpoint: The people
- What are the risks for you?
- What are you afraid of?
- What does God ask you to do?
- How does he help you?
- How do you feel after the event?

Viewpoint: The men who carry the stones
- What are the risks for you?
- What are you afraid of?
- What does God ask you to do?
- How does he help you?
- How do you feel after the event?

13

THE BIGGER THEY ARE...

THE AIM: To be encouraged that God can overcome the mighty

The aim unpacked

Here we see the people following God's command and being rewarded for doing so. In our lives we often come up against seemingly insurmountable problems or issues. Jericho would have been similarly daunting for the Israelites, but they followed God, took on the mighty and overcame them.

WAY IN

 **theGRID MAGAZINE**

WHAT: problem pages
WHY: to think about issues young people face
WITH: magazine page 89

1 Give out copies of page 89 and ask the young people to read the letter to Damien and his response.

2 Ask the young people what they think about Matt's letter, and discuss their thoughts about Damien's advice to him.

3 In pairs or threes, challenge the young people to fill in the blank 'Dear Damien' letters with other issues that young people face. Once they have done this, invite them to swap magazine pages with another pair or three and write responses to each other's letters.

4 Gather the young people back together and ask each pair to give feedback to the whole group on the issues that have been raised. (This can be a very helpful exercise in getting to know the issues your group is concerned about.)

5 Explain that everyone has problems and issues in life and that, in this session, they will see how to deal with them. There's a much more effective way than listening to frauds like Damien!

 **SCENE SETTER**

WHAT: discussion
WHY: to let the young people express their SIPs – 'Seemingly Insurmountable Problems'
WITH: whiteboard or large sheet of paper

1 On a whiteboard or a large sheet of paper, write up the heading 'SIPs' – 'Seemingly Insurmountable Problems'.

2 Discuss with your group issues and problems that they think young people face. (Encourage them to think globally as well as in their own country/culture.)

3 Invite the young people to write their answers on the whiteboard or paper. Here are some ideas in case they are stuck: relationships – friends, family; image – clothes, hair, weight; school – work, exams, teachers; free time – social life; poverty – at home and globally. This activity will need to be handled sensitively as there may be members of your group who suffer with some of these issues. If so, provide an opportunity for some one-to-one time during your session.

4 For further information on this whole topic, you could look at the websites for charities such as Save the Children, Christian Aid, Tearfund or ChildLine that offer help and advice on issues at home or abroad.

5 Explain that in today's session you'll be looking at Joshua and the Israelites who had their own 'SIP'!

 **THEMED GAME**

WHAT: graffiti wall
WHY: to establish some of the big issues facing young people
WITH: large sheet of paper, art materials, games or bricks or boxes (optional)

1 Paint the outline of a brick wall on a large sheet of paper – wallpaper is ideal (about 2 m by 2 m).

2 As the young people arrive, explain that later they'll be thinking about how we can break down the walls or barriers in our lives that can hold us back. But first invite the young people to add graffiti to the wall on the subject of 'problems and issues' that young people face in today's world.

3 Keep this on display and return to it at the end of the session. Invite the young people to pray for the situations that are listed.

4 If you have a large group, have some games of giant Jenga or Lego® or Duplo bricks around for the young people to play with while they are waiting to add to the wall, or a pile of old shoeboxes that they can use to build a 3D wall.

BIBLE EXPERIENCE

 LEVEL 1: CONNECT

WHAT: poetry, drama and art
WHY: to be encouraged that God can overcome the mighty
WITH: magazine page 90, Bibles, graffiti wall (optional)

1 If your group did either the 'graffiti wall' or 'discussion' option from *Way in*, have another look at it together and see what problems and issues the young people have written. Clarify with them if necessary what some of the issues actually are. Then explain that Joshua and the whole of Israel had another 'Seemingly Insurmountable Problem' of their own.

2 Read Joshua 6:1–20 aloud to the group, perhaps from the *Dramatised Bible* or a modern paraphrase. If your group likes acting, they could act out the events. Allocate people to be the Israelites, Joshua, the priests and the city/people of Jericho. Encourage the group to develop a football-style chant for the moment when the wall falls down.

3 Give out copies of page 90. Ask for a volunteer to read the poem 'Up the wall'. In the light of the Bible verses you have just explored, invite the young people to think, either to themselves or discussing in pairs, about what the poem is saying.

4 Discuss together what the Israelites did about their problem of entering Jericho. (They were obedient to God's instructions – although those instructions must have seemed a bit odd!)

5 Conclude this activity by saying that we can do the same. When we face issues that seem too big for us to handle, we need to have faith and trust in God and ask him what he wants us to do.

 LEVEL 2: INTERFACE

WHAT: thinking, searching and discussing
WHY: to be encouraged that God can overcome the mighty
WITH: Bibles, small prize (optional)

1 Divide your young people into pairs and give each pair a pen, some paper and a Bible.

2 Ask them to read Joshua 6:1–20 and write down all the numbers they can find in the verses. (There are numbers in verses 3, 4, 5, 6, 8, 11, 13, 14, 15 and 16.)

3 Challenge the pairs to create a 'giant' mathematical sum, using all the numbers and whatever equations they can think of. Give them a couple of minutes in which they must use all of the numbers and reach the answer '1' (or as close as they can). If your young people are not fans of numbers and struggle with this challenge, give them a minute and then use this as an example of the 'Seemingly Insurmountable Problem' Joshua was facing!

4 Let the pairs share their sums and, if you wish to, offer a prize for the most creative or the closest equation to the answer '1'.

5 Explain that Joshua and the Israelites were coming up against their first big obstacle in their conquest of the land God had promised them. But God had promised them that they would take Jericho, and had also told them how to do it. Say that we can come up against many obstacles, pressures and worries in our lives. Just as God helped the Israelites, he has promised to help us too. We can pray and ask God to help us, and he will. So when we're faced with difficult problems or situations, the answer, like the great mathematical sum, is '1' – God. We should be encouraged that God can overcome the mighty, as he did in Jericho, and he can also help us overcome our issues.

 LEVEL 3: SWITCH ON

WHAT: Bible study
WHY: to be encouraged that God can overcome the mighty
WITH: Bibles

1 In pairs or small groups, ask the young people to read Joshua 6:1–20. If they wish, they can also read verses 21–27 to find out what happened to Rahab.

2 Invite them to list all the main characters in the narrative. Discuss their answers with the whole group. They should have: God, Joshua, Israelites, priests, the people of Jericho, and Rahab.

3 Ask the pairs or small groups to think about what role each of these characters played – what they actually did during the events.

4 For all of the characters, apart from God, they should now list how they think they were feeling, at these times in the story:

- before anything happened
- during the marching
- when the walls came down

5 Bring everyone together and obtain feedback on what emotions they believe were evidenced in the narrative.

6 Now explore the emotions the story brings out in the young people. Ask them to think silently about the following:

- How does the story make you feel about problems or issues in your life that you want to overcome?

RESPOND

 MUSICAL

WHAT: writing improvised music and lyrics
WHY: to understand that God can help us overcome issues
WITH: musical instruments, soundproofed room!

1 Explain to the group that in the 1960s, protest music, such as the song 'We Shall Overcome', was popular. The idea of this was to speak out against issues, often political, through words and music. Can the group think of any current protest bands or protest songs?

2 Remind everyone of this session's Bible verses. Now invite them to improvise a dramatic interpretation of the story through music. Drums, tambourines and cymbals would be ideal, and, of course, trumpets, if anyone in your group plays one!

3 Alongside this, another group could write some lyrics based on the Bible verses, to be read between bursts of improvised sounds or to accompany it. Be prepared for a lot of noise here and allow for freedom of expression!

4 Listen to the compositions and then pray, giving God thanks for helping us overcome our 'big issues'.

5 You could also sing a song together, based on today's theme of having confidence in God's ability to overcome the mighty, or God being with us in all of life's problems and dilemmas. Encourage use of the musical instruments and improvised percussion while you sing! Some suggestions are:

- 'Everyone Needs Compassion (Mighty to save)' by Reuben Morgan and Ben Fielding
- 'Blessed Be the Name of the Lord' by Clinton Utterbach
- 'Strength Will Rise as We Wait upon the Lord' by Lincoln Brewster

 PRACTICAL

WHAT: prayer wall
WHY: to visualise how God answers our prayer
WITH: roll of plain wallpaper or large sheet of paper

1 This is an ideal follow-up activity to the graffiti wall in the *Way in* section. Alternatively, start one now by painting a brick wall on a large sheet of paper – wallpaper is ideal.

2 Invite the young people either to read what they have already written on the wall, or to bring any problems they or others may have – anything they want help to overcome – and write them on the wall. If you used this activity as a starter, ask the young people if they want to add anything to the wall after seeing what God did to the walls of Jericho.

3 Explain that Joshua and the Israelites overcame a serious barrier in their lives by trusting and obeying God. Likewise, if we trust and obey God, we can face and overcome our problems. Like Joshua, it may be in a different way to what we expect.

4 Pray together for the items on the graffiti wall, asking God to overcome the problems. You can do this either in silent prayer or, if your group is confident enough to speak out loud, each praying for one item.

5 Leave the graffiti wall up for the next few sessions and take a moment or two each session to pray for each item, or, if there has been an answer to prayer, to cross out that item. You can also add more items. Eventually you will see that God is knocking down the 'wall' and overcoming the barriers in the young people's lives.

 CREATIVE

WHAT: drama
WHY: to visualise a response to today's subject
WITH: suitable props (optional)

1 If your group is large, you may like to split into smaller groups of four or six for this activity.

2 Ask the young people to give a brief account of the events in this session's Bible verses – just to refresh their memories!

3 Now give them an opportunity to create and act out a contemporary version of this story. These improvisations could explore the subjects of faith, trust and obedience to God. Encourage them to present a piece that has a problem situation that is resolved.

4 After they've had time to prepare, draw the group back together and watch any of the sketches that the young people want to share. Finish by praying, thanking God that he is there for us to trust, and that he will help us in all our problems.

MORE ON THIS THEME:

If you want to do a short series with your group, other sessions that work well with this one are:

DEAR DAMIEN

(HE LOVES HIMSELF SOOO MUCH!)

Dear Damien

How you doin'? Me? I'm not doing so well at the moment. So many issues messing up my life! I guess I'll start at the beginning. First off – well, there's the 'parent problem'. As ever they're driving me nuts – don't like my hair, my clothes, my friends or my 'attitude' as they call it. In fact, I wonder if they like me at all some days! Being 13 is just so hard. Then all my mates tell me I'm becoming 'reclusive', just because I like to shut myself in my room and listen to my music. Ugh! Life! Please help, you are sooo cool!

Cheers, Matt

Hi Matt

This is the coolest dude on earth here getting back to a fellow 'life struggler'. Parents, eh? Who'd have 'em?! Still, hang on in there, mate. Stay calm, don't let them hassle you. Be yourself, they'll get used to it! And your mates – well, they should get some style, if you know what I mean – music is cool, music is mean, music is life!

**Checking out,
Damien**

DEAR DAMIEN

PROBLEM:

FROM:

DEAR

ANSWER:

FROM DAMIEN

DEAR DAMIEN

PROBLEM:

FROM:

DEAR

ANSWER:

FROM DAMIEN

DEAR DAMIEN

PROBLEM:

FROM:

DEAR

ANSWER:

FROM DAMIEN

UP THE WALL

My head spins,
full of so much information.
I feel like I'm going 'up the wall'!
So many issues and problems to deal with.
My mind is running amok.
What to do,
how to do it,
when to do it?
All these questions, and thousands more, fill my head.
Spinning and whirling, seemingly endless.
Who should I trust, who should I turn to?
Where in the world can I find peace?

© Jane Wade 2005

Bible bit
Joshua 6:1–20

Jericho was the first big obstacle to taking the land that had been promised by God to Israel. It probably seemed like a huge insurmountable problem, but the Israelites did what God told them to do (even if it was a bit bizarre), and were rewarded for doing so.

Are there things in your life that seem too great to overcome? With faith and trust in God, those issues can come tumbling down, just like the walls of Jericho – though perhaps not always as easily or dramatically!

WALL DIVIDERS

BERLIN WALL

– a fortified wall surrounding West Berlin, built in 1961 to prevent East German citizens travelling to the West. Its demolition in 1989 marked the end of the Cold War. (Cold War – the hostile yet non-violent relations between the former Soviet Union and the United States and its respective allies, from around 1946 to 1989.)

JERICHO

– a walled town in the West Bank in the Jordan Valley. It is regarded as the world's oldest town, with remains dating back to 8000 BC. According to the Bible, it was destroyed by Joshua after he led the Israelites back from captivity in Egypt.

HADRIAN'S WALL

– a fortified wall built from the Solway Firth to the mouth of the River Tyne in the early second century AD as a defence against invasion by the Picts. It was built on the orders of the Roman Emperor Hadrian and marked the northern boundary of the Roman Empire.

(All of the above information is taken from the *Encarta World English Dictionary*, published by Bloomsbury Publishing PLC, 1999.)

14

STARTING OUT

THE AIM: To realise that God's holiness is absolute and he is not to be messed with

The aim unpacked

In today's passage, we focus specifically upon the character and holiness of God – symbolised by the Ark of the Covenant. We see how Uzzah, through a small act, shows disrespect to God by touching what God has commanded must not be touched – and pays a high price. This incident would have been a defining event in David's reign and relationship with God.

WAY IN

 theGRID MAGAZINE

WHAT: animal quiz
WHY: to introduce the consequences of not treating things with respect
WITH: magazine pages 95 and 96

1 Give everyone a copy of pages 95 and 96, and look at the descriptions and pictures in the 'World's deadliest creatures!' quiz.

2 Divide the group into pairs or threes and challenge the young people to put the animals in order of deadliness, with number one being the most dodgy and number ten being as deadly as a cute little pussy cat (well, almost!).

3 Ask the groups to feed back what they thought. Check out the answers together and see who got the most right.

4 Make the point that we should be careful what we go round touching! Sometimes not treating certain things with respect can have deadly consequences.

 SCENE SETTER

WHAT: cola challenge
WHY: to experience something in its purest form
WITH: different brands of cola, disposable cups, labels

1 In advance, buy between three to six different varieties of cola, including one brand-named version and a number of diet or budget versions. Pour out some cups of each type and label them with numbers 1 to 6, keeping note for yourself of which is which.

2 One by one, invite the young people to have a small taste of each of the colas.

3 Give everyone some paper and ask them to write which they think was the 'real thing' – the brand-named cola.

4 Reveal the results of the vote. For an added challenge, ask them to guess some of the other ones – for example, the diet cola, a supermarket own brand, the budget/value cola, etc.

5 If appropriate, say that whether they recognised it or not, they tasted one of the colas in its purest form. Today's session will be looking at what happens when we experience true purity.

 THEMED GAME

WHAT: object game
WHY: to introduce the idea that some objects shouldn't be touched
WITH: an assortment of random objects, small prizes

1 Have an assortment of about 15 to 20 completely random objects laid out in the room (for example, a teapot, a glove, a pen).

2 Ask for a volunteer to go out of the room (and earshot). While they are out, the rest of the group chooses one of the objects that is the 'oops' object.

3 Invite the person to come back in the room and ask them to pick out three objects. If they manage to choose three that do not include the 'oops' object, they win a small prize. If they choose the 'oops' object, the entire group should shout 'Oops!' and the person fails to receive a prize.

4 Repeat the game several times if you have time, choosing different objects.

5 Ask the young people if there are any 'oops' objects in their home or school which they aren't supposed to touch. Why? Did anything bad happen when someone touched them?

BIBLE EXPERIENCE

 LEVEL 1: CONNECT

WHAT: discussion and article
WHY: to realise that God's holiness is absolute and he is not to be messed with
WITH: whiteboard or flip chart, magazine page 94

1 Make a list together of the sort of attributes and personality the most powerful being in the universe might have (for example, the power to move an entire solar system with his little finger).

2 With a different-coloured pen, circle the ideas that you feel are applicable to God – making the point about how powerful and huge God is.

3 Draw a (rough) picture of the Ark of the Covenant (or just a box). While you do this, explain to the group that God gave David power and made him king. At first he was the ruler of a place called Judah and then he took over all of Israel, which included the capital city, Jerusalem.

4 Read 2 Samuel 6:1–11 as a group. Then give out copies of magazine page 94 and invite the young people to read the article called 'What's in the box?'

5 Go back to the drawing of the Ark of the Covenant, or the box. As a group, think of words to do with the Ark of the Covenant. You might like to suggest that it was a visible symbol of God's presence, holiness, purity and power, and a reminder to treat God with respect.

6 As you do this, ask the young people if anything in this story makes them feel a bit uncomfortable – for example, Uzzah's death. Does anything make them more aware of God's holiness and power? What is their response to that?

 LEVEL 2: INTERFACE

WHAT: questionnaire
WHY: to realise that God's holiness is absolute and he is not to be messed with
WITH: magazine page 94, resource page 97, clip from *Raiders of the Lost Ark* (optional)

1 Read 2 Samuel 5:4–12; 6:1–19 together. Then ask a volunteer to read out the 'What's in the box?' article from page 94.

2 Ask if anyone has seen the Indiana Jones film *Raiders of the Lost Ark*. If so, ask someone to recap what happens when the people open the box. If possible, you might like to show this clip to the group (it's near the end of the film).

3 Explain that although the film is fiction, the idea of not messing with what is holy (ie the Ark of the Covenant and, more importantly, God himself) is real. It's easy for us to think that God is just like some kind of fluffy puppy that meets our needs. We can easily forget that the God described in this passage is the same God we worship today, and he is not to be messed with.

4 Hand out copies of the questionnaire from resource page 97 and encourage the young people to fill it in individually.

5 Reread 2 Samuel 6:1–11 to the group. Point out that Uzzah died because, in his haste, he forgot to show God the respect that God had commanded. We, too, need to take a close look at our lives and check that we are showing God the respect he deserves.

 LEVEL 3: SWITCH ON

WHAT: Bible study and discussion
WHY: to realise that God's holiness is absolute and he is not to be messed with
WITH: Bibles, resource page 98

1 Ask a couple of volunteers to read 2 Samuel 5:4–12; 6:1–19. Ask the young people if they know what was in the Ark of the Covenant and why it was so important. Explain if necessary (see the information in Levels 1 and 2).

2 Divide the young people into pairs or threes and give each a copy of resource page 98. Allocate each small group one or two of the passages to read and ask them to discuss the questions together.

3 Come back together and ask each group to feed back their answers. Conclude by making the point that God's holiness demands a respectful response from us.

RESPOND

 MUSICAL

WHAT: listening to music
WHY: to respond to God's holiness
WITH: CD or MP3 of 'Miracle Maker' by Delirious? (from the album *Now Is the Time: Live at Willow Creek*), playback equipment

1 Get hold of the Delirious? track, or another worship song about God's holiness.

2 Invite the young people to make themselves comfortable in a space on their own. Encourage them to close their eyes or look away from others and imagine that they are standing in front of the Ark of the Covenant – just as David and the others did so long ago.

3 Play the track and invite the young people to spend time in reflection and prayer as they listen. Challenge them to respond to God as they feel they should in the presence of a Holy God.

 PRACTICAL

WHAT: prayer and worship
WHY: to consider whether our lives show that we worship a holy God
WITH: pre-made box to represent the Ark of the Covenant, envelopes, worship music (optional)

1 Before the session, get hold of a largish box. The box will represent the Ark of the Covenant. If you have time, you might like to decorate it elaborately – a bit of gold paint or paper should help. Make sure the top is taped shut.

2 Then ask the group, 'Can people tell by looking at our lives that we live with respect for a Holy God? If this really was the Ark of the Covenant, how would you want to respond?'

3 Encourage the young people to consider, if they were able to respond to God's presence in some way, what their response would be.

4 Hand out pens and paper. Invite the young people, if they wish, to write a letter to God, put it in an envelope and stick it to the outside of the box. You may want to put a worship track on at this point. Remind them they can touch this box without dying!

5 After a few minutes, close by praying for the group, thanking God for his holy presence with you and asking him to help you be more respectful towards him.

 CREATIVE

WHAT: visual reminders
WHY: to make a reminder of God's holiness
WITH: small blank boxes, craft materials

1 Beforehand, gather together a wide range of craft materials – for example, paints, coloured paper/card, felt tips, foil and fabric. If possible, include recycled materials and/or objects from nature, such as pebbles, flowers, leaves and small twigs.

2 Give everyone a small blank box. Recap that the contents inside the Ark of the Covenant were reminders of God's holiness and power as shown to the Israelites.

3 Invite the young people to create something from the materials provided that will be a personal reminder to them of God's power and holiness (they don't need to explain it to anyone else). They may want to draw a picture that reminds them of a time they powerfully met with God; others may want to write a Bible verse onto a stone, and so on. If they have time at the end, they may like to decorate the box, but encourage them to spend more time on the contents.

4 Alternatively, if you don't have access to a wide range of materials, challenge the young people to find or create mementos at home during the week. You may then like to spend more time decorating the box during the session.

MORE ON THIS THEME:

If you want to do a short series with your group, other sessions that work well with this one are:

15	*Thinking big*	*2 Samuel 7*
16	*Doing well*	*2 Samuel 9*
17	*Going wrong*	*2 Samuel 11:1 – 12:15*

WHAT'S IN THE BOX?

Bible bit
2 Samuel 5:4–12; 6:1–19

Our God is really… nice. I mean REALLY nice. He's always there to give us a hug when we need one and, of course, to answer our prayers (especially those urgent ones when we've done something we shouldn't). Except, that isn't the whole truth of it…

You see, David learned that as well as being all-loving, God is all-powerful and very, very holy. In fact, he's so pure that if you mess with him – well, let's just say the outlook wasn't too good for Uzzah when he forgot to give God the full respect that God had commanded. So if you want to keep with the idea of a nice fuzzy God – best not read today's Bible bit. You might get a shock…

What do you think is in this box?

How come this box-type thing that the Israelites had was so powerful? Did it have some kind of nuclear device in it or something that gave a zillion-volt electric shock when people went near it?

Well, not exactly. You see, there was nothing particularly amazing about the box itself. In fact, it was basically… a box. It's what the box stood for that made it so powerful.

God himself had said that, right there, in between the two angel type things on the very top of the box, he would actually be present. No hologram. No cool 3D cinema illusion. God himself right there between the two angels on the box. Be careful how close you get!

This box had stuff in it that were symbols of the fact that God was (and is) number 1.
Not to be messed with. Purer than even the purest volcanic water and more powerful than a trillion nuclear power stations put together. The things inside it were reminders.

There were:
- the stone tablets of the Ten Commandments (version 2.0 – the first lot was smashed up)
- the staff that Aaron and Moses used when they needed to prove to Pharaoh who was the real boss
- some manna – the food that God miraculously provided to feed the Israelites in the desert

If the box went somewhere, it was a sign that God was there too.
No one messed with the box. If you wanted to hold it, you held it with two poles – you certainly never touched it. Touching it was like thinking you were big enough to touch God – not a good idea. In fact, they didn't even call it 'The Box'. They called it 'The Ark of the Covenant' – or as we might say, the reminder of God's promise to be with his people.

Approach with caution…

WORLD'S DEADLIEST CREATURES!

So you thought your teacher was scary! Check out the creatures below and see if you can rank them from 1 to 10 in terms of just how deadly they are (number 1 being the most scary and number 10 being still pretty scary but not quite as dangerous). The descriptions are there to help you match them up – enjoy!

1 This has caused at least 5,500 deaths since 1954. Most people die before they reach the shore. They live in the seas around Asia and Australia.

2 This is the world's longest venomous snake. One bite can kill a human. In its spare time it enjoys eating other snakes and killing elephants with just one sting.

3 This might look harmless, but one drop of this little critter's venom can kill up to 20 humans.

4 This little fella is only the size of a golf ball. Its bite is painless but it carries enough venom to kill 26 adults.

5 Despite the dodgy name, the venom of this creature is more likely to cause unbearable pain than to kill.

6 These ugly-looking things don't usually kill but can cause so much pain that people who have been bitten beg for the affected limb to be amputated.

7 This is responsible for more human deaths than any other of its kind. And it wanders all over the place…

8 This is the world's most venomous snake: one bite could kill 100 humans or an 'army' of 250,000 mice. However, the good news is that it's shy so it tends to avoid people.

9 Don't be fooled by the nice colours on this creature. It's only 5 cm long but has enough venom to kill ten humans. If you even touch this baby it could be curtains for you.

10 For some reason, despite the fact that it can kill you, some people eat this as a delicacy. Chefs have to be licensed to cook it. One slip of the knife and the poison kills you between 4 and 24 hours after eating.

- Marbled cone snail
- Death stalker scorpion
- Box jellyfish
- Stonefish
- The Brazilian wandering spider (or banana spider)
- Blue-ringed octopus
- Poison dart frog
- Puffer fish
- King cobra
- Inland taipan (snake)

Answers on page 318

REMEMBER: BE CAREFUL WHAT YOU TOUCH OUT THERE!

Put a circle around the number that is most true for you. Be honest! You don't have to share your answers with anyone else if you don't want to.

I only really pray when I really need something from God.

Not at all true				Sometimes true				Definitely true	
1	2	3	4	5	6	7	8	9	10

I try not to mention to my mates at school that I am a Christian.

Not at all true				Sometimes true				Definitely true	
1	2	3	4	5	6	7	8	9	10

I come to church because I have to; I'm not sure I really believe all this stuff.

Not at all true				Sometimes true				Definitely true	
1	2	3	4	5	6	7	8	9	10

I use God's name like a swear word without it meaning much.

Not at all true				Sometimes true				Definitely true	
1	2	3	4	5	6	7	8	9	10

I pick and choose which bits of the Bible to believe in and obey, so it doesn't mess up my life too much.

Not at all true				Sometimes true				Definitely true	
1	2	3	4	5	6	7	8	9	10

I like church more because of my mates here and the social stuff we get to do rather than all the God stuff.

Not at all true				Sometimes true				Definitely true	
1	2	3	4	5	6	7	8	9	10

Exodus 3:1–6

How can we show respect to God in our worship?

Which people in the past (or present) have inspired you to live a life that honours God?

Exodus 33:7–9

What places do you go where you know you can completely focus on God and hear from him?

How can you separate out time to do this on a regular basis?

What was the after-effect on Moses of spending all this time meeting with God?

Isaiah 8:11–13

What sorts of things are other people around you (who aren't Christians) afraid of? What do they spend their time thinking about?

In what ways should you, as a Christian, be different and why?

Revelation 15:3,4

What is God's holiness all about?

What kinds of things in the world today do you think are the opposite of God's holiness?

In your life, how could you stand up for what is holy?

THINKING BIG

THE AIM: To hear how elated David was by God's plans for, and promises to, his family

The aim unpacked

David's plan was not in line with God's — it was not the right time to build the Temple — but this was not bad news, as God used this opportunity to make a promise to David that his descendants would continue to lead Israel. Use the activities today to help the young people empathise with David and to understand that David was blown away by this promise — the promise of a secure future!

WAY IN

theGRID MAGAZINE

WHAT: discussion
WHY: to share good news!
WITH: magazine page 102

Invite everybody in the group to share a piece of good news. What has been the best thing about life over the past week/month/year?

Allow time for the young people to share stories together and then hand out copies of page 102.

Encourage the young people to fill in the three boxes at the top of the *The Daily Grid* template with their good news stories. The larger space at the bottom will be used in the *Bible experience* section.

Explain that today they will be hearing about some good news God gave to David.

SCENE SETTER

WHAT: celeb spotter!
WHY: to empathise with David's feelings of surprise at God's plan
WITH: bowl or box

1 Give out pens and paper and ask everyone in the group to draw their favourite celebrity (or any famous figure — they could be fictional or historical), without showing anyone else who they have drawn. The picture need not be accurate, but should be recognisable (they can include the person's name if necessary!).

2 Fold the drawings in half and place them all in a bowl or box in the centre of the room. Jumble them up and then invite each person to take one (it doesn't matter if they pick out their own — but they mustn't give it away!).

3 In turn, try to guess from the picture which person drew it. Some will be obvious, but look out for surprises!

4 Reveal the illustrators of each picture and then discuss whether there were any surprises. Relate this to David's feeling of surprise as he talked to God about his plans for the future.

THEMED GAME

WHAT: blindfolded!
WHY: to explore how it feels to take an unexpected change in direction
WITH: blindfolds, obstacles (for example, chairs)

1 Do this activity in pairs or, if you have a large group, ask for two volunteers to demonstrate to everyone else.

2 Let the young people look carefully around the room and explain that one person will need to be blindfolded and the other will need to guide them from a start to a finish point.

3 Blindfold the volunteer(s) and then add some obstacles to the route (making sure that the guide(s) do not give away the change).

4 The guides must then direct the blindfolded to the finish point (safely around the obstacles!) using only words.

5 Once finished, reflect with those who were blindfolded whether they were surprised by the route taken. How did it feel to face something unexpected?

BIBLE EXPERIENCE

 LEVEL 1: CONNECT

WHAT: newsflash!
WHY: to hear how elated David was by God's plans for, and promises to, his family
WITH: Bibles, magazine page 102, small rewards (optional)

1 Read the story from 2 Samuel 7 in advance and then paraphrase or retell the story to the group as creatively as possible (you could use different voices for the characters, or act it out with a co-leader).

2 Invite the young people to reflect on what they thought about the story as you discuss it with them and ask them questions. You could make this fun by explaining before telling the story that they will be quizzed on it afterwards. Then ask questions with no 'correct' answers (such as 'What was your favourite bit?'). You could offer a small reward (such as a sweet) to each person who gives an answer.

3 Invite the young people to use the bottom half of 'Read all about it!' on page 102 to summarise the story in a journalistic style using their own words. They might like to work in pairs or small groups. Alternatively, they could use the space to draw a comic strip.

4 Invite them to share their summaries, and finish by asking how they think David felt at the end of the story.

5 If you used *Way in 'theGRID* magazine', continue the discussion by asking, 'How was David's feeling of excitement similar/ different to how we felt about our good news?'

6 If you did not use *Way in 'theGRID* magazine', use the three sections at the top of the newspaper template to describe how David felt (for example, elated), why he felt like this (for example, because of God's promise), and what he did to show it (for example, he praised God).

 LEVEL 2: INTERFACE

WHAT: retelling the story
WHY: to hear how elated David was by God's plans for, and promises to, his family
WITH: Bibles

1 Divide the young people into small groups and invite them to read the passage together. If your group would prefer smaller chunks, ask half the group to read verses 1 to 17 and the other half to read verses 18 to 29.

2 Summarise the passage together by asking one person to offer two to five words about the beginning of the story. Then ask the next person to add their words about the next part. Repeat this until you reach the end of the story.

3 Give out pens and paper and ask the young people, back in their groups, to create a mind map of the passage, referring to their Bibles and writing words to describe God's promise in one colour (key words or short phrases only), and words to describe David's response in another.

4 Swap the sheets between the groups to reflect on the story together – did all the groups choose the same words? What do they like about the words/phrases the other groups used? How do God's message and David's response fit together? Can they match up words/phrases in the two colours?

 LEVEL 3: SWITCH ON

WHAT: Bible study
WHY: to hear how elated David was by God's plans for, and promises to, his family
WITH: Bibles, magazine page 103

1 Help everyone find 2 Samuel 7 in their Bible and read the passage together as a group. Where appropriate, stop for questions, encouraging all the young people to engage with the text. Let them know it is OK to ask if something needs explaining, and ask your own questions to gauge what they think or understand of the passage.

2 Share the aim of the session with the young people, and give them time to go through the passage on their own or in pairs, underlining words or verses that underpin the aim (for example, verses 9,12,13,15,16,19,25,26). After some time, invite them to feed back their choices to the rest of the group.

3 Ask the group to consider what they can learn from this passage about the Lord, and then about David. They can use 'The Lord unwrapped' and 'David unwrapped' on page 104 to record their thoughts, either in words or in illustrations.

4 Finish by looking at 2 Samuel 7:25,26. Ask the group, 'How did the fulfilling of God's promise bring glory to his name?'

RESPOND

 MUSICAL

WHAT: songs of praise
WHY: to praise God as David did
WITH: Bibles

1 Reread 2 Samuel 7:18–29 as a group, perhaps from a couple of different Bible versions.

2 Encourage the young people to choose phrases from the passage that praise God, and use David's words to produce a song of worship to God. You could use a familiar tune, changing the existing words to ones from the passage. If more appropriate for your group, write a poem or rap of praise instead!

3 If you have time, add extra verses to your song, praising God for the good news we have heard today (and for any other good news we have heard recently), just as David did.

4 If possible, you could record or perform your song of praise, or teach it to a younger children's group or the whole church congregation!

 PRACTICAL

WHAT: share and prayer
WHY: to develop listening skills, encouraging and praying for one another

1 Explain that the surprise of this passage is, in some ways, not a surprise. God's plan is full of unexpected twists and turns that don't always fit with our plans and preferences.

2 In pairs or threes, encourage the young people to talk to one another about God's plans for their lives – do they have any ideas about what they might be? Does it excite or frighten them that God has a plan? What has been great or difficult so far? Has God surprised them at any stage? Would they like to be surprised? What's good and what's hard about surprises? How is God's plan for them going so far?

3 Monitor these discussions closely, and encourage the young people as they chat. Pray together to close, asking that God would help each of us to be quick to praise God for his plan, even when it is surprising!

 CREATIVE

WHAT: praise paper chain
WHY: to create something using our words of praise to God
WITH: strips of coloured paper, Bibles

1 Starting with the Bible passage, encourage the young people to look for words to describe God or how we feel about him. Then encourage them to use these to inspire their own words about God.

2 Write each word on a strip of coloured paper. Use as many as you can!

3 Connect the strips together by forming interlinking loops for a praise paper chain! See how long you can make it by adding as many words as possible. While they are adding each word, encourage each young person to explain why they have chosen that word. This gives them an opportunity to reflect and consciously offer it as praise to God.

4 Finish by praying a prayer of praise to God, using parts (or all if you have time) of the paper chain.

5 Display the chain prominently, and if appropriate, ask other members of the church to add to the chain.

MORE ON THIS THEME:

If you want to do a short series with your group, other sessions that work well with this one are:

14 *Starting out* *2 Samuel 5:4–12; 6:1–19*

16 *Doing well* *2 Samuel 9*

17 *Going wrong* *2 Samuel 11:1 – 12:15*

Bible bit
2 Samuel 7

David was all set in his role as king, and suddenly he realised that God needed a house! However, God was quick to tell David that was not his current priority. Instead, God needed to give David some good news – that he had great things in store for David's descendants.

David was thinking about the present, but God had his eye on the future. David's plans were redirected by God, who knew that his Temple wouldn't be built for some time yet.

You might think that David would feel a bit cheesed off by this. There he was coming up with a really good idea, wanting to do something for God and to acknowledge that, although David was king, God was even greater than David. Yet God says not now. Does David feel rejected or discouraged? Not at all! Instead, he listens carefully to God's message, and then rejoices! Straight away, he makes sure he says thanks for what God has promised.

READ ALL ABOUT IT!

Congratulations! You've just been appointed as *The Daily Grid*'s top writer! What will you include on the front page of your debut edition? Fill in the three boxes at the top of the page with stories of your own good news.

THE DAILY GRID

Use the space at the bottom to tell the story of 2 Samuel 7. How would people at the time have reported this news?

15

What's the low-down on David and God? As you've been reading 2 Samuel, what have you learned? Use the spaces below to make a profile for both God and David using all that you've read and discussed. You can add to this page in future sessions as you continue to explore their story.

THE LORD UNWRAPPED

DAVID UNWRAPPED

THE LORD'S CHARACTER

THE LORD'S WAY OF DOING THINGS

DAVID'S CHARACTER

DAVID'S WAY OF DOING THINGS

WHAT THE LORD IS PLANNING

WHAT THE LORD WANTS

WHAT DAVID IS PLANNING

WHAT DAVID WANTS

16
DOING WELL

THE AIM: To see how David was overwhelmingly kind to a man who was disabled

The aim unpacked

Saul was dead. David was no longer fleeing for his life; he was now officially king of Judah. His enemies had been defeated; the kingdom was his to command, yet… his burning desire was to show kindness to someone — anyone! David emulated the indiscriminately kind nature of God, proving yet again that he really was 'a man after God's own heart'.

WAY IN

 **theGRID MAGAZINE**

WHAT: kindness quiz
WHY: to introduce the theme of kindness
WITH: magazine page 107

1 Give out copies of page 107 and pens.

2 Invite the young people, independently or in pairs, to complete the 'Random acts of kindness' activity.

3 Once completed, ask if anyone can remember the last time someone showed them an act of kindness.

4 Finish by introducing today's theme, looking at one of David's acts of kindness.

 **SCENE SETTER**

WHAT: pass-the-parcel game
WHY: to introduce the theme of giving to others
WITH: wrapped-up prize parcel, music, playback equipment

1 Prepare a pass-the-parcel in the usual way by wrapping a prize in multiple layers of paper with a sweet or small reward inside each layer.

2 Seat the group in a circle and start playing some music. Pass the parcel around the circle clockwise until the music is stopped randomly by a leader who is blindfolded or looking the other way.

3 Now explain that there is a twist! Instead of opening a layer, they have to give the parcel to someone else to open and have the sweet.

4 Start the music again and continue until someone wins the final prize.

5 Explain that the point of the activity was to show that it is often in our nature as humans to want to keep things for ourselves rather than to give things away. Sometimes to act kindly is not natural, but is something we have to work at.

 **THEMED GAME**

WHAT: sharing game
WHY: to introduce the theme of giving to others
WITH: prize, smiley faces, music, playback equipment

1 In advance, create and copy enough smileys for three or five each, then cut out the same amount again (so if you make 50 for the group make another 50 and hide them).

2 Explain that the aim is to give away all your smileys by playing 'Rock, Paper, Scissors' with others. The losing player gives a smiley to the winner then finds someone else to play.

3 If someone gives away all their smileys they are out. The person with the most smileys at the end wins the prize.

4 Try to play until one person is out. Stop playing and ask everyone to count their smileys.

5 Identify the person who is out or who has the least smileys. Remind the group that you said the person with the most smileys wins, but you also said the aim was to give them all away. Because this person gave away the most, you're going to give them all your smileys (the hidden ones).

6 Give them the prize, then say that real kindness is giving without expecting anything in return.

BIBLE EXPERIENCE

 ## LEVEL 1: CONNECT

WHAT: dilemma discussion
WHY: to see how David was overwhelmingly kind to a man who was disabled
WITH: magazine page 108, Bibles

1 Give out copies of magazine page 108 and ask everyone to look at the 'Kindness conundrum'.

2 Invite the young people to read through the activity in pairs and to consider what option they think Luke should go for. Allow time for feedback and discussion as a group.

3 Read or summarise 2 Samuel 9 to the group, explaining that David was a king who was now exercising his power to do whatever he wanted in his new kingdom.

4 Ask the following:

- What does David's kindness tell us about his relationship with God?
- What do you think David's response would be to the other driver in the scenario?
- Would God want to punish the driver for his bad behaviour or would he want to forgive him and bless him with something that he doesn't deserve?

5 Make the point that this passage about David's kind nature also shows us that God's nature is one of kindness and amazing grace. We don't have to earn God's love; we just have to accept it.

6 Finish with a short time of prayer, and offer to talk to anyone who would like to know more about what accepting God's love means.

 ## LEVEL 2: INTERFACE

WHAT: drama and discussion
WHY: to see how David was overwhelmingly kind to a man who was disabled
WITH: copies of the sketch from resource pages 109 and 110, props, Bibles

1 If possible, have competent actors rehearse the sketch beforehand. Give each person a copy of the sketch from resource pages 109 and 110.

2 Perform the sketch to the group. Alternatively, read it through in pairs.

3 Ask the young people for their reaction to the sketch. What do they think about the lawyer sacrificing himself for the criminal?

4 Read 2 Samuel 9 as a group.

5 Explain that the lawyer's kindness to the criminal in the sketch is symbolic of David's kindness to Mephibosheth. See if the young people can come up with parallels between the two. (For example, both were undesirable – the criminal was a thief, Mephibosheth was disabled; it wasn't their idea – their saviours came to where they were.)

6 Make the point that both these examples are symbolic of how overwhelmingly kind God is to us as human beings. Close with a prayer and offer a time to ask further questions if needed.

 ## LEVEL 3: SWITCH ON

WHAT: Bible study
WHY: to see how David was overwhelmingly kind to a man who was disabled
WITH: Bibles

1 Ask a few volunteers to read 2 Samuel 9.

2 Ask the young people what they think is the difference between mercy and grace. (Mercy is letting someone off something and requiring something from them. Grace is giving someone something they don't deserve and requiring nothing from them.) Ask them: which attribute does this story show? Why?

3 Explain that this passage introduces the theme of grace both to the Old Testament people and to all humankind. The instructions God had given to his people so far were all about the balance of justice and mercy.

4 Ask the young people to get into pairs or small groups and think about the following questions based on 2 Samuel 9:

- In what ways does David represent God and Jesus?
- In what ways does Mephibosheth represent humankind?
- What is the significance of Mephibosheth being disabled? (He is unable to come to where David is; he would have been shunned by society; he would have been an inconvenience to David's servants.)

5 Have time for feedback as a group. Ask the following question for the whole group to discuss: 'What does David's overwhelming kindness tell us about God?'

6 Finish with a time for prayer and reflection on how our actions should demonstrate the overwhelming kindness of God.

RESPOND

 MUSICAL

WHAT: reflection
WHY: to think about our own level of kindness
WITH: worship music, playback equipment

1 Have some appropriate worship music that speaks of God's love, mercy or kindness to create a reflective mood. Some songs you could listen to or sing together include:

- 'Great Is Your Faithfulness (Unchanging)' by Chris Tomlin
- 'All My Days (Beautiful Saviour)' by Stuart Townend
- 'Amazing Grace' by John Newton

2 Ask the young people to find a space on their own and to sit quietly. Have pens and paper available for them to use if they wish. Explain that you are going to play one of the songs again and they should use the time for some personal reflection.

3 Ask them to think honestly about their own life and whether they say or do kind things. Does their kindness reflect the kindness of God?

4 You may like to finish by singing another song to thank God for his kindness, or by praying that God would help them show his kindness to others.

 PRACTICAL

WHAT: acts of kindness
WHY: to think about showing kindness to others
WITH: whiteboard or flip chart

1 Ask for a volunteer to write down suggestions on the whiteboard or flip chart.

2 Invite from the young people ideas for practical acts of kindness that they could do over the next week – things that they wouldn't normally do, such as saying something encouraging to someone, or offering to do a household or garden chore.

3 Once you have a few suggestions, decide the best (and most appropriate or realistic) two or three and suggest them as practical acts of kindness for the whole group to try and do over the next week or so.

4 Repeat the exercise using a different colour on the same flip chart sheet or whiteboard. This time, come up with ideas for people you could show kindness to. By the end you should have a few appropriate ideas for acts of kindness with suggested names of who to do them for.

5 Finish by reminding the group that any act of kindness they do for someone else is actually an act of worship towards God.

 CREATIVE

WHAT: making wristbands
WHY: to remember God's kindness and show it to others
WITH: bracelet/wristband-making materials, arty person or instructions

1 If you, another leader or a confident young person in your group is into craft, or you know someone who could come along to instruct the group, choose a technique you know for making bracelets or wristbands. Alternatively, look in a craft book (from a craft shop or look up instructions online), and make sure you practise the technique before you demonstrate it to the young people.

2 Gather the materials you need. This could be coloured wool or embroidery thread for knotting or plaiting in the style of friendship bracelets, or recycled fabric or plastic bands with buttons or pop fasteners on the ends. Make sure you have enough materials for at least one wristband each.

3 Show the group how to make a wristband.

4 Get the young people into pairs or threes and encourage them each to make a wristband for someone else in the group. Make sure that everyone has a wristband made for them.

5 Encourage the group to wear their wristband to remind them of the kindness God has shown to them, and to remember to show kindness to others.

MORE ON THIS THEME:

If you want to do a short series with your group, other sessions that work well with this one are:

RANDOM ACTS OF KINDNESS

Ever helped an old woman across the road?
Ever helped a mum with a pushchair on the bus?
Well, here's your chance to have your moment of recognition.
Which of the following have you done?

- Given someone else the biggest slice of cake
- Helped someone across the road
- Told someone they had some food stuck in their teeth
- Donated money to charity
- Sat next to someone who looked lonely

- Helped someone on or off the bus
- Given someone your last sweet or chocolate
- Not uploaded an embarrassing picture of someone onto the web
- Given up some of your time as a volunteer
- Not looked at a disabled person as if they were from another planet
- Told someone something nice about themselves

- Given up your seat for someone else
- Held the door open for someone
- Did some fundraising for charity or something in your community
- Bought someone a present even when it wasn't their birthday
- Given a homeless person your gloves

SO HOW DID YOU DO? WHAT ELSE HAVE YOU DONE THAT WAS KIND?

If you ticked most of these then give yourself a pat on the back.
You're either very kind or just happened to be in the right place at the right time.
If you didn't do so well, don't worry... there are opportunities every day for showing kindness.

Give it a go!

KINDNESS CONUNDRUM

Luke was driving to work one morning when someone drove through a red light and smashed into his car. Fortunately no one was hurt, but both vehicles were beyond repair. When Luke went to see if the other driver was OK, the other driver accused Luke of being the one who went through the red light. Fortunately for Luke, the driver behind him saw the whole thing and offered to be a witness.

A few months later, the other driver took Luke to court and falsely testified against him so they could try to sue him for thousands of pounds in compensation. Thanks to the witness, however, Luke's innocence was proven and the case was dismissed. But the insurance claims still had to be settled, so Luke now had a decision to make…

What should he do next?

Bible bit
2 Samuel 9

Despite being God's true anointed king, David spent several years on the run from the ever-jealous and murderous King Saul. Everybody in Saul's family had been turned against David, except for Saul's son Jonathan who made a secret friendship with David. Although it would not have been popular with those in his new court, David decides that he wants to show extreme kindness to Saul's family out of honour for Jonathan, who had sadly died because of his father.

The only descendant that can be found is Mephibosheth, the son of Jonathan, who David discovers is heavily disabled. In biblical times, anyone with a disease or disability would have been looked down upon. David not only gives Mephibosheth's household all their land back, but he invites him to 'eat at his table' from that day forth – an honour that only the son of a king would normally receive.

Mephibosheth was from the family of David's greatest enemy who had repeatedly tried to murder David – yet David still chooses to go out of his way to show overwhelming kindness and acceptance. This was an act of amazing grace!

WHAT DO YOU THINK?

Some of the options may seem a bit too kind and extremely unlikely. Option 5 is particularly unthinkable, but in 2 Samuel 9 we see an example of this level of kindness from King David to Mephibosheth, the grandson of Saul. Saul had been David's greatest enemy and had caused him a lifetime of suffering, yet David had only kindness in his heart. Pretty incredible, huh?

1 Luke should play the other driver at their own game and lie about having a neck injury to receive extra compensation.

2 Luke should take the other driver to court and try to sue them for reasonable compensation.

3 Luke should forgive the driver and not take him to court, but demand that his insurance excess is paid by the other driver's insurance company.

4 Luke should settle for a 50/50 compensation where both drivers have their insurance excess increased.

5 Luke should buy the other driver a new car as a gift.

Drama sketch: Ultimate kindness

Scene: *Person 1 is a guilty criminal (wearing prison-type jacket with convict number 31617 pinned to the back) in a foreign police cell awaiting their sentence.*

Person 2 is a legal representative (wearing smart jacket). They haven't met before.

Props: *Table, chair, contract (a sheet of paper), telephone.*

Set-up: *Two chairs on opposite sides of a table with a phone on the table. Person 1 is sitting down at the table.*

Person 2: *(Comes in and goes to shake 1's hand.)* Good morning, I'm your legal representative.

Person 1: *(Stares with attitude, ignoring 2's gesture.)*

Person 2: *(Takes jacket off, puts it on the back of the chair and sits down.)* I'm here to inform you of the government's verdict.

Person 1: *(Ignores 2.)*

Person 2: Look, you may as well speak to me. I could be the last English person you speak to.

Person 1: Unlucky me, huh?!

Person 2: Oh, you do speak then. See, that wasn't so ba…

Person 1: *(Interrupting)* Just give me my phone call.

Person 2: Phone call! I'm afraid you don't get a phone call.

Person 1: But there's a phone.

Person 2: That's for internal use only.

Person 1: Look, I know my rights, and I'm entitled to a phone call.

Person 2: You're not in Britain any more; the law is different here.

Person 1: So how do I get out of here then?

Person 2: I'm afraid it's not that easy. The man you stole from is very important over here… and very powerful.

Person 1: So?

Person 2: So he wants to make an example of you… he wants you…

Person 1: What?

Person 2: He wants you executed.

Person 1: Executed! *(Standing up, angrily)* NO! THEY CAN'T DO THAT! *(Then more scared...)* Tell them they can't do that.

Person 2: I can't! It's the law over here; every sin must be punished.

Person 1: Why did you come to see me then?!

Person 2: Because there may be a way out. I have here a document of confession. *(Takes the paper out of his jacket pocket and slides it across the table.)* If you sign it, it should sort things out.

Person 1: What do you mean? How will it sort things out?

Person 2: Don't worry about the details; I don't have time to explain. Do you want to go free or not?

Person 1: Well, of course I do, but what's the catch?

Person 2: Look, in one minute they will be coming for you. They will torture you in public and then execute you!

Person 1: OK, fine... give me that thing then. *(He signs it.)* There. OK... now what? *(Looking scared.)*

Person 2: Now you go. Just walk through that door. I've already made the arrangements.

Person 1: But how...?

Person 2: That's my job.

Person 1: *(He goes to walk off.)*

Person 2: Oh, one more thing – don't forget to leave your jacket.

Person 1: *(He takes his jacket off but feels that something isn't quite right, but eventually hurries off.)*

Person 2: *(Waiting until 1 has gone, he picks the phone up.)* This is cell 14. Prisoner 31617 is ready for execution. *(Then he takes the confession and rips it up, puts on 1's jacket which has the numbers 31617 on it and sits down to wait.)*

(Lights go dim – if possible.)

THE END

Bible: 2 Samuel 11:1 – 12:15

GOING WRONG

THE AIM: To hear that God did not give up on David, even when he broke God's rules

The aim unpacked

David is famous for having done a lot of stuff right. But wow, when it came to Bathsheba, he went very, very wrong! In a moment of weakness and arrogance, David utterly abused his God-given authority and had a good man murdered just so he could steal his wife and have a child with her. One of the key messages in this passage is that God forgives the sin, but David must still live with the consequences.

WAY IN

theGRID MAGAZINE

WHAT: rules activity
WHY: to introduce the theme of rules and their importance
WITH: magazine page 114

1 Give out copies of page 114 and pens.

2 Ask the young people to work individually or in pairs to complete the 'Following the rules' activity.

3 Ask the group, 'Was it easy or difficult to follow the rules? Did you break any, and if so, how did you feel about breaking them?' While these rules were silly, talk together about rules that the young people think are important, and find out what their attitudes towards keeping or breaking them are.

4 If appropriate, explain to the group that today's passage looks at some severe consequences of breaking rules.

SCENE SETTER

WHAT: secret rule game
WHY: to think about following rules
WITH: chairs

1 Seat everyone in a circle on chairs.

2 Say, 'I'm going to the seaside and I'm taking a… [bucket and spade].'

3 Going clockwise, ask the person next to you to repeat the first part of the phrase and then say what they will bring to the seaside.

4 Tell them whether they are coming or not. Explain that there is a rule concerning who goes and who doesn't, but you can't say any more. (The rule is that anyone who has their legs or arms crossed while saying the sentence is going to the seaside.)

5 Go on to the next person and repeat the same thing. Keep going round the circle until most people have figured out what the hidden rule is and are going to the seaside too! If no one has figured it out after a while, give big hints by exaggerating your movements.

6 Explain that in the game, they got somewhere by following a rule, even though they didn't know what it was. Say that in today's Bible passage, King David knew what the rules were, but didn't follow them.

THEMED GAME

WHAT: game with a twist
WHY: to build upon the theme of rules and the need for them
WITH: any necessary game equipment

1 Play a game that your group are familiar with, such as football, dodgeball or tag. If you have a smaller group or less space, you could play a card game such as Uno, or a board game. Start by playing as normal with all the usual rules.

2 After every minute or so, stop the game and change or get rid of one of the rules.

3 Continue like this until finally you say that there are no longer any rules for this game.

4 There will be (and should be) pandemonium – that's the idea! Keep a close eye on general safety and call an end to the game before it is too out of hand.

5 It will probably be quite obvious, but make the point about how this game illustrates the importance of rules. Without rules there would be chaos.

6 If appropriate, explain that in this session they will be looking at the chaos caused when King David acted as if there were no rules.

111

BIBLE EXPERIENCE

 LEVEL 1: CONNECT

WHAT: magazine activity
WHY: to hear that God did not give up on David, even when he broke God's rules
WITH: magazine page 115, Bibles

1 Read 2 Samuel 11:1 – 12:15 together as a group.

2 Ask the young people for their initial reactions to the passage. What parts stick out for them? Are they surprised at all? Why?

3 Explain that although David suffered the consequences for his actions, God still allowed him to be king. David broke nearly all of God's rules (the Ten Commandments) in one go, but God did not give up on David; he forgave him and continued to be with him.

4 Ask the group to think about these two rhetorical questions:

- If you or a friend did something really terrible, like David did, do you think God would forgive you/them?
- Do you think God would ever give up on someone? Do you think he ever has?

5 Give out copies of page 115 and get everyone to read through the 'If God gave up on us' activity individually.

6 Bring everyone back together and discuss their thoughts together.

7 Close in prayer for the group. (There will be an opportunity in the *Respond* section for the young people to respond further.)

 LEVEL 2: INTERFACE

WHAT: Bible study and discussion
WHY: to hear that God did not give up on David, even when he broke God's rules
WITH: Bibles, resource page 116

1 In small groups, invite the young people to read 2 Samuel 11:1 – 12:15 together.

2 Ask them:

- On a scale of 1 to 10 (10 being worst) how bad was David's sin?
- How is it made worse by the fact that he was the king?
- Do you think God's punishment was a bit harsh?

3 Give out copies of resource page 116 that lists 'The Ten Commandments'. Read Exodus 20 and explain that everyone in Israel at that time would have known these rules.

4 Back in their small groups, ask the young people to look back through the passage to see which of these rules David broke. Hopefully, the conclusion should be that David broke more than half of the commandments in one go.

5 As a group, ask: 'Do you think David should have continued to be king? Why do you think God kept David as king?'

6 Wrap up by saying that when we make mistakes, like David, we have to live with the consequences. But if we turn to God, he will forgive our sin. Just like with David, God will not give up on us.

 LEVEL 3: SWITCH ON

WHAT: discussion and sharing
WHY: to hear that God did not give up on David, even when he broke God's rules
WITH: Bibles, whiteboard or flip chart

1 Ask a couple of volunteers to read 2 Samuel 11:1 – 12:15.

2 Ask the group where they think David broke the rules in this passage. Why? List all their ideas on the whiteboard or flip chart.

3 Say that David actually first went wrong in verse 1. Can they see how? (He stayed in Jerusalem.) Explain that, as king, David should have been leading his army – he did in every other instance and was successful. He wasn't where he was supposed to be. The first rule he broke was not an obvious one or a really sinful one.

4 Ask the young people to get into pairs or threes and share a time when they were in trouble.

5 Now ask them to think back to where the trouble started. Where or when did it first start going wrong for them? Are there any patterns? If possible, feed back as a whole group, without requiring the young people to share anything too personal or specific.

6 Say that temptation can often come at us when we are at our weakest or most vulnerable. In David's case he was in his palace, probably bored, and he did not have his men around him; he was alone.

7 Ask the young people to think about the areas in their lives where they are weakest. What makes them vulnerable? Is it when they are bored? When they are on their own? When they are angry? Disappointed? Sad?

8 Back in their pairs or threes, encourage the young people to share these areas and think together about what they might be able to do to help prevent temptation, or to deal with it. Have a short time when they can pray for each other in their groups.

RESPOND

 MUSICAL

WHAT: musical reflection
WHY: to know that God forgives sin and is still with us, despite what we've done
WITH: CD or MP3 of 'Ocean Floor' by Audio Adrenaline, playback equipment, song lyrics

1 Invite the young people each to find their own space to relax in.

2 Explain that the song is called 'Ocean Floor' and talks about how God not only takes away our sin, but he also forgets it. When we give our sin to God it is gone for ever, just like something thrown into the ocean and never seen again.

3 Play the song and encourage the young people to close their eyes and imagine a deep, dark ocean as they listen to the words. You might like to invite them to confess any sins they are worried about and imagine God throwing their sins into the dark waters.

4 Play the song again and encourage the group to sing along with the chorus in worship to God, thanking him for his amazing forgiveness.

 PRACTICAL

WHAT: forgiveness prayer
WHY: to confess sin and know God's forgiveness
WITH: envelopes, paper or card

1 In advance, prepare enough envelopes for one per person, with the words 'I have sinned against the Lord' written on them. Also prepare some sheets of paper or card with these words on: 'The Lord has taken away your sin' (2 Samuel 12:13). Put one sheet of paper or card into each envelope and seal them.

2 Invite the young people to sit on the floor in a space of their own. Give everyone an envelope and say that they should not open it yet.

3 Explain that you are going to say a prayer of confession and if anyone would like to echo that prayer, they can repeat each phrase after you – either silently or out loud.

4 Read the following prayer (or use one of your own), pausing for the young people to echo each phrase:

- Dear God… I confess that I have sinned… Please forgive me… for all the things I have done wrong… Help me to be right with you again… Thank you for never giving up on me…

5 Then say that everyone can open their envelopes. Encourage anyone who said that prayer to keep what's inside as a reminder of what God has done for them today.

 CREATIVE

WHAT: painting
WHY: to show how continuous God's forgiveness is
WITH: large sheets of white paper, black paint, paintbrushes, floor protection

1 Make two posters in advance. One sheet of paper should have the words 'I have sinned against the Lord' as large as possible printed across it, in white lettering with a black background. The second sheet of paper should have the words 'The Lord has taken away your sin' printed across it, in black lettering on a white background.

2 Give everyone two sheets of paper and make sure everyone has access to pencils, paint and paintbrushes. You may want to put down newspaper or plastic sheeting to protect the floor.

3 Invite everyone to make their own versions of the two posters. Make sure you end up with an equal number of each.

4 Once they are finished and dry, display the posters alternately – preferably in a circle around a room, or in a long line. Explain that this is a symbol of how continuous God's forgiveness is.

5 Close with a short prayer, thanking God that he forgives, no matter how many times we make mistakes.

MORE ON THIS THEME:

If you want to do a short series with your group, other sessions that work well with this one are:

FOLLOWING THE RULES

See if you can follow these simple instructions and rules... as best you can:

1. Grab a pen and write your name in the space below with your non-writing hand.

2. Keep hold of your pen for the rest of this activity.
3. Write your age in the top right corner of the big square above.
4. Cross your legs and keep them crossed for the rest of the activity.
5. Write your shoe size in the top left corner of the square.
6. Shout out your name as loud as you can.
7. Write the number of pieces of clothing you are wearing in the bottom left corner of the square.
8. Close one of your eyes and keep it closed for the rest of the activity.
9. Add all the numbers in the square together and write the answer in the bottom right corner.
10. Turn to the bottom of this page for the last rule.

So how did you get on?

Did you follow all the rules?

Was it easy or difficult to follow them?

Were there any rules you ignored completely?

Do you generally follow rules or do you break them?

OK, so these rules were just a silly test, but some rules are important, and there are consequences if they are broken.

Have a think about some of the different rules that surround your life.

Are rules necessary?

11 Completely ignore instructions 1–10.

IF GOD GAVE UP ON US

WE DO SOMETHING REALLY BAD (SIN AGAINST GOD BY BREAKING HIS RULES)

God will never give up on us. God's love, acceptance and forgiveness are some of life's greatest constants. But because they are always there, sometimes they can be taken for granted. Sometimes to appreciate the things we have, it helps to think about what life would be like if we didn't have them.

Below is a flow chart to show the contrast in our lives if God were to give up on us.

GOD GIVES UP ON US

God lets us carry on as we are –
We carry on unaware of our mistakes or why we feel guilty

God ignores us –
Any prayers we might make are ignored

God does not forgive us –
We are not forgiven

God does not take away our sin –
We are left with our feelings of guilt and sadness

God chooses to remember our sin –
We can never escape what we did

God does not comfort us –
We are left feeling worthless and a failure

God rejects us as his children –
We do not know his love

God refuses to give us any more guidance –
We are not allowed to read the Bible any more

God will never speak to us again –
We can't feel God's Spirit any more

God wipes us from the face of the planet –
We are wiped out from the Earth

God condemns us for all eternity –
We cannot enter heaven to be with God

God has completely given up on us

GOD DOES NOT GIVE UP ON US

God shows us where we have gone wrong –
We have the chance to accept and understand our mistakes

God allows us to approach him –
We can pray to God for forgiveness

God forgives us –
We are forgiven

God takes away our sin –
We are free from guilt and sadness

God chooses to forget our sin –
We can start afresh

God comforts us –
He gives hope and tells us he has a plan for us

God reaffirms us as his children –
We can know his unconditional love

God guides us and helps us –
We can read the Bible and learn to be wise

God continues to speak to us –
He speaks to us through his Spirit

God reaffirms his commitment to humankind –
We will never be wiped from the Earth

God offers us salvation for all eternity –
We can enter heaven and be with God

God will never give up on us

The Ten Commandments

From Exodus 20, here are the Ten Commandments that God gave to Moses. All of God's commands and instructions (hundreds of them) were summed up in these ten straightforward rules for all of humankind to follow.

1 Do not follow any other God.

2 Do not worship idols.

3 Do not misuse the name of the Lord.

4 Keep the Sabbath holy.

5 Honour your mother and father.

6 Do not murder.

7 Do not commit adultery.

8 Do not steal.

9 Do not lie or deceive.

10 Do not want what isn't yours.

18

MY WAY OR THE HIGHWAY

THE AIM: To learn that worship of our Holy God is a serious matter

The aim unpacked

Solomon, the wise king, was now in a position to build the Temple which was to be the focus of the worship of God. The Temple was a mega-construction project and required only the best materials and workers. As we try to live holy lives for God, we should strive to offer the best in our holy worship of him.

WAY IN

 **theGRID MAGAZINE**

WHAT: art
WHY: to think about a place for worship
WITH: large sheets of paper, magazine pages 120 and 121

1 Imagine you have been commissioned to design a new church building. Tell the young people that they have been asked to help as junior architects.

2 Set a few parameters, such as size of the congregation, cost, sound system and visual aid needs, how much parking will be necessary, catering requirements and so on. (You could simply make it for your current congregation if you wish.)

3 Refer the group to pages 120 and 121, with its list of ecclesiastical terms. The young people may wish to use some of these for labelling their diagrams.

4 Give the young people time to work on their designs in small groups. After a while, gather everyone back together and invite each group to present their design.

 **SCENE SETTER**

WHAT: discussion
WHY: to think about how we address people

1 With the group together, explain that we all have different roles in our lives. We are all sons and daughters. When the young people are at school they are students. They all have parents or guardians, and so on.

2 Ask the young people, in pairs, to list as many roles as they can. Challenge them to find roles for which the people concerned must be addressed in particular ways. For example, a king or queen is addressed as 'Your Majesty'; a local doctor is addressed as 'Dr [Whatever]'.

3 Invite them to feed back their lists to the whole group. Explain that the roles people hold sometimes demand that they be addressed in a certain way. In this session, we'll be looking at how we should address God.

 **THEMED GAME**

WHAT: building game
WHY: to have fun with the theme of building
WITH: building blocks, wind-up kitchen timer or similar, prize (optional)

1 Challenge the young people to build the highest tower by balancing bricks on each other. They can do this as a head-to-head challenge – individually or in teams. Don't give them any idea how long they have for the exercise. Give them between ten seconds and two minutes, timed with a wind-up kitchen timer or an egg timer. If you cannot find one of these, use some other way to stop after a short, random amount of time (like a dice or a blindfolded volunteer shouting 'stop').

2 The winner is the team or person with the highest tower when the timer goes off. If you play this a few times you will need to keep score so that you can award a prize to the person who wins overall.

3 If appropriate, explain that you'll be looking together at a big building project this session.

BIBLE EXPERIENCE

 LEVEL 1: CONNECT

WHAT: re-enactment
WHY: to learn that worship of our Holy God is a serious matter
WITH: ceremonial music (such as 'Pomp and Circumstance', 'Zadok the Priest' or 'Fanfare for the Common Man'), fancy Bible, streamers, ornate cushion, smoke or dry ice (optional)

1 The verses in 1 Kings 8:1–13 show the culmination of the magnificent lengths to which Solomon and his people went to provide an appropriate place for the Ark.

2 Explain that the people in Solomon's day felt that the Ark was the most holy thing and deserved a holy ceremony, so it was kept in a holy place. Today, we believe that God's Word, the Bible, is the most holy of things.

3 Recreate a pompous procession carrying a Bible (opened at 1 Kings 8) on an ornate cushion. Shout acclamations (choose some from Psalm 84); wave the streamers and play the ceremonial music. If possible, use smoke or dry ice effects. March round the room a few times.

4 Invite someone to read 1 Kings 8:1–13 out loud, with due splendour.

5 Discuss what these ceremonial activities say about how the people felt. Do we manage to recreate such splendour today? If so, when? If not, why not?

6 End with a further ceremony to read 1 Kings 8:61.

 LEVEL 2: INTERFACE

WHAT: worship
WHY: to learn that worship of our Holy God is a serious matter
WITH: flip chart or whiteboard, marker pens

1 Make a list on the flip chart or whiteboard of all the things the young people can think of that God has done for them, beginning with the general things he has done for all people and moving on to specific things he has done for them as individuals. Make sure the work of Jesus (as summarised by John 3:16, for example) is covered here.

2 Now come up with as many ways as the young people can think of to say thank you to somebody, or to respond to a nice gesture. Encourage them to come up with imaginative answers – for example, skywriting 'Thank you' or composing a song of gratitude.

3 In pairs, invite the young people to discuss this question for a couple of minutes:

- Worship is an imaginative act of thanks. Given what you know God has done for you, how would you like to respond?

4 Ask a volunteer to read 1 Kings 8:54–61 to everyone and then ask if they can add any more ideas to the flip chart or whiteboard.

5 Working in small groups, ask the young people to devise a realistic act of worship of about one hour in length. They should take about 15 minutes to map this out, going into as much detail as they can in that time.

6 Bring them together to share their ideas. Might you have an opportunity to use any of these plans in services or acts of worship at your church or with your group?

 LEVEL 3: SWITCH ON

WHAT: Bible study
WHY: to learn that worship of our Holy God is a serious matter
WITH: magazine page 122, Bibles, art materials, large sheets of paper or lengths of wallpaper

1 Explain that the Temple was built by King Solomon, the Old Testament king most identified with being full of wisdom. Suggest that the wisdom of mockers and cynics is often more readily heard these days than the wisdom of prophets or preachers. Give out copies of page 122 and invite the young people to read the sneering, anti-Christian (but funny) comments that are scattered around the page.

2 Invite the young people to think of some wisecrack answers in response to these statements, beginning with the expression, 'Yeah, but…'

3 Ask a volunteer to read 1 Kings 8:1–13, 54–61 aloud to the group.

4 Encourage everyone to think of a decoration to go in a church that summarises biblical wisdom. The aim is to produce a piece of high-class, imaginative, biblical art to rival the sneering in the magazine. Hand out art materials and large sheets of paper or lengths of wallpaper. Invite the young people to turn their thoughts into artwork on the banners.

5 Look together at 2 Chronicles 2–6, the parallel passage to the verses from 1 Kings. Rather than reading the whole section, ask the young people to skim through it and point out to each other any remarkable things they see about the complexity and ornate nature of Solomon's Temple.

6 Explain that Solomon's Temple showed how seriously the Israelites took the worship of God. Similarly, we should take worship very seriously. But serious doesn't mean boring. In this context, 'seriously' means giving our best – our best responses to the mockers and our best worship to God.

 MUSICAL

WHAT: shouting
WHY: to make a loud and glorious worshipful noise to the Lord
WITH: Bibles or copies of Psalm 84, backing music or musical instruments (optional)

1 Give everyone a copy of Psalm 84 or a Bible.

2 Go on a march around the room (or outdoors if you can) shouting the words of Psalm 84 as loudly as possible.

3 If you have musical instruments or percussion, you might like to use these to set a beat. You could also use instrumental music – a good accompaniment could be the tune to 'Another Brick in the Wall' by Pink Floyd, without the vocals (by using a karaoke track) or looping the opening few bars.

 PRACTICAL

WHAT: journey
WHY: to think about the church building in which you meet
WITH: magazine pages 120 and 121

1 If you belong to a church with a consecrated building (consecrated means 'set aside for a special purpose'), take a trip round it. Alternatively, plan a trip to a cathedral and do this activity.

2 Using the glossary on pages 120 and 121, encourage the young people to see how many of the terms they can spot in the church building.

3 As you journey around the building, explain that it is because people felt that church buildings and their contents were so special that a separate vocabulary was formed – so a seat became a pew, a kneeler became a hassock, and so on – to set them apart from everyday objects.

4 Thank God in prayer for the buildings we have to show our love of God, and that this love is much more than just the buildings we make. Ask God to help everyone to worship him by making our whole lives set apart for him.

 CREATIVE

WHAT: worship
WHY: to give our best to God
WITH: business-card-sized pieces of card, Bibles

1 Explain that Romans 12:1,2 describes worship as service – offering ourselves as living sacrifices. This is because there are two New Testament words for worship, one to do with a special act of reverence and one to do with living day to day.

2 Discuss with the young people:

- What is the best you have? A special possession? A special skill?

- How might you worship God with it or incorporate it into worship? If the skill or possession does not easily fit into an act of worship, ask how the young person might remember to acknowledge God each time they use it or it is seen. How can they remember God with their football skill, culinary expertise or child-minding technique?

3 Give everyone a business-card-sized piece of card and encourage them to write the words of Romans 12:1,2 on one side. On the reverse, ask them to write the following: 'My special skill/thing is …' followed by, 'I will offer this to you, Lord.'

4 Encourage them to decorate the cards and take them home to use as bookmarks.

MORE ON THIS THEME:

If you want to do a short series with your group, other sessions that work well with this one are:

Bible bit
1 Kings 8:1–13,54–61

Solomon had built a huge Temple for God (2 Chronicles 2–6) and now it was time to put it to use. The Temple was to be where the Ark of the Covenant was kept. (This Ark was the symbol of God's presence with his people.) The Temple needed to be dedicated, or set up, in just the right way before the Ark could be kept there. As you read the Bible, you'll see that our proper response to God is to treat him in a special way, and that's why Solomon wanted to make sure everything was just right...

Rood screen

Altar

FOUND IN SOME CHURCHES

Old-school churches can be funny things. Whether you've been going to one all your life or you've just turned up and are maybe used to something more modern, or not used to anything at all, you probably won't know all the strange names for obscure parts of the building! Not to worry though, cos *theGRID* is here to help with this handy A to... erm, V of ecclesiastical (that means 'of the church') lingo.

Belfry

Belfry
Place (usually tower) where the bells (and sometimes bats) live.

Aisle
Often used to describe the centre gangway but technically means the areas of seating to the left and right of the centre blocks.

Altar
A raised table or surface used as the focus of a communion service where bread and wine are shared.

Architrave
Horizontal beam across the top of two columns.

Baptistry
Place where baptisms are carried out.

Buttress
Support structure built against a wall to hold the wall up. A flying buttress arches down from a wall to carry roof pressure downwards.

Chancel
The narrower area beyond where people usually sit, before the altar.

Choir
The part of the building where the singers sit. In many churches this is the chancel.

Church
Should mean 'people' but often used to describe the building where the church meets.

Cloister
A covered walkway between different buildings in a church complex (or, indeed, a complex church).

Column
Pillar supporting something, usually the roof.

Crucifix
Cross with the figure of Christ on it.

Crypt
Under-church burial chamber.

Dome
Rounded roof (like the one at St Paul's Cathedral).

Font
Place where infants are baptised (old fonts are large because infants, too, were baptised by full immersion).

Frontal
Embroidered altar covering.

Gallery
Raised area providing extra seating.

Chancel

Choir

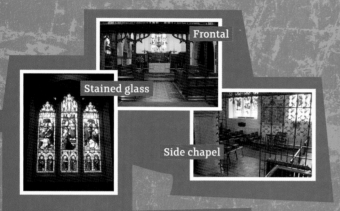

Frontal

Stained glass

Side chapel

Aisle

Hassock

Sanctuary
Originally the holy of holies; now refers to the part of the church containing the main altar.

Side chapel
Smaller worship area off the main building.

Stained glass
Coloured glass in windows often depicting Bible stories or characters.

Stall
Minister's seat.

Tower
Flat-topped tall roof.

Transept
Seating areas to the left and right of the main area, at right angles to it.

Vestry
Robing room.

Organ

Porch

Hassock
Cushion to kneel on.

Lectern
Reading desk for Bible, often ornate.

Monument
Any structure to commemorate someone who has died. A memorial is a plate or brass work for the same purpose.

Nave
Central area where most people sit.

Organ
Musical instrument commonly used in churches or cathedrals. Produces sound by driving pressurised air through pipes selected via a keyboard.

Pew
Uncomfortable bench seat, usually erected in times when people were shorter.

Porch
Covered entrance.

Pulpit
Raised area, visible from the whole church, from where the preacher speaks.

Rails
Used in some churches to mark off the area in front of the altar (originally put in place to stop animals fouling there).

Rood screen
Screen separating nave from chancel.

Spire

Pew

Column

– WHAT WOULD YOUR PERFECT CHURCH BUILDING LOOK LIKE?
– WOULD IT INCLUDE ALL, SOME OR NONE OF THESE THINGS?
– WHAT DO YOU THINK GOD'S PERFECT CHURCH BUILDING WOULD LOOK LIKE?

GOD, THE CHURCH, THE UNWISE

What some unwise people said about God, the church and all things in between:

'A church is a place where clergymen who have never been to heaven preach about it to people who will never get there.'
HL Menck

'Some people say there is a God; others say there is no God. The truth probably lies in between.'
WB Yeats

'Thank God I'm an atheist.'
Luis Buñuel

'Few sinners are saved after the first 20 minutes of a sermon.'
Mark Twain

'Vouchsafe, O Lord, to keep us this day without being found out.'
Samuel Butler

'Perhaps the most lasting pleasure in life is the pleasure of not going to church.'
Dean Inge

'If you want to make God laugh tell him your future plans.'
Woody Allen

'I don't pray because I don't want to bore God.'
Orson Welles

'I have spent a lot of time searching through the Bible for loopholes.'
WC Fields

'God is love, but get it in writing.'
Gypsy Rose Lee

YEAH, BUT....
...WHAT WOULD YOUR RESPONSE BE?

19

THE TEARS OF A CLOWN

THE AIM: To live in a holy way because our actions have far-reaching consequences

The aim unpacked

Solomon's holy life starts to slip, and it doesn't affect just him. The leader of this great nation, through his own actions, leads the people into division. As a result of his actions, Israel is torn in two. The way we act affects others. This is true in every aspect of our lives, especially in our relationship with God.

WAY IN

 theGRID MAGAZINE

WHAT: discussion
WHY: to think about distractions and temptations
WITH: magazine pages 126 and 127

1 Give out copies of pages 126 and 127 and invite everyone to read 'Positively not'.

2 Discuss these opening questions:

• What pressures are there in your life that tempt you to do unwise things?

• Are any of the ideas in the magazine workable? How could they be made to work?

Use this final question if your group is fairly committed. If not, keep it simply about doing positive things at this time.

• How, if at all, can our friends turn us away from God?

3 Explain that today the young people will be looking at how the wise King Solomon was distracted to do unwise things, which led to far-reaching negative consequences for his kingdom.

 SCENE SETTER

WHAT: collage
WHY: to think about partners
WITH: men's and women's style magazines (check them first), backing sheets

1 Say that, in Solomon's day, the king had the pick of the beautiful women. What if today you could assemble your perfect partner based on appearance only?

2 Gather some men's and women's fashion magazines (check beforehand that the content is appropriate for your young people). Working in small, same-gender groupings, invite the young people to make a collage of their perfect date by cutting out bits of the various models in the magazines.

3 Invite the groups to comment on each other's work.

 **THEMED GAME**

WHAT: drama
WHY: to think about the trappings of success
WITH: flowers for a prize

1 Explain that this is a drama, so it isn't about using any real talents the young people have. Offer an opportunity to be selected for fame and fortune. Say that everyone who wishes to enter needs to prepare a fictional 20-second audition (singing, dancing, acting, or other skill or talent). They can do this in groups if they wish. Give the young people a few minutes to prepare. This is just a bit of fun, so encourage them to ham it up as much as possible.

2 Watch the auditions and vote for the winner, or vote to remove one person at a time and ask for a different audition for the next round, and so on. (Even though this is a fun activity, be sensitive when you offer feedback.) Make a big thing of the final.

3 Reward the eventual winner with the flowers. Interview them about how they will try to avoid being carried away by the trappings of success.

4 Briefly discuss:

• Why are so many people anxious to become 'idols'? (You can do this with reference to any TV programmes that offer fame, such as *Britain's Got Talent* or *The X Factor*.)

BIBLE EXPERIENCE

 LEVEL 1: CONNECT

WHAT: Bible study
WHY: to live in a holy way because our actions have far-reaching consequences
WITH: Bibles, magazine page 128, flip chart or whiteboard, marker pen

1 Give out copies of page 128 and invite everyone to look at the 'Decisions and consequences' activity. Challenge the young people to work in pairs to match up the decisions with their consequences.

2 Chat together about any decisions group members may have taken in their lives which seemed clever at the time, but turned out to be not so smart. Start off with a personal example.

3 Remind the young people of 1 Kings 3:12, which shows God giving Solomon a wise and discerning heart. Now ask a volunteer to read 1 Kings 11:1–10.

4 Explain the cultural differences between then and now. In those days it was perfectly normal for important men to have many wives. With 700 wives and 300 concubines (other women living with him who were not married to him), Solomon had a lot of variety of companionship. The trouble was that these women all came from different countries that worshipped different gods, and Solomon wanted to please them, so he went along with worshipping their gods.

5 Encourage the young people to share any ways in which they have been, or might be, tempted by their peers to do things against their better judgement.

6 Invite the young people to think of the sorts of things that distract people today from worshipping God. Write these down on a flip chart or whiteboard, perhaps making them into a top ten.

7 Encourage the young people to think of some ways in which they can help each other to make good decisions.

 LEVEL 2: INTERFACE

WHAT: discussion
WHY: to live in a holy way because our actions have far-reaching consequences
WITH: flip chart or whiteboard, marker pen

1 Hand out small pieces of paper and pens. Ask everyone to write down what they value most in their life, or their most treasured possession.

2 Collect the answers in and number them. Give everyone more paper and, as you read the answers out, ask the young people to guess who chose what. Find out the answers and see who got the most correct.

3 Ask the young people how they would feel if what they valued most had to be forfeited at the request of their husband/wife/boyfriend/girlfriend, or even best friend.

4 Read 1 Kings 11:1–13. Explain that the passage suggests that anything that spoils God's control in our lives is idolatry. Solomon was guilty of idolatry even though all he was doing, it appears, was trying to keep his wives and girlfriends happy. He forfeited what should have been what he valued most – his relationship with God. It led to the division of his kingdom.

5 Discuss with the young people:

- Do you like, love or worship what you value most – your most treasured possession? Where should the line be drawn?

- In what circumstances might you part with it?

6 Finally, write this unfinished sentence up on the flip chart or whiteboard: 'The best way to be holy with your possessions is to …' How many ways can the young people think of to complete the sentence?

 LEVEL 3: SWITCH ON

WHAT: Bible study
WHY: to live in a holy way because our actions have far-reaching consequences
WITH: Bibles

1 Split the young people into small groups. Give out pens and paper and ask the young people to divide their sheet of paper into four quarters.

2 Ask them to write these titles in the sections on the left-hand side of the page: 'Things that pleased God' and 'Things that displeased God'. The right-hand sections should be headed 'Consequences'.

3 Allocate one of the following passages to each group: 1 Kings 11:1–13; 1 Kings 11:26–43; 1 Kings 12:1–24; 1 Kings 12:25–33; 1 Kings 13:1–10. Invite them to sort the actions in their passage into the two sections of their paper: 'Things that pleased God' or 'Things that displeased God'. For each entry they should then write what the consequence of that action was. After they've had time to do this, come together to feed back the results.

4 End by making the point that for every action of ours, whether pleasing or displeasing to God, there is a consequence. David's actions were so pleasing to God that God's judgement on Solomon was restrained. Solomon's actions were so displeasing to God that the whole kingdom ended up divided. God wants our hearts in the right place, and then sin can be dealt with.

RESPOND

 MUSICAL

WHAT: songs
WHY: to think about putting God first
WITH: worship songs, musical accompaniment or playback equipment

1 If your group likes to sing, use some songs which focus on putting God or Jesus first, such as:

- 'All to Jesus (I surrender all)' by Judson Wheeler Van DeVenter
- 'How I Love You; You Are The One' by Keith Green
- 'Jesus Shall Take the Highest Honour' by Chris Bowater

2 You could read the lyrics of some of these songs over instrumental music or listen to the songs on CD or MP3 if your group doesn't enjoy singing.

3 Finish by saying that putting God first is more than just singing about it. We need to take this into every aspect of our lives. Pray that God will help the young people stay focused on putting God first in their lives.

 PRACTICAL

WHAT: writing
WHY: to focus on a partner who is holy
WITH: local newspaper

1 Read some of the partner-seeking adverts from a local newspaper or magazine to the young people (make sure you check that they are appropriate first).

2 Divide the young people into pairs or threes and ask them to draft a lonely hearts 'wanted' advert which focuses on more spiritual than physical qualities, such as prayer life, meditation, worship or lifestyle.

3 Share the results and talk briefly about how such a partner might help keep one's mind focused on God.

4 Finish by saying that we should think about all aspects of relationships with others when choosing a boyfriend or girlfriend – and even when choosing friends. Pray that God will help the young people see the 'whole' person, including the spiritual side, when looking for friends.

 CREATIVE

WHAT: penitence
WHY: to restore a holy relationship with God
WITH: Bibles

1 Explain that the only way to get right with God is to accept that, in Jesus, our sins are forgiven. Before Jesus' death, Psalm 1 was a way for people to acknowledge their sin and to repent.

2 Give out Bibles or printouts of Psalm 1. Repeat verse 1 together until everyone has memorised it; then put the Bibles or sheets down.

3 Ask a volunteer to read the psalm with everyone joining in to recite verse 1 as a chorus or refrain between each verse. As they repeat it they should mime the actions of verse 1 – walking; standing; sitting.

MORE ON THIS THEME:

If you want to do a short series with your group, other sessions that work well with this one are:

18 *My way or the highway*   *1 Kings 5–7; 8:1–13,54–61*

POSITIVELY

Bible bit
1 Kings 11:1–13,26–43;
12:1 – 13:10

OK, we may be on the lookout for Mr or Miss Right. It's fairly natural for us to want a close relationship with a special someone (if you don't think so at the moment, trust me – one day you will!). Solomon seems to take this to extremes, though; just have a look at the number of girls he is interested in!!! But that isn't the main problem here. The problem is what these relationships lead him into. Solomon turns away from God by allowing other gods to be worshipped, and that has far-reaching consequences.

AN AGGRESSIVE PURSUIT OF WHOLESOMENESS IS POSSIBLE! SO: ·······>

Hey Jez, this is Luke's gym bag. Let's throw it in the trash!

Wicked, OK.

Christians don't want a reputation for saying 'No' to everything! We're not spoilsports or completely averse to having fun. But we do have to say 'no' occasionally. If you need to, you can say 'no' more positively with phrases such as:

I'm already committed to ... Why don't you join me?

My kind of thing is more ...

I'd rather do [something else just as fun!]

You really think that's a good idea, don't you?

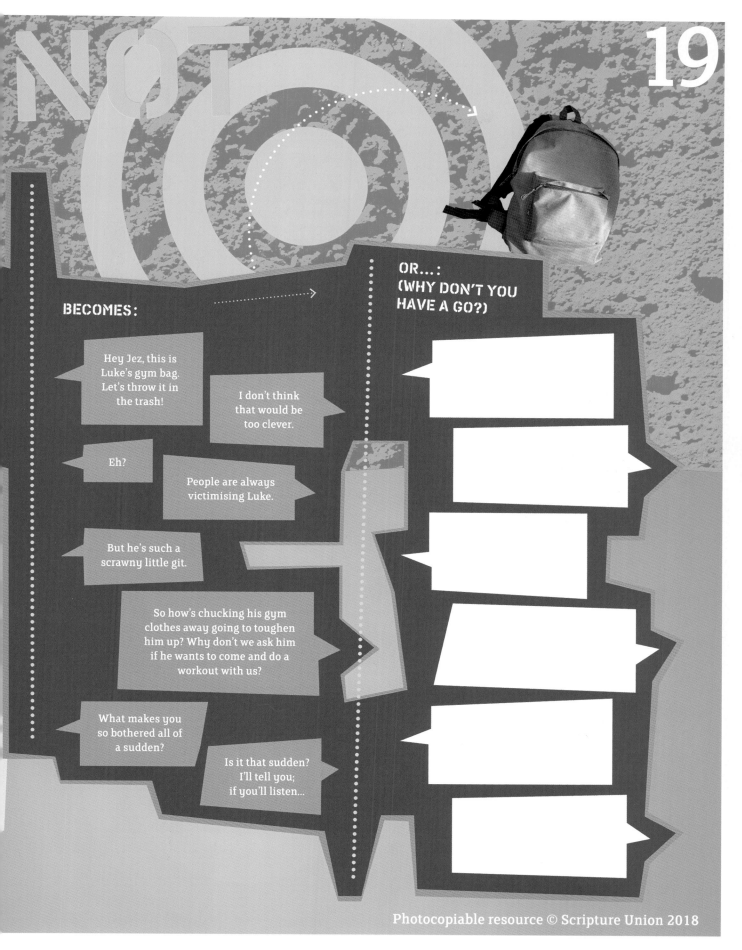

1 I needed to burst my blood blister as it was really hurting …

2 As the ball came over I ran round the back of the defender to get on the end of the cross …

3 I had to flatten a nail sticking up out of the floor …

4 My little brother was annoying me with his favourite cuddly toy …

5 I caught the 18.24 to Milton Keynes …

A … I gave it a couple of thumps with a hammer.

B … I went to see my boss to ask for more money to compensate for the stress before doing any more.

C … I asked my teachers and parents for advice.

D … I buried it in the back of the goal and ran to receive the worship of the fans.

E … the person sitting next to me lent me some money for food.

6 The teacher told me to leave the class for the rest of the lesson …

7 I couldn't decide which GCSEs to take when I looked through the book of options …

8 I walked across the tarmac and boarded the plane that would take me to a new life …

9 I needed to borrow some cash for a school dinner …

10 The pressure at work was really getting to me …

F … three hours later I was relaxing on a sun-drenched Mediterranean balcony.

G … so I stuck a pin in it.

H … I arrived in Milton Keynes at 19.00.

I … I had to go to speak to the head teacher at break.

J … I went and sat in my bedroom to chill out for a bit.

Answers on page 318

MATCH THE DECISION TO THE CONSEQUENCE!

DECISIONS AND CONSEQUENCES

HOMEWARD BOUND

THE AIM: To discover that God restores his honour through the prayers and work of his people

The aim unpacked

The wall around Jerusalem was vital to the honour of God's name, as well as being vital to the protection and function of the city. Everyone was involved in the building and, although they met with opposition, God was with them and protected them as they restored the wall. God is constantly in the process of restoring his people, both individually and as a community.

WAY IN

 theGRID MAGAZINE

WHAT: mime
WHY: to introduce things that go together

1 Divide the group into pairs and ask them to think of something that goes with something else in order to work. Give them several minutes to think of what their items could be (for example, torch and batteries, horse and jockey, bowler and batsman).

2 Now each pair should come up with a mime to demonstrate their items to the rest of the young people, who have to guess what they are. (It is best not to have told them this before, as now their mime skills will be tested more!)

3 If you have time you could do this several times, especially if you have a small group.

4 Explain that there are many things that go together. In this session we'll be looking at a couple: prayer and work, and cities and walls.

 SCENE SETTER

WHAT: house of cards
WHY: to introduce the theme of building
WITH: several decks of playing cards, flat surfaces, prizes (optional)

1 This can be done as an individual challenge or in teams. Hand out the playing cards and challenge the young people to build a playing-card house. Decide on a time limit and set everyone to work.

2 Award a prize for the biggest or the most imaginative, if you want to.

3 If appropriate, explain that you'll be looking at a major building project in this session.

 THEMED GAME

WHAT: quiz
WHY: to introduce the topic of protection
WITH: prize (optional)

1 Tell the group that you are going to have a quiz on the subject of things that protect. You can do this individually or in teams if your group is large enough.

2 Explain that you will call out an item and they must write down the thing it protects and what it protects against. Use the items in the list below:

- a firewall – a computer network against hackers
- a shin pad – shins against bruising
- sunglasses – eyes against sun damage
- pesticide – a plant against insect attack
- a plaster – a cut or abrasion against further damage or infection
- an immobiliser – a car against theft
- a seat belt – a person in a car crash against more serious injury
- traffic lights – pedestrians against cars
- a suit of armour – a knight or soldier against injury
- a defence lawyer – the accused against unfair judgement

BIBLE EXPERIENCE

 LEVEL 1: CONNECT

WHAT: drama sketch
WHY: to discover that God restores his honour through the prayers and work of his people
WITH: magazine page 133

1 If you want to perform the sketch from page 133, practise it with some volunteers before the session.

2 Perform the sketch, or hand out copies of page 133 and invite the young people to read through the sketch on their own or in groups of three.

3 Explain that this sketch covers part of the story of Nehemiah, who heard about the state of repair that Jerusalem was in. He set out to rebuild the city walls and gates, after having prayed to God. In ancient times, the walls of a city were important for protection and status. If the walls were rubbish, then the god of that city was also seen as rubbish.

4 Discuss as a group what things might make a city look good to other people these days. Are there ways in which Christians could get involved to improve their city in God's name? You might like to do some research online about examples where this is already happening, such as the Eden Network, Street Pastors or local Christian soup kitchens and food banks.

5 If appropriate for your group, you could read the full account from Nehemiah 1, 2 and 4. *The Message* version of the Bible has a particularly good way of telling this story.

 LEVEL 2: INTERFACE

WHAT: Bible study
WHY: to discover that God restores his honour through the prayers and work of his people
WITH: magazine page 132, Bibles

1 Make sure everyone has a Bible, a pen and a copy of page 132. The page is set out as a planning application form. It contains all the relevant questions that someone would need to answer in order to obtain planning permission from the Ancient Israel Planning Board.

2 The young people, working in pairs if they wish, must fill in the application form using information from Nehemiah 1, 2 and 4. (You might prefer to split the passage between the groups so that you cover the whole story.)

3 Share the results.

4 Explain to the group that in ancient times, and up until quite recently, cities had walls to protect them. If a city did not have a wall, it meant that it was not well protected. Jerusalem was seen by the Jews as God's holy city. If this city didn't have a wall, then it was dishonourable to the city and to God himself. It also meant that it was seen to be weak among the surrounding people who didn't believe in God. It would make them think that God was weak.

5 Make sure the young people realise that it was through the prayers and hard work of Nehemiah and others that God restored his honour, and Jerusalem once again became an honoured city.

 LEVEL 3: SWITCH ON

WHAT: Bible study
WHY: to discover that God restores his honour through the prayers and work of his people
WITH: Bibles, Bible commentaries

1 Divide your young people into pairs and make sure each pair has a Bible. Make some Bible commentaries or study Bibles available if possible.

2 Ask the pairs to look at a chapter each of Nehemiah 1, 2 or 4 and to answer the following questions (the same questions for each chapter):

- What is happening in this chapter?

- Who are the main characters in this chapter? What are their motivations for acting in the way they did?

- Is there something we can learn from this chapter and incorporate into our lives – an action or a way of thinking?

3 Once the groups have spent some time going through the chapters, come together to share all that they have learned and discuss any questions they found. Invite the other groups to ask questions too.

4 Make sure the young people realise that, because Nehemiah prayed and then acted, the walls were built and God's honour was restored.

RESPOND

 MUSICAL

WHAT: musical prayer and proclamation
WHY: to ask God to restore his honour throughout the world
WITH: music and lyrics for 'Our God Is an Awesome God' by Rich Mullins, playback equipment or musical accompaniment

1 Explain that God answers our prayers today, just as he answered Nehemiah's prayers. We believe that God is powerful and can do anything, therefore we can ask him to restore his honour throughout the world.

2 Ask each young person to write on a sheet of paper an area of the world where they would like to see God's power in action.

3 Using the song 'Our God Is an Awesome God' as a refrain, invite each young person to read out what they have written, then sing together the chorus to proclaim God's awesomeness. If you don't have musicians, you could listen and sing along to a recorded version and fade the chorus in and out each time.

4 Say that we don't know how God will answer our prayers, but we trust that God will do what is best in the bigger eternal picture. But we do know that if Nehemiah hadn't prayed, nothing would have been done.

 PRACTICAL

WHAT: prayer pattern
WHY: to have a pattern of prayer we can use in our daily life
WITH: Bibles

1 Explain to the group that God's honour had been restored in the eyes of nations when the city walls had been rebuilt. This all started with the prayer of one man – Nehemiah. Say, 'Each one of you is an individual – one person – and yet what things could your prayers accomplish?'

2 Make sure everyone has access to a Bible. Ask them to turn to Nehemiah 1 and look for the prayer that Nehemiah prayed.

3 Invite the young people to write a prayer pattern based on Nehemiah's prayer. This only needs to be in the form of section headings and then a short explanation why. For instance, the pattern would start with 'Praising God' and the explanation would be 'because God is the one we should be praising'.

4 Once they have done this, see if they have finished with a line similar to, 'Be with me as I go about my day'. If they haven't got something like this, suggest that they add it.

5 Finish by encouraging some silent prayer based on the young people's prayer patterns and, as you close, remind them that they can use this pattern whenever they need to.

 CREATIVE

WHAT: poster collage
WHY: to see where God's honour is at stake in our lives
WITH: selection of teen magazines, flip chart or large sheets of paper, marker pens, glue

1 Explain that God's honour was restored through the prayers and work of Nehemiah. God's honour can still be restored in our lives.

2 Hand out the magazines, large sheets of paper, glue and pens and ask the young people to create individual or group collages. The images should represent any aspect of life where people are not honouring God. It could include a visual representation of others who mock us for what we do and believe, just as Nehemiah was mocked.

3 As the young people create the collages, pray that they will honour God's name in their lives.

MORE ON THIS THEME:

If you want to do a short series with your group, other sessions that work well with this one are:

20

ANCIENT ISRAEL PLANNING BOARD

Bible bit
Nehemiah 1,2,4

Nehemiah's journey was a dangerous one, from his visit to the king to the opposition he faced from the rulers of the lands around Judah. But God kept him safe and protected him as he set about restoring the walls of Jerusalem. While he did that, God took on the business of restoring his people…

Fill in this form for Nehemiah, looking at Nehemiah chapters 1, 2 and 4 for some clues.

Place for application: Name of applicant:

Why did you decide to do the work?

What was your first step in planning?

What changes to the current building(s) do you wish to make?

Who will be doing the building?

What security measures do you have in place against potential attacks?

Where will the building materials come from?

Why do you want to make the changes to the current building?

Do you have the backing of any important people?

Is there anyone who might object to this building work being carried out?

Why?

Is there any other information you feel is relevant to your application?

GRAND DIY DESIGN SOS

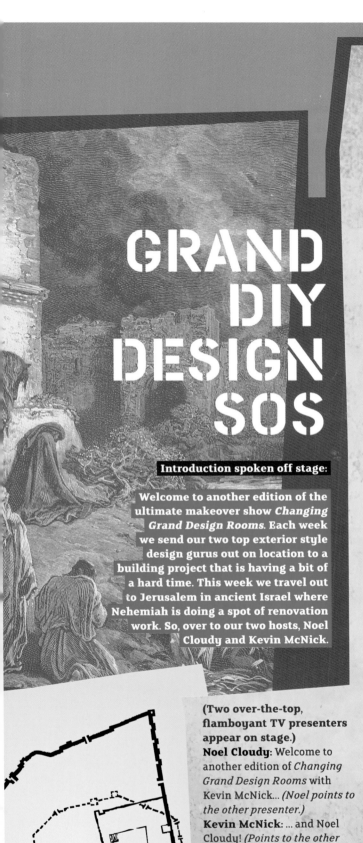

Introduction spoken off stage:

Welcome to another edition of the ultimate makeover show *Changing Grand Design Rooms*. Each week we send our two top exterior style design gurus out on location to a building project that is having a bit of a hard time. This week we travel out to Jerusalem in ancient Israel where Nehemiah is doing a spot of renovation work. So, over to our two hosts, Noel Cloudy and Kevin McNick.

(Two over-the-top, flamboyant TV presenters appear on stage.)

Noel Cloudy: Welcome to another edition of *Changing Grand Design Rooms* with Kevin McNick… *(Noel points to the other presenter.)*

Kevin McNick: … and Noel Cloudy! *(Points to the other presenter.)*

Noel Cloudy: Well, today we've come all the way to ancient Israel to see a very interesting project.

Kevin McNick: Yes, I've had to put the factor 50 on or my skin would simply roast, the sun is that hot.

Noel Cloudy: We're here to see the rebuilding of the city walls of Jerusalem. So let's get going and talk to the chief architect, Nehemiah.

Nehemiah: Well, actually, I'm not the…

Kevin McNick: Hi, Nee, do you mind if I call you that? Of course you don't; hey, you're wearing some really trendy threads. *(Pulls a mock being-sick face to the audience.)* So, how did you become the chief architect?

Nehemiah: *(Slightly annoyed at being spoken over.)* Well, as I was trying to say, I'm not actually the chief architect on this build.

Noel Cloudy: Oh, that's amazing! Are you the slightly wacky but ever so loveable interior, I mean, exterior designer?

Kevin McNick: Are you sure? That robe is so last year, and as for the hairstyle: that went out with the ark.

Nehemiah: No, I'm not a designer.

Kevin McNick: Told you so.

Noel Cloudy: Well, what exactly are you?

Nehemiah: Well, actually I'm the king's cup-bearer: when he asks for a drink I get it for him.

Noel Cloudy: So how come you've got a job rebuilding the walls of this city?

Kevin McNick: Yeah, he's certainly not over-qualified.

Nehemiah: Well, I heard that the city was in a bit of a state – its walls falling down and its gates burnt. As this is God's city…

Noel Cloudy: God's city? So God's the client, the one you have to answer to if you get the colour scheme wrong?

Kevin McNick: I bet he's easier to work for than some of those rich toffs in Mayfair.

Nehemiah: Well, not exactly; it's his city, his Temple is here, and if his city is in a mess, it looks like he is in a mess too. Therefore I want to rebuild the walls and get things looking great, because God is great.

Noel Cloudy: I see, so you started with some detailed plans, costed the whole project up and went to visit the bank.

Kevin McNick: I hope you took the bank manager a drink; that's the only way you'd get any money.

Nehemiah: Well, no, I started where all people who follow God start: I prayed.

Noel Cloudy and **Kevin McNick:** *(Together.)* You prayed?

Nehemiah: Yes, I prayed to God and asked for his help.

Kevin McNick: And then he sent you to the bank?

Nehemiah: No, I was given the opportunity to talk to the king, to explain everything and ask for his help.

Noel Cloudy: And he asked for another glass of wine?

Nehemiah: He gave me all that I needed, gave me the right contacts and gave me his full support. And now here we are, rebuilding the walls, and not in need of two ridiculous presenters who know nothing about building to comment on what is happening. When you've got God on your side, and your people are praying and working, then you can do amazing things.

Noel Cloudy: Oh, all right, I suppose that put us in our place.

Kevin McNick: Yes, s'pose we should be going then.

Noel Cloudy: That's all from us here in Jerusalem.

Kevin McNick: Next week we'll be in Italy with some advice for a young lad building a tower in a place called Pisa.

21

Bible: Nehemiah 6:15,16; 12:27–43

GIVE IT BACK TO GOD

THE AIM: To celebrate the work God does among his people

The aim unpacked

Now the wall of Jerusalem is finished, and the people celebrate by marching around the walls, praising God with songs of thanksgiving and different musical instruments. This is an unrestrained response to what God has done for the people of Jerusalem – he has kept them safe from their enemies, provided the means to rebuild the walls and restored them to honour among the nations who surround them.

WAY IN

 **theGRID MAGAZINE**

WHAT: phrase matching
WHY: to introduce the theme of celebration
WITH: magazine page 137

1 Hand out a copy of page 137 to each young person and ask them to look at 'Celebration time'. They are to match the celebration phrases with the people and events they relate to.

2 Once they have finished, bring the group together and check their answers. Encourage them to share any thoughts they have about the events.

3 Ask the group if they know of any other ways in which people have celebrated.

4 Explain that in this session you'll be looking at how Nehemiah and the Jewish people celebrated when the city walls were completed.

 **SCENE SETTER**

WHAT: discussion
WHY: to introduce the idea of responding to good events

1 Divide the group into pairs and ask each pair to discuss a time when something nice or good happened to them.

2 Then ask the pairs to discuss whether or not they said 'Thank you' to the person, or people, who brought about that good experience or event.

3 Bring the group back together and obtain feedback from the pairs about those good events. How often did the young people say 'Thank you'?

4 Talk about times when we always (or nearly always) say 'Thank you', and the ways we say 'Thank you' at those times. For example, this might be a card, a phone call or a text message to say 'Thank you' for a Christmas or birthday present.

5 Explain that today you'll be looking at a really big thank-you that involved a whole city having a big celebration.

 **THEMED GAME**

WHAT: team game
WHY: to look at how we celebrate
WITH: sporting equipment for your chosen game

1 Divide the young people into teams and play a team game in which points are scored. The most obvious are football or basketball, but something like 'rag hockey' would work as well.

2 The aim is to score points against the opposing team. However, say that there will be extra points awarded for the most unique celebrations after each score.

3 Award the extra points depending on how unique and over the top the celebrations are.

4 If appropriate, explain that you'll be looking at a celebration later.

BIBLE EXPERIENCE

 LEVEL 1: CONNECT

WHAT: putting together a celebration
WHY: to celebrate the work God does among his people
WITH: Bibles, creative materials

1 Recap the story of Nehemiah from the previous session. Nehemiah, having heard about the state of Jerusalem's walls and gates, prayed to God. God provided the means to rebuild the walls and make Jerusalem a proper city again.

2 Ask someone to read Nehemiah 6:15,16.

3 Now that the walls have been rebuilt, it is time to celebrate. Divide the group into pairs and ask them to devise an opening ceremony for the city's new walls and gates. They should create a VIP list of people they would like to invite, write a speech to be read out and think of some activities and events to go with the celebration. Have as many creative resources available as possible for the group to use and encourage the young people to look together at the Bible passage for ideas.

4 Invite each pair to present their ideas and then, if you wish, ask everyone to vote on which ceremony they think is the best.

5 Explain that the celebration following the building of the walls and gates involved everyone in the city. People were invited to lead praise and thanks to God, and they also marched around the top of the walls before meeting at the Temple and worshipping and thanking God.

6 Read Nehemiah 12:27–43 to the group and explain that when God does something, his people celebrate.

 LEVEL 2: INTERFACE

WHAT: guided meditation
WHY: to celebrate the work God does among his people
WITH: resource page 139

1 Invite the young people to sit down and make themselves comfortable.

2 Recap the story of Nehemiah from 'Level 1 Connect'.

3 Encourage the group to close their eyes, listen to the words of the meditation and think about the questions raised. Then read the meditation from resource page 139.

4 When the meditation is finished, remind the young people that they are now back in the session.

5 Ask them if any of the feelings they experienced during the meditation were similar to how they feel when they celebrate anything in the real world.

6 Say that whenever God does something good in our lives, we should take the time to celebrate and say 'Thank you'.

 LEVEL 3: SWITCH ON

WHAT: discussion
WHY: to celebrate the work God does among his people
WITH: Bibles, Bible commentaries, Bible dictionary, Bible atlas, laptop with internet access (optional)

1 Recap the story of Nehemiah as in 'Level 1 Connect'.

2 Ask someone to read Nehemiah 6:15,16 and then Nehemiah 12:27–43.

3 Use the following questions to make sure everyone has understood the passage. If possible, stay in one group and look up any information in the relevant books, or online if you have internet access.

- Who were the Levites?
- How far away from Jerusalem were the towns mentioned?

4 Look at a map of Jerusalem at the time of Nehemiah and notice the route of the marchers on top of the walls.

5 Use the following questions to help the young people apply the passage to their lives (only use the questions that are relevant to your group):

- Are there any celebrations that involve the whole community where you live?
- What celebrations do you have in your church?
- On a scale of 1 to 10 (1 being sombre and 10 being joyful), how joyful are your church celebrations? What do you celebrate and why?
- What is the balance that we should aim for between reverent worship and joyous celebration? Why?
- Do we include celebration in our own personal times with God? How could this be done?
- Do our churches tend to focus on 'bad things' or 'the work God does among his people'? Why? Does that need to change?

RESPOND

 MUSICAL

WHAT: celebration
WHY: to thank God for all that he has done
WITH: music, musicians and instruments or playback equipment

1 This activity totally depends on your group. Ask them what is going on around them that they would like to celebrate. Then ask how they would like to celebrate – whether they would like to sing, dance, listen to some worship and celebration songs or make up their own!

2 Depending on what they want to do, choose some celebration songs to use. You could sing the song 'My Lighthouse' by Rend Collective, or others that your young people know.

3 Try to think about taking your celebration further. Why not record the singing, or video the dance and post it on YouTube or similar (ensure you keep to your church's safeguarding policy). We'd love to see anything you create!

 PRACTICAL

WHAT: prayer wall
WHY: to pray and thank God for answered prayers
WITH: large sheet of paper (wallpaper would be ideal)

1 Explain that Nehemiah and the Jews celebrated because the city walls had been rebuilt. The walls had been rebuilt because of the prayers and hard work of Nehemiah and the others.

2 Say that you are going to create a prayer wall to act as a visual reminder of prayers made and also to remind the group to celebrate when prayers are answered, just as Nehemiah and the rest of the Jews did.

3 On a large sheet of paper, write the title 'Prayer Wall'.

4 Invite the young people to write prayer requests on smaller pieces of paper or sticky notes and stick them onto the prayer wall.

5 The prayer wall could become a regular fixture at your group's meeting place. If you don't use the same room or space each time you meet, you could mount the wall on a board and transport it between meetings.

6 Make sure you add to and monitor the wall each time you meet, and celebrate when a prayer is answered.

 CREATIVE

WHAT: guided prayer
WHY: to think about how we respond to God in our lives
WITH: magazine page 138

1 Hand out copies of page 138.

2 Explain that the picture shows some blob people who represent different feelings.

3 Ask the young people to relax and think about their relationship with God. Let them meditate on the things that have happened in their lives, everything they have, the things they don't have, the good times and the not-so-good times. Also remind them that Jesus loves us all and wants to be a friend to each and every one of us.

4 Then ask them to look closely at the blob pictures and silently think about which blob best represents them. As they think about this, ask them whether they would prefer to be another blob in the picture. As they think about this, encourage them to pray and to ask God for his help and power to move from one blob to another as they grow in confidence in God.

5 Close in prayer, thanking God that he can restore us like he restored the walls and gates of Jerusalem, wherever we are and whoever we are.

MORE ON THIS THEME:

If you want to do a short series with your group, other sessions that work well with this one are:

CELEBRATION TIME

Match the celebration phrases with the person who said them and the event they relate to. Each phrase should be joined to two other boxes. (Answers on page 319.)

Bible bit
Nehemiah 6:15,16; 12:27–43

What do you do when God answers your prayers, does something for you or blesses you? Do you take it for granted, or do you thank God for what he has done? In this passage, the wall of Jerusalem is finished and Nehemiah leads the people in a big knees-up to thank God and celebrate! Do you ever do the same thing?

Rose Tyler, you were fantastic. And you know what? So was I.

That's one small step for man, one giant leap for mankind.

A record is nothing if not shared.

WORLD CUP FINAL, 1966

WINNING AN OSCAR

NEIL ARMSTRONG

KENNETH WOLSTENHOLME (COMMENTATOR)

BECOMING THE FASTEST PERSON TO SAIL SOLO NON-STOP AROUND THE WORLD

A MESSAGE SENT TO THE ROMAN GOVERNMENT AFTER A GREAT VICTORY

LUKE SKYWALKER

THE DOCTOR (DOCTOR WHO)

GWYNETH PALTROW

LANDING ON THE MOON

They think it's all over; it is now.

ELLEN MACARTHUR

JULIUS CAESAR

I love you all!

Woo-hoo!

Veni, vidi, vici. (I came, I saw, I conquered.)

DESTRUCTION OF THE DEATH STAR

BEFORE HIS TENTH REGENERATION

Meditation

[Make sure the young people are comfortable. Invite them to close their eyes and imagine they are in the story you are reading.]

The sun is high in the sky and is warming you through. You have been working hard for almost two months, but today you won't be sweating through work. Today is a day of rest for you; your body won't be cutting stone and building today.

You are resting. Feel the sun on your body and the relaxation in your muscles. *(Pause.)*

The Levites have been arriving for most of the morning to join with those who have arrived over the previous few days. There are people everywhere and there are loads of instruments too – cymbals, harps and other stringed instruments that you've never even seen before.

You are overawed by the amount of religious leaders and with the anticipation of hearing all the music. *(Pause.)*

The priests and the Levites are doing their religious bit now. They are going through the rituals to make themselves holy before God. They are also doing it for you, making you holy, an ordinary citizen of Jerusalem.

You feel clean. You are not anyone special, not a VIP, and yet here you are, one of God's holy people. *(Pause.)*

It is not just the people that are being made holy. The walls and gates that you have been building are also being dedicated, handed over to God. They are his walls and gates in his city, where you live.

You are proud of your work and the fact that it is God's too. You realise everything you do is, or should be, God's. *(Pause.)*

Nehemiah, who has been in charge of the building project, is now dividing the Levites, singers and leaders into two groups. One group is marching one way along the top of the completed wall and the other group is going the other way. They are singing and praising God as they go.

You feel, as well as hear, the sound wash over you. The celebration covers the whole city; the city is singing with one voice. *(Pause.)*

You are now outside the Temple, where God himself has his home among his people. The noise is tremendous; trumpets join with the singers' voices.

You realise that the joy you feel is from God. All that has happened is because of God. Your voice joins with the priests, leaders, Levites, singers, women and children to praise God, and to celebrate everything he has done in your life. *(Pause.)*

22
EZRA

THE AIM: To assess the value of leadership and to think about the leaders God gives us

The aim unpacked

Ezra was a leader. In many ways he 'coached' the Israelites and helped them be the best they could be. And he helped them work well together, reforming the people into a team after they had been apart for so long. As we think about the value of leadership, we'll also be thinking about how we should be followers. To function well, teams require a combination of good leaders and good followers.

WAY IN

 **theGRID MAGAZINE**

WHAT: personality quiz
WHY: to start thinking about being a leader and a follower
WITH: magazine page 143

1 Hand out copies of magazine page 143 and pens.

2 Ask the young people to spend some time completing the leader and follower questionnaires on their own.

3 Either in small groups or as a whole group, ask the young people to discuss their results. Do they agree with what the questionnaires suggest? Do they prefer to be leaders or followers, and why? Encourage them to share with the group times when they have displayed these traits.

 **SCENE SETTER**

WHAT: sports commentary
WHY: to think about why leadership is essential
WITH: microphone with sound recorder (optional)

1 Divide the young people into small groups and ask them to imagine they are commentating on a hockey match.

2 Get each group to write a script of the commentary, explaining that one team has a really good coach and captain and the other team has an extremely bad coach and captain. Tell them that their commentaries should reveal this, and that they should make lots of comments on the differing leadership displayed within both teams.

3 Either provide appropriate equipment for the groups to record their commentaries or invite them to perform them live in front of the wider group.

4 Conclude by asking the young people to talk about their experiences of being in teams where the captains or coaches were particularly good or bad. What makes a captain or a coach good or bad?

 **THEMED GAME**

WHAT: team task
WHY: to introduce the challenges of leadership
WITH: newspaper, string, other equipment as needed

1 In teams of about three or four, challenge the young people to have a go at each of the 'team tasks' you've set up around the room. The team should choose a different team member to act as the leader for each task.

2 Here are two suggested tasks, but you can come up with others:

Crossing the river

• Only the leader is told the objective, but they are not allowed to talk.

• Mark out a river, and give the leader two sheets of newspaper (boats). The team leader has to get all their team from one side of the 'river' to the other. If any team members 'get their feet wet', they must start again.

Making a net

• Only the leader is told the objective, and only they are allowed to talk.

• In the designated time, the team has to make a net using only string and scissors. The net should let a golf ball through, but stop a tennis ball.

BIBLE EXPERIENCE

LEVEL 1: CONNECT

WHAT: imagination exercise
WHY: to assess the value of leadership and to think about the leaders God gives us
WITH: large sheets of paper, item of sports equipment (optional), magazine page 144

1 Ask the young people to imagine some of the situations from page 144. Encourage them, in small groups, to present their thoughts to the rest of the group through one of the following ways:

- drawing 'with' and 'without' pictures
- writing descriptive stories
- acting out short sketches

2 Explain that good leadership is important to ensure that groups of people function well together. As the leader of this group, you want to make sure that everyone has the opportunity to share and get something out of the session. Discuss together ways in which good leadership is important for the group and ask them for suggestions on how best to work together. What might happen if the group didn't have a leader?

3 Introduce the group to the character of Ezra by saying something like, 'When the Israelites returned to their homeland, after they had been taken and forced to live in other countries for hundreds of years, Ezra helped get things back in order. He was their leader, almost like their manager and coach.' Then ask volunteers to read the following passages: Ezra 7:6,8–10,24–26; Nehemiah 8:1–3.

4 Reflect on the Bible passages together by identifying in which ways Ezra was a good leader. Then, in small groups, ask the young people to imagine what might have happened if the Israelites hadn't had a leader like Ezra at this critical stage in their history. After a few minutes, invite them to present their thoughts to the rest of the group using one of the methods in point 1.

LEVEL 2: INTERFACE

WHAT: leader profiles
WHY: to assess the value of leadership and to think about the leaders God gives us

1 Divide the young people into twos and threes and ask them to put together a profile for the coach of an Olympic hockey team. Explain to them that their profile should include the tasks the coach would need to carry out and the characteristics they should display.

2 Next, still in their small groups, ask the young people to read Ezra 7 and Nehemiah 8:1–10. Challenge them to put together a profile for Ezra's job. Hint that it is likely that the profiles will contain many similarities.

3 Bring the group back together and get the young people to feed back on their profiles, noting any similarities or differences. Make sure they have picked up the main points of the Bible passages concerning Ezra's role and that they have understood the background history (see 'Level 1 Connect' point 3).

4 Explain that even the best leaders need good followers. A hockey team will only function well if the team members follow the advice of their coach or captain. The same was true for Ezra – things would only go well if the Israelites followed his lead. As a whole group, quickly put together profiles for a member of a hockey team and also for an Israelite at the time of Ezra. What does a good follower look like?

5 To conclude, spend some time discussing with the group what leadership qualities make them want to follow a leader or not. Identify the 'leaders' that the young people are currently following, or who they think they should be following more.

LEVEL 3: SWITCH ON

WHAT: Bible study and team talk
WHY: to assess the value of leadership and to think about the leaders God gives us
WITH: resource page 145, film clip (optional)

1 If possible, show your group a clip from a sports film of a coach giving a 'team talk'. There are plenty of options! Alternatively, challenge your group to remember scenes like this from films they have seen and to describe them to the group.

2 Spend a few minutes discussing why a 'team talk' from the coach can be so significant and game changing. See if any members of your group have had any real-life experiences of team talks.

3 Introduce Ezra to the group. Explain that he was one of the leaders of the Israelites when they returned to their homeland after many years in captivity. Then give everyone a copy of resource page 145 and make sure everyone has a Bible. Ask them to read Ezra 7 and Nehemiah 8:1–10 in small groups.

4 Encourage the small groups to make some notes about why Ezra was a good leader to the Israelites. Challenge them to follow Ezra's example in giving a 'team talk' to the three people on resource page 145, referring back to the Bible passages for tips on good 'coaching'.

5 Gather the group together for feedback. Then ask them to chat about the key leaders in their lives. Who are the people they follow, look up to and turn to when they need guidance and advice?

141

RESPOND

 MUSICAL

WHAT: praise anthem
WHY: to think of God as our ultimate Leader
WITH: lyrics to your national anthem

1 Start talking with the group about your country's national anthem. You might want simply to show them a copy of the lyrics, you may be brave enough to get them or your fellow leaders to sing it, or alternatively show them a clip of it being performed.

2 Make the point that national anthems are often about the person to whom the country looks for leadership and guidance – in the UK's case, it's about the monarch.

3 In pairs or threes, ask group members to write an anthem to God, reflecting on him as the ultimate Leader and us as his followers.

4 After they've had a good amount of time to do this, gather the young people together and ask each group to read or sing their anthems.

 PRACTICAL

WHAT: encouragement
WHY: to encourage the leaders that you know

1 Suggest to your group that being a leader is not always easy. If a hockey team, for example, were to do really well at the Olympics, it would probably be the players who would get all the credit. However, if the team were to do really badly, it would be the coach who would get the blame!

2 Give everyone in your group a sheet of paper and a pen. Suggest that they write a letter to a leader they know, to encourage them. This could be a group leader(!), a church leader, a leader of a team or club they're part of, or even the local MP.

3 After everyone has written their letter, encourage the young people to get into pairs and to share with one another who they've written to and why they chose that person.

4 Then ask the young people, in their pairs, to pray for the people they've written to.

 CREATIVE

WHAT: pass the prayer
WHY: to creatively encourage everyone to pray
WITH: hockey sticks and a ball (actual or improvised)

1 Get everyone to stand in a circle and give each group member a hockey stick.

2 Explain that every time someone passes the ball to them they should say a short prayer – either out loud or silently – then pass the ball to someone else.

3 In order to give this activity some structure, you could have three parts to it:

Part 1 – Get the young people to say single words about why God is so great.

Part 2 – One-sentence prayers of thanks.

Part 3 – One-sentence prayers of requests.

MORE ON THIS THEME:

If you want to do a short series with your group, other sessions that work well with this one are:

FOLLOWING THE LEADER

Answer these questions to find out what sort of leader and follower you are.

WHAT KIND OF LEADER ARE YOU?

1

There's a big job that needs doing. What do you do?

a) Find a group of people and tell them to do it. While they do the work, you sit down and relax.
b) Prepare a mini-speech to get people excited about doing it.
c) Ask if anyone would like to help you do it.
d) Go home, pretend you didn't notice.

2

You're working with some classmates on a school project. There's a disagreement about how you should undertake the task that has been set. What do you do?

a) Shout that your way is best and they really must listen to you because you know what you're talking about.
b) Tell the group that they must focus on what you're trying to achieve and not worry about the detail so much.
c) Suggest that you should make a list of the positives and negatives of each approach to discover which way is best.
d) Stay quiet and just do what you're told when the rest of the group has made a decision.

3

You've been asked to help organise a youth camp and you need to decide who's going to do what job. What do you do?

a) Decide by yourself who should do what, and present it to the group at the meeting.
b) Suggest to the group that before you decide who needs to do what, you really ought to figure out what the aim of this camp is. After all, do some of these jobs actually need doing?
c) Ask everyone to say which jobs they'd like to do and why they think they best fit with their strengths.
d) Sit back and let someone else decide. You're happy to do whatever.

4

You're now on the youth camp and the toilets need to be cleaned. What do you do?

a) Go and tell someone that they have to clean the toilets or they won't be getting any dinner.
b) At dinner, ask for volunteers, giving a short speech on how this is an excellent opportunity to serve and bless others – like when Jesus washed the disciples' feet!
c) Say you're going to clean the toilets and ask if anyone is willing to help you.
d) Go and hide in the toilets!

WHAT KIND OF FOLLOWER ARE YOU?

1

You're on a school trip and have to do a series of team-building activities. The leader of your team is doing a good job. What are you thinking?

a) You're thinking about how bored you are. You don't want to be part of these team-building activities – they're stupid!
b) You're thinking that if you were the leader you'd be doing things so much better.
c) You're not thinking much, you're just doing exactly what you're told. You are just really pleased you're not the team leader, because that would mean you'd have to think.
d) Thinking! You haven't got time to think! You're getting stuck into all the activities. You're encouraging everyone, helping those who are finding it difficult and generally keeping everyone's spirits up!

2

Your youth group leader has asked you to photocopy some worksheets. What do you do?

a) You're annoyed that they asked you, so you decide to do the task as slowly as possible. Hopefully they won't ask you again in the future.
b) You protest, saying that photocopiers always seem to jam on you and it would be better to just share anyway.
c) You go and do it. A couple of copies come out a bit wonky, but you can't be bothered to do them again.
d) You do the job and are delighted that you've been given the opportunity to help. You make sure it's done well and even sort the worksheets into separate piles.

3

Your parents have asked you to clean your bedroom. What do you do?

a) Refuse to do it; you just can't be bothered right now.
b) You explain that you don't really think it's that messy at the moment, and try to persuade them to let you do it later.
c) You do it, but only as little as you can possibly get away with, hiding as much under the bed as you can.
d) You clean your room thoroughly. You even use a duster and vacuum cleaner!

4

You're on holiday and you are on a guided tour. The tour guide isn't very good. What do you do?

a) You wander off by yourself, causing the guide to have to stop the tour and come and find you.
b) You try adding your own funny commentary, but you just end up annoying the tour guide, who doesn't appreciate you implying that they're boring.
c) You keep quiet, do the tour and spend the time thinking about what you're going to do next.
d) You try and encourage the tour guide by nodding lots as they speak and try to make things more interesting by asking questions.

22

Bible bit
Ezra 7; Nehemiah 8:1–10

Ezra may not seem the most exciting, dynamic Bible character: he doesn't kill enemies or work miracles. However, his role is essential in holding the no-longer-exiled Israelites together as a nation and as God's people.

The coach of a sports team has an important role. They not only help the players improve as individuals but also enable the team to play well together. Ezra was like a coach to the Israelites. He led them to be the best that they could be and to work together to become even greater than the sum of their parts.

A FILM WITH NO DIRECTOR

A HOCKEY TEAM WITH NO COACH

AN ORCHESTRA WITH NO CONDUCTOR

NO DIR EC TION

A COMPANY WITH NO MANAGER

A BUILDING SITE WITH NO FOREMAN

Pick two of these situations and use the spaces here to draw or write descriptions of what you think would happen.

A CHURCH WITH NO LEADERS

Read Ezra 7 and Nehemiah 8:1–10. What do you think would have happened to the Israelites when they returned home after years of captivity, if they hadn't had a leader like Ezra?

WHAT LEADERSHIP QUALITIES AND TOP TIPS CAN YOU SEE FROM EZRA'S EXAMPLE IN THE BIBLE PASSAGES?

Team talk

These three young people are in a desperate need of a 'team talk' from their coach – YOU! What would you say to them to guide them and encourage them to keep going?

For some tips on how to be a good leader, read Ezra 7 and Nehemiah 8:1–10 to learn from Ezra's example. Scribble down some notes and pieces of advice to yourself around the page as you read the Bible passages and then apply them to each of the profiles below.

I'm useless!

Everything I try and do is a disaster. I failed to get into the school football team, so I decided to stop playing football and started playing the drums instead, but there was this other drummer at school and he was so much better than me, so I quit. Someone suggested I start running, so I did, but that was hard work, so I gave that up too. Last week I was helping my dad do some DIY, but I slipped and broke a window. I'm now trying to revise for my exams, but I just can't get my head around any of the subjects. I just seem to be useless at everything.

Quitting God?

I hate going to school on Mondays. Every week my so-called friends bully me for going to church on Sundays. Things aren't much better on Tuesdays, Wednesdays, Thursdays or Fridays either. Everyone takes every opportunity to make a joke about how I believe in God and try to follow him. I think I might just give up. I'll stop going to church. I'll say I don't believe in God. I'll stop trying so hard to live a Christian lifestyle in front of my friends. At least that will make the bullying stop.

Future panic

I'm 14 next month and I have no idea what I want to do with my life. I have no idea what job I want. I have no idea what I want to study at university. And – eek – what if I don't do well in my exams and can't go to university? I'm panicking. I'm scared I'm going to make bad decisions and make mistakes and ruin my life. I want to get married, but what if no one wants to marry me? I don't want to be alone.

23
WHATEVER

THE AIM: To understand that some people will not accept God

The aim unpacked

In this session we look at the prophet Jeremiah. Although Jeremiah's message is one of pending disaster, it is delivered in the hope that the people will return to God. God shows Jeremiah how his people are like clay in a potter's hands. God is in control because he is the Creator; his people are his creation. But he knows that some people will always reject God.

WAY IN

 theGRID MAGAZINE

WHAT: discussion
WHY: to show that you just can't get through to some people
WITH: magazine page 149

1 Hand out copies of page 149. Invite everyone to look at the *Blind Date* cartoon strip.

2 Discuss these questions with the young people:

- Do you think the young women in the story deserve a date?
- Why? Why not?

3 Make the point that relationships can only work if both parties are prepared to make an effort! This is true for every relationship – not just romances!

 SCENE SETTER

WHAT: discussing adverts
WHY: to introduce the idea that people respond differently to the same message
WITH: selection of current glossy magazines

1 Ask the young people each to pick an advert they like from the magazines.

2 Invite each young person to explain why they picked their particular advert. What do they like about it? Does it make them want to buy the product?

3 Pick one or two of the adverts and make sure everyone can see them. Ask:

- Who thinks this advert is a good one? If so why, and if not, why not?
- What is it about this advert that you like, or don't like?

You could hold a vote when you have finished the discussion.

4 Make the point that however clever an advert is, not everyone who sees it will want to buy the product. We all respond differently to the same messages.

 THEMED GAME

WHAT: modelling clay game
WHY: to introduce the idea of shaping clay
WITH: modelling clay, list of objects to be modelled

1 Divide the young people into two teams. Each team must choose a modeller to go first.

2 Secretly show the modellers from each team the same item from your list. On your signal, they should go back to their teams and model that item for the rest of their teams to guess. The first team to guess correctly wins a point. You can impose a time limit to make it more exciting if you wish!

3 Continue playing until everyone has had a turn at modelling.

4 If appropriate, explain that you will be looking later at a story about someone who modelled clay.

BIBLE EXPERIENCE

 LEVEL 1: CONNECT

WHAT: drama and discussion
WHY: to understand that some people will not accept God
WITH: magazine page 150

1 Give out copies of page 150 and get everyone to find the script for *The Jerry Zinger* Show. Choose someone to play each character.

2 Read Jeremiah 18:1–12 so that everyone is familiar with the story. Then read through the sketch.

3 Discuss the sketch with the young people. Do they want to add in any dialogue of their own? Talk about any changes they want to make, without removing the central story.

4 Invite the young people to act out the sketch together. Encourage your group to improvise a stage set and invite everyone who is not in the sketch to be the audience.

5 When you have finished, chat together about why the people of Judah didn't want to listen to God. Talk about the chance that God was giving them. You may want to ask:

- Which is easier to do: what you want to do or what someone else wants you to do?
- What difference do you think the illustration of the potter made to the people of Judah?
- What chance was God giving them?

 LEVEL 2: INTERFACE

WHAT: Bible reflection
WHY: to understand that some people will not accept God
WITH: resource page 151, quiet music (optional)

1 Ask the young people to find a comfortable place to sit. Explain that you are going to read out a meditation based on a passage of Jeremiah, but first you are going to read the Bible passage.

2 Read Jeremiah 18:1–12. Then read the meditation from resource page 151. You may find it helpful to play some quiet music in the background.

3 Ask the young people to discuss these questions in small groups, and then obtain feedback:

- What adjectives would you use to describe God's message to the people of Judah? Loving? Harsh? Unfair? Just?
- How would you describe the reaction of the people of Judah?
- Think about your own reaction to the message. If you had been in the crowd, what would you have thought?
- Would you be open to being remoulded by God?
- Why is it that some people don't want to hear God's message for them?

LEVEL 3: SWITCH ON

WHAT: Bible study and discussion
WHY: to understand that some people will not accept God

1 Read Jeremiah 18:1–12 together and discuss what God was trying to say to the people of Judah. Focus on verses 7–10. Try to draw out that the chosen people could be made to start again if it all went wrong; also that if people who had ignored God were to turn back to him, God would lovingly start again with them.

2 Ask the young people to think about how it feels to have God take you back to the start and begin again with you. It might be helpful here to share a time when God has started again with you over an issue. Maybe a friendship was all wrong, or perhaps you had made a lifestyle choice that wasn't part of God's plan for you. Make sure you choose an appropriate issue to share with the group. Often these times are painful – if your example was, let the group know!

3 Read 2 Corinthians 5:17–19 and discuss these questions with your group:

- What do you think it means to be a 'new creation'?
- What makes it possible for God to renew us in this way?
- How does the image of the clay in Jeremiah affect your understanding of this passage?

4 Encourage your group to read the passages again quietly and to reflect on the following questions. They may wish to write a journal entry or draw a picture to help them.

- What do you do that makes it hard for God to shape your life?
- What action do you need to take to change this?
- Why do some people say no to God?

147

RESPOND

 MUSICAL

WHAT: singing
WHY: to state that you have accepted God
WITH: words of creeds, words and music for creed-based songs, playback equipment or musical accompaniment

1 Gather together some creeds and creed-based songs and invite the young people to read and listen to them (for example 'I believe in Jesus'). Chat about whether there's anything in these creeds that might prevent people accepting God.

2 If everyone in your group is in agreement, sing one of the songs or say one of the creeds together to state what you as a group believe about Jesus. Make sure people can opt out without pressure if they aren't sure.

3 With music playing in the background encourage the young people to spend some time thinking and praying for people they know who have not yet accepted God.

 PRACTICAL

WHAT: prayer
WHY: to remember and pray for those who have not yet accepted God
WITH: tea lights, permanent marker pens, sand tray, matches

1 Set up a tray of sand large enough for each of your group to place a tea light in. Place one lit tea light in the centre of the tray.

2 Explain that you are going to spend some time thinking about and praying for people you know who do not yet know God or who have rejected him.

3 Give each person a tea light and make available some permanent marker pens. Encourage the young people to spend some time quietly praying and then to write the name(s) or initials of those they are praying for around the metal part of the tea light.

4 Allow time for each person to light their tea light from the centre candle and place it in the sand tray. Make sure you have properly assessed any risks involved in allowing the group to light candles and that you have adequate safety measures in place.

5 When all the candles are lit, say a simple prayer of blessing – for example, 'Thank you, God, that you know all these people far better than we do. We pray that you would open their eyes to see you, their ears to hear you and their hearts to love you. Amen.'

6 Blow out the candles and allow the wax to cool. Encourage everyone to take their candle home and use it to continue praying for their friends.

 CREATIVE

WHAT: clay modelling
WHY: to explore the response to the idea that some people reject God
WITH: coloured modelling clay, tools for shaping (skewers, forks, knives)

1 Divide up the modelling clay (Fimo is ideal) and give some to each person.

2 Invite the young people to make something like a pot or bowl. While they are doing this, ask them to think about how God shapes our lives. Remind them that if what they are making doesn't go to plan, they can squash it down and start again.

3 While they are still working on their pots, ask them to think about how willing they are to be squashed down and reshaped by God if they go off course. Ask them to think of one thing that God might want to reshape in their lives. Encourage them to pray about this now, asking God to squash and remould that part of their life.

4 Ask them to think about why some people reject God. Why do these people not want to be moulded by God? Invite the young people to tell God about someone they know who has said no to God.

MORE ON THIS THEME:

If you want to do a short series with your group, other sessions that work well with this one are:

24   *Hope springs eternal*   *Jeremiah 31:1–6; 32:1–15*

25   *'I'm not listening'*   *Jeremiah 36*

26   *Well, fancy that*   *Jeremiah 38:1–13*

Have you ever found that some people just aren't interested?

Bible bit
Jeremiah 18:1–12

It's obvious, blatant, impossible to miss and interpret in any other way. If you continue to mess up, things will get bad, very bad. So what do you do? Hopefully not the same as those who heard Jeremiah's words in this passage.

THE JERRY ZINGER SHOW

Jerry Zinger

Jeremiah

Boo Boo

Down WITH JEREMIAH

JU-DAH

The People of Judah

Mr Potter

THE CHARACTERS:

Jerry Zinger: Irrepressible talk show host
Jeremiah: Slightly tattered prophet of God
The People of Judah: The stubborn people of God
Mr Potter: The simple potter at whose house Jeremiah first received his message from God

Jerry: Good evening and welcome to *The Jerry Zinger Show*! On the show tonight: the crazy prophet of doom who is driving Judah mad – Jeremiah! *(Jeremiah enters and takes a seat.)*

Jerry: So, Jeremiah, just what is it you have to say that is driving God's people so crazy? Why are you so deeply unpopular?

Jeremiah: Well, Jerry, I guess it's because I won't tell them what they want to hear. I tell them what God wants me to say.

Jerry: And just what is it that God wants you to say, Jeremiah? Or can I call you Jerry?

Jeremiah: Er, yes, I suppose you can. *(Clears his throat.)* This is the word of the Lord. *(Reads Jeremiah 18:6–12.)* *(Silence for a moment after he finishes reading. Jerry looks puzzled.)*

Jerry: Well, that's certainly fascinating. What does it all mean? Here to give us the other side of the story, please give a big Jerry Zinger welcome to… The People of Judah! *(The People of Judah enter in a group and take their seats.)*

Jerry: So, Judah, what have you got to say to Jeremiah?

Judah: He's just an old misery. He's always coming up with prophecies about our destruction. And look, we're still here! If God is so mad with us, why doesn't he just smite us right here and now? Eh? Eh?

Jeremiah: *(Trying to be patient.)* Because for some reason far beyond my understanding, he wants to give you the chance to change your ways. He wants you to submit willingly to him. He wants you to be obedient to him and show him your love

so that he can bless you.

Judah: You just want to try and control us. You don't want us to be ourselves. You want everyone to be miserable, like you.

Jerry: OK, people, let's keep calm now. There's just one other person who might be able to help us understand this situation. Please welcome… Mr Potter! *(Mr Potter wanders in, looking a bit confused.)*

Jerry: Hello, Mr Potter. I understand that it was at your house that Jeremiah received this message from God.

Mr Potter: Ar, I believe he did.

Jerry: So, Mr Potter, what we're all dying to know is, what does he look like?

Mr Potter: Who? Jeremiah?

Jerry: No, not Jeremiah! The big G. GOD!

Mr Potter: I don't rightly know. I didn't see 'im or nuffin.

Jerry: You didn't see him?

Mr Potter: No…

Jerry: So, this message, how did it arrive?

Mr Potter: Don't rightly know. Thar I was, working on me pots, and suddenly Jeremiah

starts talkin' about how we's all a bit like clay in the 'ands of God. I thought about it, you know, thar at the wheel, and I says to meself, 'e's not wrong. No, 'e's not wrong about that. *(Warming to his theme.)* You know, sometimes a pot just goes wrong and I have to stop, roll it back into a ball and start again. Often the second time round, the pot is perfect!

Jerry: *(Clearly exasperated by the lack of drama in this story.)* Well, there you have it, folks. Jeremiah watched Mr Potter at work and thought he heard God speaking to him. Judah isn't keen to listen to him, and frankly I'm not surprised! But what do you think? You decide! *(Audience applauds, show ends, all leave the stage except Jeremiah.)*

Jeremiah: *(Looking up.)* I'm sorry. I tried, I really did. *(Jeremiah gets up and dejectedly walks offstage.)*

Meditation

Imagine you are at the house of the potter with Jeremiah. Try to think of what you might see around you. Bags of clay, water, shaping tools, a potter's wheel. Maybe there are some pots waiting to be put into the kiln. You can see the kiln and feel the heat coming from it. On the other side of the room you might see some glazed pots that are ready to be sold, or perhaps some pots which broke while they were being fired.

You and Jeremiah watch the potter for a while. He makes one, two, maybe more pots that are perfect. You can see he is a very skilful man. As the wheel turns in front of him, he shapes the pot with ease and makes the pot grow out of a shapeless lump of clay before your eyes. Have you ever had a go on a potter's wheel? What was it like? Was it easy?

You are watching the potter when suddenly you realise that not everything has gone well. The pot has become lopsided and misshapen. The potter stops the wheel, cuts the clay from it and moulds it into a round lump. He then places it back on the wheel and starts again.

Now imagine that you are with Jeremiah before the people. He is telling them what the Lord has told him to say. The people are like the clay and God is the potter. He shapes them into beautiful creations, if they follow his ways. But if they disobey him, he will gather everything up and start again. Jeremiah's message speaks of God's love and his discipline. He wants the people to follow his ways so that they can live lives that are happy and fulfilled. But the people don't want to know. They are stubborn. They realise that following what God wants means that they won't be able to do what their evil hearts' desire. So they refuse to listen.

They don't know (or don't want to know) that the Lord is about to hand them over to their enemies – to bash the clay down and start again.

24

Bible: Jeremiah 31:1–6; 32:1–15

HOPE SPRINGS ETERNAL

THE AIM: To know that we can live with hope because of God's knowledge and power

The aim unpacked

Although Jeremiah's message is one of pending disaster, it is delivered in the hope that the people will return to God. God's people weren't going to change their ways — well, not all of them. However, here we see that there is hope for the future. Even though the times ahead will be tough and traumatic, there is light at the end of the tunnel — however dark the tunnel may be.

WAY IN

 theGRID MAGAZINE

WHAT: discussion
WHY: to think about situations that can make us feel hopeless
WITH: magazine page 155

1 Invite the young people to read through the section called 'Nightmare on your street?!' on page 155. Ask them to rank the situations listed on a scale from 1 to 10 (10 being the worst and 1 being the easiest situation to handle).

2 Encourage the young people to feed back their answers to the rest of the group. Discuss how each of these situations would make them feel and how they might handle it if it were their problem.

3 Sensitively ask if anyone has ever been in a situation where they felt completely hopeless. If anyone would like to share what it was, ask them how they dealt with the problem and what happened in the end. You or another leader might like to share an example of your own with the group.

 SCENE SETTER

WHAT: sorting and problem solving
WHY: to consider what situations, if any, are without hope
WITH: copies of resource page 156

1 Organise the young people into groups of about three and give each group a set of the cut-up scenarios from resource page 156.

2 Explain that they have a few minutes to sort the scenarios into two groups: 'Hopeless' (those without any chance of improving) and 'Hopeful' (those that have a chance of improving).

3 After a few minutes, invite each group to feed back to the others. Does everyone agree?

4 Explain that they should now try to think of something practical that someone could do in each situation to show that there is hope. For example, for the person who failed all their exams, someone could buy a congratulations card in advance for doing well in the next set of tests. Give them a few minutes to complete this.

5 Invite feedback from each group. Were some situations harder to find hope for than others? Why?

 THEMED GAME

WHAT: game
WHY: to understand how it feels when the odds are against you
WITH: sweets as prizes

1 Ask for a volunteer who is good at talking. Explain that they have to talk for one minute about a subject of their choice. If they manage to keep talking for a minute without hesitating or repeating themselves, they will win a few sweets.

2 To add to the fun, the rest of the group has to do all they can to distract the person who is talking, to make them either hesitate or repeat themselves. They can do anything within the boundaries of decency(!) but are not allowed to go closer than 1 metre to the person speaking and must not say anything insulting to them. If any of these rules are broken, the person speaking automatically wins. If the group succeeds in distracting the person, everyone in the group gets a sweet.

3 Play the game again and give a few people a chance to try to complete the challenge. If appropriate, ask the people who tried to talk how it felt when everyone else was against them. Did they feel like giving up at any point?

BIBLE EXPERIENCE

 LEVEL 1: CONNECT

WHAT: battle re-enactment
WHY: to know that we can live with hope because of God's knowledge and power
WITH: large sheet of paper with the word 'Jerusalem' written at the top, resource pages 158 and 159 with the pictures cut out in advance

1 Put the paper on the floor and ask the young people to imagine that it is a map of Jerusalem. Explain that we are going to lay out on the map the situation that Jeremiah was facing in today's passage, to help us understand what things were like for him.

2 Hand out the pictures from resource page 159 so that everyone has at least one (but keep the script for your use). Explain that you are going to read out a summary of today's Bible passage and that each person should place (and remove) their picture on the paper at the point in the story where it is mentioned.

3 Read out the summary from resource pages 158. You may want to stop halfway through the story and ask the young people how they think they might have felt if they had been stuck in prison in the middle of Jerusalem at the time the soldiers were surrounding it. Then continue to read out the Bible summary.

4 When you have finished, ask the young people why they think Jeremiah bought a field in the middle of a siege. What was this a sign of? Ask two volunteers to read Jeremiah 32:1–15 and Jeremiah 31:1–6.

5 Make the point that, if we are living to please God, God promises that, although things may be hard and seem hopeless at times, ultimately he will bring good things to those who trust him (Revelation 21:3–5).

 LEVEL 2: INTERFACE

WHAT: sorting and discussion
WHY: to know that we can live with hope because of God's knowledge and power
WITH: sets of cards from resource page 157

1 Split the young people into groups of about three and give each group a set of the information cards about Jeremiah from resource page 157. Read Jeremiah 32:1–15 together.

2 Ask each group to divide the information cards into two sets: things that were 'For' Jeremiah and things that were going 'Against' Jeremiah. Give them a few minutes to complete this.

3 Ask each group to feed back to everyone else. Overall, do the young people think Jeremiah was in a good situation or not?

4 Explain that sometimes we can be in situations where it can seem that we are up against things. Ask the young people if they have ever felt like everything was going against them and that things were hopeless. If appropriate, ask one or two to share their experiences with the rest of the group.

5 Ask the group what choices Jeremiah had in his situation. Suggest that he had at least three choices:

    a) to give up all hope

    b) to fight against the army

    c) to trust that God had it all under control

Ask the young people what they would have done in Jeremiah's situation. Then ask which, out of the three options, they normally do whenever they feel things are against them.

6 Remind the young people in your group that you are always there for them to talk to and pray with whenever things are hard.

 LEVEL 3: SWITCH ON

WHAT: Bible study
WHY: to know that we can live with hope because of God's knowledge and power
WITH: flip chart or whiteboard (optional)

1 Organise the group into twos or threes and ask each group to read the following Bible passages: Jeremiah 32:1–15 and Jeremiah 31:1–6.

2 Explain that you are going to start off by looking back at what the situation was like for Jeremiah. Ask each pair or three to discuss the following questions.

• What things were against Jerusalem and Jeremiah? (See Jeremiah 32:2,3.)

• Why were they in this situation? (See Jeremiah 26:1–6.)

• What was God's promise despite this? (See Jeremiah 31:1–6.)

(It may work better to ask them just one question at a time rather than asking them all at once. Alternatively, you may want to write the questions on a flip chart or whiteboard so the groups can see them.) If there is time, ask them to feed back and discuss their thoughts with the rest of the group.

3 Explain that you are now going to think about our lives today and how the situation Jeremiah was in and God's promise to him are still relevant to us today. Ask them to discuss, back in their pairs or threes:

• In what ways or areas of your life do you feel that things are stacked against you?

• Are there any reasons why you are in this situation?

• Look up Psalm 139:23,24. This is a good prayer to say at difficult times in our lives.

• What hope can you ultimately have when you are in difficult situations? (See Matthew 10:28–32; John 10:27–29.)

4 Remind the young people in your group that you are always there for them to talk to and pray with whenever things are hard.

RESPOND

 MUSICAL

WHAT: musical reflection
WHY: to remember that Jesus' light always shines in the darkness
WITH: 'There Is a Light' by Delirious?, playback equipment, inextinguishable candle

1 In advance, get hold of the song 'There is a light' by Delirious? (from *Live and in the Can*, track 15, labelled as 'Spontaneous Song 8'), and an inextinguishable candle (available from card shops). If you can't access this track, you could use the song 'Light of the World' by Tim Hughes, or 'I Will Praise You (no matter what)' from the *Great Big God 2* album. (This is a children's CD, but the song is relevant to this activity and is not too childish.)

2 Explain that you are going to listen to a song which reminds us that no matter what happens, Jesus' light will always shine in the darkness.

3 Make the room as dark as possible and light the candle. Play the music track and after a few moments try to blow out the candle – it should relight itself. You can do this several times.

4 Read out Jeremiah 31:1–6 and remind the young people that the God of Jeremiah is the same God we worship today, and that he sent his Son Jesus so that we do not have to live in darkness. We have the Light that gives life (John 8:12)!

 PRACTICAL

WHAT: verse reminders
WHY: to provide a reminder of the hope we can have in God
WITH: credit-card-sized pieces of card, laminator (optional)

1 Give out the cards and invite the young people to decorate their card with a Bible verse. They can either use one of the following suggested verses or use their own favourite verse to remind them that no matter what they face, God is still in control. Suggested verses are:

- John 10:28
- Revelation 21:4
- Psalm 23:5,62

You may want to laminate the cards so they are more durable.

2 Encourage the young people to take their cards home with them this week and look at them any time they are struggling. Depending on your group, the young people could email or text each other the verses during the week. You could encourage each member of the group to be responsible for encouraging another person by sending a card, an email or a text. If you choose to do this, you may need to organise it so that no one is left out.

 CREATIVE

WHAT: creative prayer
WHY: to put into practice living in hope because of God's power
WITH: sheets of green paper, quiet music (optional)

1 Give out the sheets of green paper, saying that they represent the field that Jeremiah bought. Remind the young people that the field was a symbol of hope for Jeremiah and the people of Judah. They were going through really tough times, but God was going to save them soon.

2 Ask the group to write any worries they have on their paper. You might want to play some quiet background music as they do this.

3 Pray together about these worries, as appropriate for your group. They could pray all together, in small groups or in pairs.

4 After everyone has finished praying, encourage the young people to swap sheets and take someone else's home (make sure this is optional). Encourage them to continue praying for the items on each other's 'fields' throughout the week.

MORE ON THIS THEME:

If you want to do a short series with your group, other sessions that work well with this one are:

23	*Whatever*	*Jeremiah 18:1–12*
25	*'I'm not listening'*	*Jeremiah 36*
26	*Well, fancy that*	*Jeremiah 38:1–13*

Bible bit
Jeremiah 31:1–6; 32:1–15

God loves his people; we can see that in the first reference here. But his people are going to go through a really tough time, all will be lost and any hope will seem futile. But Jeremiah gives a practical demonstration of faith and hope for the future. One day things will get better.

NIGHTMARE
ON YOUR STREET?!

Rank on a scale from 1 to 10 (10 being enough to make you want to hide in a cave for the rest of your life and 1 barely making you flinch) just how much of a nightmare each of these situations would be to you.

An elderly relative sits you down to explain the importance of safe sex.

1 2 3 4 5 6 7 8 9 10

You get into a conversation with someone where you end up saying some really cruel things about your best friend. You turn round to see your best mate standing behind you.

1 2 3 4 5 6 7 8 9 10

Your grandma insists that you wear a jumper that she knitted for you (with fluffy white sheep on the front) to the youth club party.

1 2 3 4 5 6 7 8 9 10

Your teacher informs you that he is looking forward to parents' evening and explaining how you haven't done any work this term.

1 2 3 4 5 6 7 8 9 10

Your Head of Year gets you out in assembly to talk about how you won an award for ballet dancing at primary school.

1 2 3 4 5 6 7 8 9 10

You find out your ex is going to be at a party you are going to – with the person they dumped you for. You are going alone.

1 2 3 4 5 6 7 8 9 10

You secretly try out some hair dye but unfortunately it makes you look like you've had a blue rinse. According to the bottle, it takes six weeks to wash out.

1 2 3 4 5 6 7 8 9 10

You have to read a section from a Shakespeare play out to the rest of the class.

1 2 3 4 5 6 7 8 9 10

Your school trousers are just that little bit too short but your parent or guardian won't buy you new ones.

1 2 3 4 5 6 7 8 9 10

You accidentally send a text about a person you secretly fancy to that person.

1 2 3 4 5 6 7 8 9 10

An African child is diagnosed with HIV.	A Year 8 boy has failed every test he has taken this school year.
A footballer badly injures his knee during training. The doctor says he will never play again.	A young person is always getting dragged into doing things that they don't want to do by their so-called friends. Anyone who isn't 'in' with this group of friends gets really picked on.
A teenage girl wants to be a doctor when she is older but her family are dead set against it.	A teacher at school seems to have got it in for one particular pupil. No matter what happens, this pupil gets blamed – often when they are not at fault.
A 14-year-old wants to go on holiday with their best friend in the summer but it will cost £400 and they haven't got £400.	A young man is paralysed in a road traffic accident.
A young person is bullied at school. They have tried telling a teacher but it hasn't helped.	A politician tries to persuade two groups to stop a war against each other that has been going on for 20 years.
Hopeless	**Hopeful**

The Babylonian army is surrounding Jerusalem (where Jeremiah is) and is ready to attack.	The Babylonian army is surrounding Jerusalem (where Jeremiah is) and is ready to attack.
There is no way out of Jerusalem.	There is no way out of Jerusalem.
Jeremiah's cousin comes to visit him in prison and offers to sell him a field in the area.	Jeremiah's cousin comes to visit him in prison and offers to sell him a field in the area.
God has told the people that Jerusalem will be destroyed by a huge army.	God has told the people that Jerusalem will be destroyed by a huge army.
The king in Jerusalem (Zedekiah) can't stand Jeremiah or his preaching.	The king in Jerusalem (Zedekiah) can't stand Jeremiah or his preaching.
The king locks Jeremiah up in prison.	The king locks Jeremiah up in prison.
God tells Jeremiah to buy the field as a way to show people that, although Jerusalem will be destroyed, one day it will be rebuilt and become valuable again.	God tells Jeremiah to buy the field as a way to show people that, although Jerusalem will be destroyed, one day it will be rebuilt and become valuable again.

Battle re-enactment

Give out the pictures. Read out the following script and invite the young people to carry out the actions that are described in italics.

So, this is the scene: Jem is having a seriously bad day. There he is, sitting in the middle of Jerusalem. *(The young person who has the picture of Jeremiah should put it in the middle of the paper.)* There are houses all around him. *(The young people who have the pictures of the houses should scatter them around Jeremiah.)* The next thing he knows, the king throws him in the prison in the middle of Jerusalem. *(The prison picture should be put in the middle of the piece of paper and Jeremiah on top of it.)* His crime? Telling people what God is saying. This is not a good day.

Just when we think things couldn't get any worse, our mate Jem remembers that being in prison isn't his only problem.

The city is surrounded by Babylonian soldiers. *(The pictures of soldiers should be placed on the paper so they surround all the houses in Jerusalem.)* They stretch all the way around the city, and at any moment they are going to invade. There is no way for anyone to get out – the city and everyone in it seem doomed.

Then, in the middle of all this, God tells Jem to do something that seems really... well... er... odd. God tells Jem to buy a field in Jerusalem. *(The picture of the flower should be placed in the Jerusalem area – inside the area surrounded by the soldiers.)* So that's exactly what he does. While he's in prison in a city that's surrounded by an army that's about to rip the city to shreds, Jem buys a field in the city.

This is the reason why: Jem says, 'God has told me, "Things are going to be tough. This city is going to be invaded by the army *(move the soldiers inwards on the paper)* and loads of houses will be destroyed. *(Rip up the houses.)* But I have told Jem to buy a field as a way of showing you that even though many houses will be destroyed and loads of people will be killed, this is still a place worth investing in. There is hope for this city. *(Remove the soldiers and the prison so only Jeremiah and the flower remain.)* One day people will want to buy the land here again. Though times are tough now, things will get better."'

USE WITH SESSION 24 BIBLE EXPERIENCE 'LEVEL 1 CONNECT'

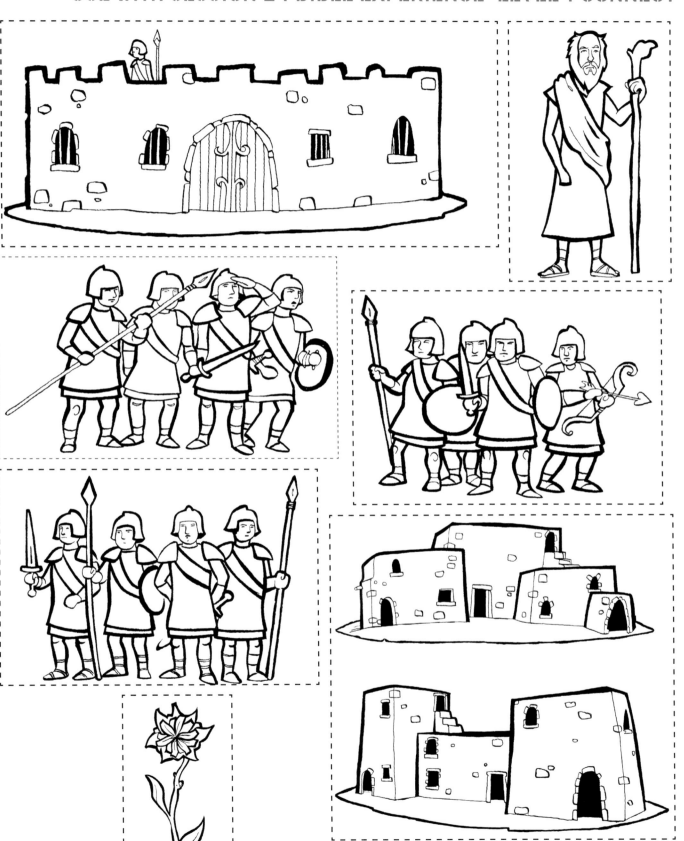

Photocopiable resource © Scripture Union 2018

25

'I'M NOT LISTENING!'

THE AIM: To realise that ignoring God won't change anything

The aim unpacked

Although Jeremiah's message is one of pending disaster, it is delivered in the hope that the people will return to God. People often treat God with an 'out of sight, out of mind' attitude, particularly younger people; eternity appears a long way off for your average 11- to 14-year-old. The king thought he could ignore God too, by burning Jeremiah's message of disaster, but he couldn't; it changed nothing.

WAY IN

 theGRID MAGAZINE

WHAT: scenarios
WHY: to introduce the idea that not listening can have consequences
WITH: magazine page 163

1 Give out copies of page 163 and look at 'I'm not listening!' In pairs, the young people should complete the scenarios with what happened next. Encourage them to use their imagination!

2 After a few minutes, invite the young people to share their responses with the rest of the group. Who had the most creative or imaginative suggestion?

3 Discuss the value of listening and not listening. When do the young people always listen? When do they deliberately not listen? Is it always when they want to avoid doing something?

4 Use the concept of the consequences of not listening to introduce today's session and the message that God gave Jeremiah to pass on to the people of Judah (including the king), that if they didn't listen and change the direction of their lives, disaster would surely follow.

 SCENE SETTER

WHAT: choices activity
WHY: to reinforce the idea that God knows everything
WITH: resource page 165

1 Divide the young people into pairs or threes and give each group a copy of resource page 165.

2 Draw the young people's attention to the questions and situations at the bottom of the page, one at a time. Give each group 30 seconds to choose up to three people from the list who they think would be the most appropriate person or would know most about that situation.

3 Bring the young people together. Use feedback from the activity to think about how certain individuals may know quite a lot about some situations but not very much about others.

4 Explain that in today's session we are going to hear how Jeremiah recorded a prophecy from God for the people of Judah. Jeremiah couldn't have known what was going to happen in the future, but he trusted in God's 'bigger picture'. It wasn't a comfortable message or one that was going to be easy to deliver, but he trusted in God.

 **THEMED GAME**

WHAT: game
WHY: to think about some of the barriers to listening
WITH: resource page 166, small prize

1 Prepare enough of the 'chat cards' from resource page 166 for the young people to have one each.

2 Arrange the young people in pairs. Hand out one 'Person A' and one 'Person B' card to each pair, ensuring they don't see what the other person has.

3 Start with Person A. Give them one minute to do what it says on the card. Then give Person B 20 seconds to recall what their partner said. Discreetly give a point every time Person B mentions one of the words Person A has on their card.

4 Then repeat the exercise, reversing the roles and letting Person B speak for one minute. Award a small prize to the pair that scored the most.

5 Ask the young people how easy they found it to listen to the other person. What were some of the things that made it difficult?

BIBLE EXPERIENCE

LEVEL 1: CONNECT

WHAT: mime
WHY: to realise that ignoring God won't change anything

1 Organise the young people into groups of three or four. Give each group one of the following scenarios, without telling the other groups what they are. You may want to add some of your own:

- ignoring instructions
- lying to a parent
- playing truant from school
- stealing from a shop
- not listening to a warning

2 Give the groups five minutes to come up with a 30-second mime to portray their scenario.

3 Encourage all the groups to present their mimes to each other. Ask the other groups to guess what each scenario is.

4 Use the scenarios to encourage the young people to think about the consequences that these situations can lead to. You may want to use the following questions:

- What are some of the possible consequences of the situation in this scenario?
- Do you think there is a way out of these consequences?
- Do the choices we make affect how God views us?

5 Read Jeremiah 36:1–3, 21–25 and 28–31. Depending on your group, you may want to summarise part of the story. Explain to the young people that Jeremiah's message was a warning to the king and his people to change their ways.

6 Ask the young people to identify what would happen if the king were to ignore the warning. What would they do in that situation?

LEVEL 2: INTERFACE

WHAT: discussion
WHY: to realise that ignoring God won't change anything
WITH: magazine page 164

1 Give out copies of page 164.

2 Read through the descriptions of Jeremiah (the listener) and King Jehoiakim (the ignorer). Ask the young people, in pairs, to come up with some words to describe each man.

3 Read Jeremiah 36 together. This is a long passage so you might want to do a combination of reading selected sections and summarising, depending on your group. Ask:

- Does the passage prove you were right about the adjectives you chose for both men?
- How might Jeremiah have felt when he heard that Jehoiakim had destroyed the scroll?

4 Read verses 27–31 again and ask the young people what the consequences were for Jehoiakim. How did ignoring God's Word help the king?

5 Ask the group to refer back to page 164 and challenge them to fill in the section 'Who are you like?' Would they say that they listen to God (through the Bible, prayer, what is said in church and *theGRID* group), or do they ignore God when it isn't convenient to listen to him? Where do they sit on the scale between Jeremiah (completely faithful to God) and King Jehoiakim (a nasty piece of work who didn't care about God at all!)?

LEVEL 3: SWITCH ON

WHAT: Bible study
WHY: to realise that ignoring God won't change anything
WITH: cards from resource page 167

1 Split the young people into three groups. Give each group a section of Jeremiah 36 to read:

- Group A: Jeremiah 36:1–10
- Group B: Jeremiah 36:16–26
- Group C: Jeremiah 36:27–32

Give each group a set of the cards from resource page 167.

2 Ask each group to sort the cards into things which feature in their passage and those that do not, and to summarise their part of Jeremiah 36 so everyone is aware of the whole passage. These are the main points:

- God gives Jeremiah a warning message for the people of Judah.
- Baruch writes this message on a scroll.
- Baruch reads out the message in the Temple.
- The people who hear the message are frightened and take it to the king.
- As sections of the scroll are read, the king cuts them up and throws them on the fire.
- God tells Jeremiah to write another scroll.
- God tells Jeremiah what will happen to the king because he did not listen to the message.

3 Encourage each group to briefly feed back their summaries and results to the rest of the group.

4 Continuing in their groups, ask the young people to consider the following questions:

- What did King Jehoiakim hope to achieve by burning Jeremiah's scroll?
- What was going to happen to Jehoiakim and his family?
- How do people ignore God these days?
- Are there times when you ignore God?

RESPOND

 MUSICAL

WHAT: reflection
WHY: to reflect on God's knowledge and love for each of us
WITH: copies of Psalm 139, highlighters, background music (optional)

1 Give out copies of Psalm 139:1–16,23,24 from *The Message* paraphrase of the Bible (this is available on www.biblegateway.com). Ask someone with a good reading voice to read it aloud slowly and reflectively. You may want to play some gentle background music.

2 Invite the young people to highlight or make a note of any verses that stood out for them as the psalm was being read. Ask the group then to make up a tune or a rhythm for one or more of the verses. See if they can create a song or rap from the verses that stood out for them.

3 Encourage the group to remember the song or rap they have made up and to use it as a reminder throughout the week of how valuable God thinks they are, even in the midst of tough times.

 PRACTICAL

WHAT: Bible reading
WHY: to think about taking notice of God's Word
WITH: Bible notes or printouts (optional)

1 In advance, gather some examples of different types of Bible-reading guides, daily notes, devotional books, journals.

2 Chat together about reading the Bible and how it is a valuable way for us to learn more about God and to hear him speak to us. Invite the young people to share any questions or difficulties they find that put them off reading the Bible at home, and talk them through as a group.

3 Challenge the young people to read the Bible every day for a week, saying that you are all going to do it together (leaders included!).

4 Throughout the week, encourage the young people to talk together about their Bible reading through texting, emailing or social networks (only join in as appropriate, bearing in mind your safeguarding policy with regard to contacting the young people).

5 Remember to round up the session's Bible reading the next time you meet, and see how the group got on with reading the Bible. Make time to discuss any questions the week's readings brought up, or to share anything the young people found really interesting.

 CREATIVE

WHAT: listening to God
WHY: to encourage young people to listen to God
WITH: background music

1 Hand out sticky notes and pens. As you play some quiet background music, encourage the young people to close their eyes and try to listen to what God might be saying to them. Explain that God speaks to people in many different ways, and not necessarily in the same way to every person! God can speak through our thoughts, emotions, the words of others, everyday objects, the beauty around us, the quiet and the loud! Give an example of how God has spoken to you to start them thinking.

2 Encourage the young people to write on their sticky notes anything they think God might have been saying to them. Have extra available if needed.

3 If appropriate, give space for the young people to share what they have written. Encourage them to keep their sticky notes in their Bibles, or somewhere safe, as a reminder. If anyone feels God has said something to them for someone else, exercise a little caution and judge whether it would be good to share that with the other person. Be sensitive to anyone who may feel that God did not say anything to them. Reassure them of his love and encourage them to keep listening in many different ways – God speaks to everyone, but sometimes it takes time for us to recognise it and to hear what he is saying!

4 Close with a prayer, asking Jesus to continue to speak to us and to help us create the time and space to listen.

MORE ON THIS THEME:

If you want to do a short series with your group, other sessions that work well with this one are:

23	*Whatever*	*Jeremiah 18:1–12*
24	*Hope springs eternal*	*Jeremiah 31:1–6; 32:1–15*
26	*Well, fancy that*	*Jeremiah 38:1–13*

CHEERS, EARS!

Listening to other people is overrated... or is it?
'It's at times like this, I wish I'd listened to my mother!'
'Why, what did she say?'
'I don't know; I wasn't listening!'
Arthur Dent and Ford Prefect in
The Hitchhiker's Guide to the Galaxy

I'M NOT LISTENING!

**WITH A FRIEND, HAVE A LOOK AT THE SCENARIOS BELOW AND DECIDE WHAT HAPPENED NEXT!
WRITE TWO POSSIBLE CONSEQUENCES:**
- **ONE IF THE PERSON PAID ATTENTION TO WHAT THEY HAD HEARD OR READ**
- **THE OTHER IF THEY DID NOT PAY ATTENTION TO WHAT THEY HAD HEARD OR READ**

Joe's parents have gone away for a fortnight's holiday to Bognor (why Bognor? no one knows!) leaving Joe to be looked after by an elderly relative. As Joe's parents leave, they call back to Joe, 'Don't forget to give the hamster food and water!'

LISTENED

NOT LISTENED

Just as Tom's dad announces he had better go as his flight leaves in three hours' time, Tom hears a news flash on the radio about flights being cancelled at the nearby airport.

LISTENED

NOT LISTENED

You are cycling in the local woods and your friend encourages you to go and explore off track with them. You remember noticing several warning signs around the trail.

LISTENED

NOT LISTENED

At school in Science, you're doing some practical experiments with chemicals. Your textbook tells you to make sure safety goggles are worn at all times.

LISTENED

NOT LISTENED

WHO ARE YOU LIKE?

THE LISTENER

Jeremiah was called by God to be a prophet when he was still very young. He was faithful to God and listened to everything that God told him, even though it nearly always put him in danger. God had some very angry stuff to say to the kings of Judah, and the kings often took it out on Jeremiah. However, no matter how tough life was for him, Jeremiah stayed faithful to God.

THE IGNORER

Jehoiakim was a nasty piece of work. A man called Josephus described him as 'unjust and wicked by nature ... neither reverent toward God, nor kind to man'. He completely forgot the work that had been done by his father, Josiah, and he went back to worshipping idols and generally being really evil. He killed lots of people, including another prophet, Uriah. He met his end on his way to being a slave in Babylon.

How would you describe yourself? Are you like Jeremiah, listening to God even when it's hard to do so, or do you ignore what God is saying because you don't like the sound of it? Write a couple of sentences to describe yourself here:

_____
_____
_____
_____
_____
_____

BIBLE EXPERIENCE

 **LEVEL 1: CONNECT**

WHAT: photo story
WHY: to see that an unpopular message can be helped by unlikely means
WITH: magazine page 172

1 Give out copies of page 172. Read the story and discuss all together what happens.

2 Discuss why they think Ed may have helped Jez. He didn't have to at all; it wasn't even his school.

3 Read Jeremiah 38:1–13. Ask the group to find the similarities between the Bible passage and the photo story:

- Jeremiah was being unfairly punished by some officials.
- Ebed-Melech was a foreign servant, not one of God's people. (Cush was what is now Ethiopia.)
- Jeremiah was released, thanks to the intervention of an unlikely person.

4 Explain to the group that this is all we know about Ebed-Melech the Cushite. What is their impression of this minor character in the Bible?

5 Remind the group that, if Jeremiah had died in the well, God's message, unpopular as it was, would have gone unheard.

 LEVEL 2: INTERFACE

WHAT: interactive Bible story
WHY: to see that an unpopular message can be helped by unlikely means
WITH: long sheet of paper, marker pens

1 Spread a long sheet of paper (wallpaper or lining paper is ideal) on the floor. Draw around a volunteer and comment on how there are no features on this 'person' at the moment. Explain that you are going to look at a character in the Bible who only appears very briefly.

2 Read Jeremiah 38:1–13 together. Ebed-Melech is a character who only appears for a short time in the Bible, yet he plays a major part in the story of Jeremiah.

3 Encourage the young people to find as many details of Ebed-Melech as they can from the passage and write them on the 'person' on the paper. Guide them through any of these that they may have missed:

- Country of origin (Jeremiah 38:7)
- Job (Jeremiah 38:7)
- Bravery (Jeremiah 38:8,9)
- Thoughtfulness (Jeremiah 38:11,12)
- Effectiveness (Jeremiah 38:13b)

4 Explain that this servant, Ebed-Melech, leaves the palace (something a foreign slave serving in the palace would not be allowed to do), approaches the king (something else slaves were not allowed to do), and tells him that his own countrymen are wicked. What does this say about the character and bravery of this minor character in the Bible?

5 Ask the young people to think about what difference it would make to their lives to have some of the characteristics of Ebed-Melech. Chat about this. Some examples of bravery may be to start a Christian Union at school (or help with the existing one) or to invite friends to a youth group or a family to a church service.

 **LEVEL 3: SWITCH ON**

WHAT: Bible study
WHY: to see that an unpopular message can be helped by unlikely means

1 Split the group into pairs. Ask them to read Jeremiah 38:1–13, looking out for the characteristics of Ebed-Melech. Ask the group to rate how likely Ebed-Melech was to succeed. When the pairs have finished reading and rating, discuss what they have decided. Why do the young people think God used Ebed-Melech to help Jeremiah and let his message be heard?

2 There are other examples in the Bible of non-Jews being used by God. Ask the young people to look at these examples, back in their pairs:

- Rahab (Joshua 2) – Rahab helped the Jewish spies when they were gathering information about Jericho. She was saved from being killed because of this.
- Ruth (Ruth 1) – Both Ruth and her mother-in-law Naomi had been widowed. Naomi returned to Bethlehem; Ruth went with her because of her great love for Naomi, and became one of Jesus' ancestors (Matthew 1:5). (We'll be looking at Ruth's story in the next two sessions.)
- King Artaxerxes (Nehemiah 2) – Nehemiah learned of the destruction of Jerusalem when he was in Persia. He went to Artaxerxes to ask his permission to go back to Jerusalem and rebuild the city.
- The wise men (Matthew 2:1–12) – The wise men worshipped Jesus and gave him gifts.

3 Ask the groups to consider for what purpose these unlikely non-Jews were being used. Was the message they were helping to put across unpopular like Jeremiah's?

4 Chat about why they think God chooses to use the weak, the feeble and outsiders to make his will come about. Ask:

- What does it mean for you?
- Have you ever been called upon to help announce an unpopular message?

RESPOND

 MUSICAL

WHAT: singing
WHY: to worship God and ask where he might want to use the group
WITH: worship songs, playback equipment or musical accompaniment

1 Choose some familiar songs about spreading God's Word for the group to sing together. Some suggestions are:

- 'Let Your Word'
- 'I, the Lord of Sea and Sky'
- 'There's a Calling to the Nations'
- 'These Are the Days of Elijah'

2 Have a time of worship through singing, focusing on the theme of these songs.

3 At the end of this worship time, explain that the message of Jesus is sometimes an unpopular message, but God will use the young people in unlikely ways to help, if they are open to being used by him!

4 To finish, sing a quieter song, encouraging the young people to focus on asking God how he wants to use them.

 PRACTICAL

WHAT: challenge
WHY: to think about helping God's message
WITH: 'Salt 'n' Shake' crisps

1 Ask the group to find and read Matthew 5:13, where Jesus challenges his disciples to be the 'salt of the earth'.

2 Give out the crisps and invite everyone to taste one before putting the salt in (be aware of any food allergies and dietary restrictions and offer an alternative, if necessary). Ask them to add the salt, shake the bag and then taste another crisp. Encourage them to think about the difference in flavour. In the same way, we are to affect the world around us. Salt has an effect on everything it touches. So we should have an effect on everything we touch.

3 In pairs or threes, ask the young people to think of some ways in which they can help spread God's message. Ask them to think laterally and not go for the obvious ways. In what unusual ways could the young people help to spread God's Word?

4 Gather the young people together and obtain feedback from the groups. Build up a list of possible ways for the young people to spread God's message, and challenge them to do one thing from the list this week. Give everyone a crisp packet or salt packet to take home as a reminder to be willing to be used by God.

 CREATIVE

WHAT: creative prayer
WHY: to help the group understand what part they can play in God's plans
WITH: quiet music

1 Chat with the young people about how we can sometimes feel that we are at the bottom of the school, the youngest in our church, the quietest in the youth group. We may feel that God could never use people like us. However, remind the young people that in the story of Jeremiah, God used an unlikely person to save an important prophet.

2 Ask the young people to take a sheet of paper each and to think about the important people in their lives: head teachers, teachers, vicars, ministers, parents, friends, politicians. Ask them to write down the names of these people on the paper. As they write, encourage them to pray for each person, asking God to help each one to hear him, and for courage for themselves to speak God's Word to these people.

3 Finish with the following prayer: 'Lord, help me to be open to you and your leading. Help me to be as faithful to you as Ebed-Melech was. Show me the people you want me to speak to and help. Amen.'

4 Ask the group to take their paper home and to carry on praying for the people whose names they have written down.

MORE ON THIS THEME:

If you want to do a short series with your group, other sessions that work well with this one are:

RESCUE RANGERS!

Imagine you are a very accident-prone person. If you lived in America, you might be one of the 400,000 people a year who are injured by their own duvet (or mattress, pillow or their bed in general). Which of these rescue rangers would be the most likely to help you in each of the following situations?

26

Bible bit
Jeremiah 38:1–13

Political bloggers have been censored in some countries. If they speak out about the government, they can get into trouble. Jeremiah was in a similar position, but he didn't have his internet access cut – he was thrown down a well to keep him quiet. Yet God's message was helped by a most unlikely source.

1 You are making a sandwich while watching the TV. As you cut the bread, you are distracted by the latest goings-on in the Square and accidentally slice through your little finger. Bleeding profusely, you are rushed to the hospital.

2 While on holiday in an exotic location, you are taken captive by a group of terrorists.

3 You are crossing the road on your way home from school when you drop your favourite novelty pencil. As you bend down to pick it up, you are run over by a milk float.

4 You are swimming in the local pool and you (of course) decide to show off by diving backwards from the highest diving board. As you jump off, you hit your head on the board and are knocked unconscious.

Skilled in combat, bomb-making, weapons training, survival and hand-to-hand combat. Fluent in five languages, can adapt to other cultures and terrains. Highly trained and skilled soldier.

A

SAS COMMANDO

Trained to see potential dangers, skilled in rescue and first aid, fit and athletic. Carries a rescue float and dresses in rescue clothing (trunks!). In radio contact with helicopter rescue and coastguard.

LIFEGUARD

B

Highly trained in medicine, able to save lives, able to treat wounds, cuts and broken bones, and a highly respected member of society. Years of experience in medical problems; has many other health professionals on hand, if needed.

C

DOCTOR

D

BLOOD DONOR

Anyone who gives blood saves a life. They could be of any age, any religious background and any social class (a murderer serving life in prison could easily be a blood donor!).

ZERO HERO!

JEZ AND ED GO TO DIFFERENT SCHOOLS AND HAVE NEVER MET, SO WHAT HAPPENS NEXT SEEMS VERY UNLIKELY…

There was always trouble between St Joseph's and Bramshore High…

'Jez, how dare you damage school property! Detention for the week, and you'll have to pay for the window.'

'It wasn't Jez; it was a lad from my school. The other teacher wouldn't believe that Jez didn't do it.'

'I believe you were put in detention for something you didn't do, Jez.'

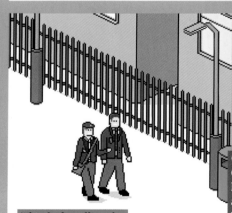

'Thanks for telling the truth, Ed!'

Check out Jeremiah 38:1–13.
Can you find any similarities between the Bible passage and the story?
Why do you think Ed helped Jez?
Why do you think Ebed-Melech, a foreign servant, helped Jeremiah?

Bible: Matthew 9:9–13

27

COULD TERRORISTS GO TO HEAVEN?

THE AIM: To recognise that God's forgiveness is available to all

The aim unpacked

This session focuses on God's forgiveness and acceptance. Matthew, although not quite in the same league as Hitler or any other leader guilty of genocide, would have been someone the religious elite believed was not loved or accepted by God, and yet Jesus broke through to make a relationship with him. Today many of our young people feel alienated and unloved, perhaps that they are too bad to be loved by God, and yet his love reaches deeper than we ever imagine.

WAY IN

 **theGRID MAGAZINE**

WHAT: discussion
WHY: to think about entry requirements to different events or clubs
WITH: magazine page 176

1 Make sure everyone has a copy of page 176 and a pen. Introduce the activity. What would they have to be, do or have to get into these exclusive events or clubs? Invite everyone to fill in their ideas, and then obtain feedback.

2 Divide the young people into pairs and ask them to discuss whether they would actually like to be a part of any of these group events or clubs and whether they would qualify for any of them.

3 Being part of God's family obviously stands out as different from the others. On the one hand, it should feel even more prestigious to be one of God's people than to be involved in any of the other things listed – but it's often something that we take for granted. On the other hand, there are no special requirements, there is nothing that we need to do to impress God. Everyone is welcome and God's forgiveness is available to all, if they ask him for it. Don't worry if the young people don't quite grasp this at the start – that's what this session is for. You could revisit this question at the end.

 **SCENE SETTER**

WHAT: list-making
WHY: to consider who are the worst villains of all time and whether God's forgiveness is available to them
WITH: flip chart or whiteboard, marker pens

1 Encourage everyone to discuss in pairs who they think are the worst five villains of all time – people who have done really evil things.

2 Invite feedback from the groups and write up their suggestions on the flip chart or whiteboard, making a note of people who are voted for more than once.

3 Discuss the suggestions and agree on a 'top ten villains of all time'. Encourage the young people to argue for who they think should be in and why.

4 When the list is complete, look at it together and reflect on whether God would forgive these people if they were sorry and asked him to forgive them. Make a note of the group's initial reactions and come back to the list later in the session.

 **THEMED GAME**

WHAT: categories game
WHY: to think about feeling excluded
WITH: chairs

1 Invite everyone to sit on a chair in a circle.

2 Read out a category from the following list. (Check these are appropriate for your group and think up some more so that you have a long list.) Everyone who falls into that category has to get up and swap places with someone else. While they are moving around, you or another leader need to remove a chair or two so that the circle gets smaller each time. People who don't get a chair are eliminated from the game:

- Everyone whose name begins with S
- People who go to _____ school (insert name!)
- People with brown eyes
- Everyone who has been to America
- Everyone who has a pet

Every so often, throw in a category that applies to everyone to get them all moving, such as 'Everyone who has two eyes' (assuming that they all have!).

3 Play until there are only two people left and declare them the winners. Discuss the game: how did it feel to be excluded? Introduce the theme – God's forgiveness is available to all, so no one needs to feel excluded.

BIBLE EXPERIENCE

LEVEL 1: CONNECT

WHAT: story
WHY: to recognise that God's forgiveness is available to all
WITH: magazine page 177, Bibles

1 Discuss with the group:

- When did you last forgive someone?
- What kind of things do you find it easy to forgive?
- What would you find difficult to forgive?

2 Distribute copies of page 177 and ask everyone to read the story of John Plummer, a helicopter pilot in the Vietnam War who dropped napalm on a village and caused incredible suffering to its inhabitants, including a 9-year-old girl whose pain was caught on camera. Twenty-four years later, John met the girl, and she forgave him for what he did to her and her village. Ask for reactions to the story:

- Could you do what Kim did?
- What difference did it make to John?
- What difference do you think it made to Kim?

3 Read together or tell the story of Matthew 9:9–13. Explain that tax collectors were Jews who were employed by the Romans to collect taxes for them. They were seen as traitors by their own people and hated. Yet Jesus was happy to be seen with them and to eat with them. He knew that God's forgiveness was available to all, no matter what they had done. (You may need to explain what tax is.)

LEVEL 2: INTERFACE

WHAT: drama
WHY: to recognise that God's forgiveness is available to all
WITH: Bibles

1 Read together Matthew 9:9–13, explaining the background to the story and why tax collectors were seen as 'sinners'. Discuss with the group:

- Why do you think Matthew followed Jesus?
- What impact would Jesus eating with the tax collectors and 'sinners' have had on his followers, and on the Pharisees?

2 Divide everyone into groups of three or four. Challenge them to come up with a modern-day equivalent of this story – of Jesus meeting with a group of people and asking one of them to follow him. Which people these days are hated in our society or seen as evil? Who would be most likely to criticise Jesus if he were here and were to share a meal with those people? Give the groups some time to create a drama sketch around this.

3 Invite the group to perform their sketches and discuss them:

- Do we really believe that Jesus can accept and forgive such people?
- What do these people need to do to receive that forgiveness?

Make sure the young people understand that sin is turning away from God, not just doing 'bad' things. We have all sinned and we all need God's forgiveness, even if we think we lead pretty 'good' lives. The good news is that his forgiveness is available to everyone!

LEVEL 3: SWITCH ON

WHAT: Bible study
WHY: to recognise that God's forgiveness is available to all
WITH: Bibles, Bible dictionaries

1 Give some background to why the Romans ruled Palestine and why the Jews had to pay taxes to them. In the centuries before Jesus' birth, Palestine was politically unstable. After the Jews returned from exile in about 538 BC, the Persians ruled them. They were kicked out by Alexander the Great and the Greeks. In 168 BC, the Greek ruler Antiochus IV Epiphanes (great name!) tried to put a statue of a pagan god in the Temple, which the Jews were unhappy about. Judas Maccabeus led a successful rebellion and for nearly 100 years the Jewish people were in charge of their own land. Then in 63 BC, Roman troops, led by Pompey, invaded Palestine and it came under Roman rule. The Jews had to pay taxes to the Romans to support the empire. Some Jews became tax collectors for the Romans, but they weren't popular!

2 Read together Matthew 9:9–13. Who were the Pharisees? Discuss how Christian communities today can be like the Pharisees, labelling certain people as not good enough for God. What types of people tend to be labelled in this way, or are told they can only belong to the church if they change?

3 Read the following Bible passages. What did the prophets say were the most important elements in a worshipping community? (Prophets are people who bring words from God about particular situations.)

- Hosea 6:6
- Isaiah 1:11–17
- Amos 5:21–24

4 From these verses, what do you think the church needs to watch out for so that they don't become like the Pharisees? Create a five-point charter that you think churches need to take note of. Could you present this to the leadership of your church?

5 Explain that God's forgiveness is available to everyone – whoever they are and whatever they are like.

RESPOND

 MUSICAL

WHAT: prayer for forgiveness
WHY: to give young people an opportunity to ask God for forgiveness
WITH: song about forgiveness ('Nothing but the Blood' from *Face Down* by Matt Redman, or 'You Led Me to the Cross' by Matt Redman from *Soul Survivor Worship 1999*), playback equipment, electric paper shredder, Bible

1 Set up the shredder in the middle of the room and check that it works. Encourage the young people to find a space where they are comfortable. Make sure everyone has a pen and some paper. Play the track and invite the young people to spend some time in prayer, explaining to God that they know they have sometimes done things they shouldn't have. They can write or draw symbols on their sheet of paper to represent the things that they are praying about.

2 Lead everyone in a general prayer for forgiveness. Remind them that God's forgiveness is available to everyone, no matter what they have done. Then, when they are ready, invite everyone to come and put their sheet of paper into the shredder to symbolise God destroying their sin and making them like new. Make sure that there is a leader supervising the shredder at all times.

3 Read Psalm 51 to the group over some background music. This is David's prayer for forgiveness. Assure them that God has heard their prayer and they are forgiven. Remember that each member of your group will be at a different stage of their journey with Christ, and saying sorry for something is only part of this journey.

 PRACTICAL

WHAT: forgiveness cards
WHY: to provide a way to ask God for forgiveness throughout the week
WITH: blank business cards and erasers or small 'magic slates', one for each person, Bible

1 If you can, get hold of some cheap 'magic slates'. A magic slate has an area for writing on with a stylus, and a lever that moves across which erases what you have written. Alternatively, use business cards, as explained below.

2 Hand out the blank business cards and pencils. Encourage everyone to find a space. Invite them to think back over the past week and recall things they have done wrong. Remember where your group are here. Do they know what things they need to be forgiven for? You may have to suggest ideas, if they are not very far along their spiritual journey. For each thing, they should make a small mark on their card – but tell them not to press too hard. Invite them to spend a few moments in prayer thinking about those things and asking for God's forgiveness.

3 Then hand out the erasers. Read 1 John 1:9 and assure them of God's forgiveness. Invite them to rub out the marks they have made on the card to show that they are forgiven and can start again.

4 Encourage the group to take their cards away and use them through the week. Each time they do something wrong they should mark their card. At the end of each day they should pray, asking for God's forgiveness, read 1 John 1:9, and then rub all the marks out. As the week goes on, are they marking it less or more as they grow in their relationship with God?

 CREATIVE

WHAT: clay modelling
WHY: to underline the fact that God's forgiveness is available to all
WITH: clay or play dough, worship music and playback equipment, cross, cloth

1 It can be hard to believe that God could forgive everyone, even people like terrorists, if they were to ask for God's forgiveness. This activity will help to make this truth more tangible.

2 Talk about the fact that God's forgiveness is available to everyone, and revisit some of the people and situations that need forgiveness that you have talked about during the session. Set up a small cross in the centre of the group.

3 Invite people to make symbols or models of things or people that they find it hard to believe that God could forgive. These could be things in the news, or overseas, or things that affect them personally. Play some music in the background as they make these things and place them round the cross, as a way of acknowledging that God can forgive that thing or person.

4 Lead the group in prayer, thanking God that he is able to forgive anyone who comes to him in prayer. You could encourage the group to name some of the situations and people they have created symbols and models of, or just let their artwork speak for itself.

MORE ON THIS THEME:

If you want to do a short series with your group, other sessions that work well with this one are:

HOW DO YOU GET IN?

There are lots of exciting things going on that ordinary mortals like us don't get to be a part of. But could we? Would we want to?! How would you get into these exclusive clubs and events? What are the entry requirements? Write down three things that you would have to do, have or be to get in.

BACKSTAGE

PHOTOGRAPHED IN HELLO MAGAZINE

1
2
3

PREMIER LEAGUE FOOTBALL SQUAD

1
2
3

ED SHEERAN'S BIRTHDAY PARTY

1
2
3

HOLLYWOOD FILM PREMIERE

1
2
3

ACCESS TO BACKSTAGE AT GLASTONBURY

1
2
3

BEING PART OF GOD'S FAMILY

1
2
3

GUEST AT A ROYAL WEDDING

1
2
3

OPENING NIGHT OF A WEST END MUSICAL

1
2
3

Bible bit
Matthew 9:9–13

Being a tax collector meant you were a fairly bad person, at least as far as the religious people of Jesus' day were concerned. In basic terms, tax collectors took money from the Jewish people, which was then used to keep the Roman invaders in charge. As far as the majority of people were concerned, Matthew was part of the oppressive regime that was ruining their country. Surely someone like him couldn't be forgiven and allowed to follow Jesus?

FORGIVENESS

One of the most striking images to come out of the Vietnam War was of a 9-year-old girl running naked down the street, her arms outstretched and her face contorted with shock and pain. The girl's name was Phan Thi Kim Phuc and she was known as Kim. She lived in a village called Trang Bang in northern Vietnam.

The war was originally between North and South Vietnam, but then the USA and 40 other countries came in to support South Vietnam, while China and the USSR supported the Vietcong in North Vietnam. The people who suffered the most were the civilians caught in the fighting between the two.

The day that the photo was taken in 1972 started like any other. Kim got up and played with her friends as usual, while an American helicopter pilot, John Plummer, finished off his plans to drop napalm on her village. Napalm is a highly flammable jelly-like substance that sticks to whatever it lands on and then catches fire. Kim was caught in the raid, and the photographer caught the scene on camera to show the world what was going on.

For 24 years John Plummer was haunted by the picture, knowing that he had been the cause of the girl's suffering. He was not even sure whether she had survived the raid. His friends and family tried to reassure him that he had just been doing his job, and reminded him that he had tried to make sure the village was clear of civilians before he had dropped the bombs, but he still carried a heavy weight of guilt. He wished he could find the girl and say sorry.

Then in an amazing coincidence, John did meet Kim. It happened on Veterans Day in 1996. Kim had gone to the Vietnam Memorial in Washington DC to lay a wreath for peace, and John was there with a group of former pilots. Kim gave a speech to the crowd and said that although she still suffered from her burns, she was not bitter and she wanted people to remember that others had suffered even more than she had. She said that she forgave the men who had bombed her village.

John pushed his way through the crowd and explained who he was. He said, 'I'm sorry, I'm sorry', over and over again. Kim held out her arms and embraced him.

They met again later that day and Kim affirmed her forgiveness. Twenty-four years of anguish and regret were wiped away by that two-minute meeting in the crowd. They have since become good friends and still keep in touch.

Having met Kim, John still regrets what happened in the war, but he has been able to forgive himself for inflicting pain and suffering on others and has found peace. He says that forgiveness is a gift – he could never have earned it or deserved it, but it was given to him freely by Kim.

[Source: rewritten from *RE in Practice – Living with Others*, published by Christian Education.]

Check out the Forgiveness Project website for some amazing stories of forgiveness:
www.theforgivenessproject.com

Bible: Matthew 15:21–28

28

ACCEPTED, WHOEVER YOU ARE

THE AIM: To be sure that we are accepted by God

The aim unpacked

Despite Jesus' initial response in this passage, we see here that the forgiveness and acceptance offered by God are available to all through faith. It's good to stress that being accepted by God doesn't mean conforming to a 'Christian' stereotype. The woman was accepted because of her faith, not her race, style of clothing or anything else.

WAY IN

 **theGRID MAGAZINE**

WHAT: relationships activity
WHY: to think about groups that traditionally don't get on
WITH: magazine page 181, answers for the situations on page 319

1 Distribute copies of page 183 to everyone. Challenge them to work in pairs to link up the words that go together in the 'I hate you!' activity. Discuss the results as a whole group and identify the context of each broken relationship.

2 Discuss with the group how these broken relationships may have come about and how they get perpetuated. Point out that not every Israeli will hate every Palestinian, for example. In fact, many of them are working together to bring about peace in their land. But there is a tradition of hatred and distrust between them.

3 Introduce the theme of the session: Jesus accepted people regardless of the traditional feelings between his people and theirs.

 SCENE SETTER

WHAT: exercise scale
WHY: to discuss how we can be sure of something
WITH: plain wallpaper, marker pens

1 Prepare a separate strip of wallpaper with a long line labelled 0% to 100% for each of the statements below, and other statements that you know are relevant to your group's interests. Fix the strips to a wall or spread them out on the floor.

2 Read out each of the statements below and ask the young people to take a thick pen and sign their name somewhere on the line to show their response. Ask, 'How certain are you that [the event] will happen?'

- Chelsea will win the Champions' League next season.
- It will rain tomorrow.
- I will go to university when I am older.
- I will have plastic surgery before I am 50.
- Church will be boring next Sunday.
- God accepts me as I am.

3 Talk about how we can be sure of things. If we have seen or experienced something, we can be completely sure. For other things, we have to weigh up what we already know and take a guess. Discuss the response to the last statement. This session will explore how we can be sure that we are accepted by God.

 THEMED GAME

WHAT: spelling game
WHY: to explore what it feels like to be left out
WITH: water-based marker pen

1 Write one letter on everyone's palms. The letters and words you choose will depend on how many people are in your group. If you have between five and ten, you can use the letters A, E, I, O, S, T, N, R, G, Z. (For five people, write one letter on each of their hands; for ten, write one letter on one hand of each person; and for a number in between, write one letter on some people and two on others.)

2 Call out the following words one at a time: staring; grain; roast; string; gate; great.

3 The young people have to get their hands in the correct order to spell each word. Use one letter such as 'Z' that doesn't appear in any of the words that you ask them to spell, so that someone experiences what it is like to be left out – choose someone who will cope with this!

4 Discuss when you have finished:

- What did it feel like to never be involved?
- What did it feel like to be a letter that was hardly used?

Say that it's horrible to be left out, but when it comes to God, no one is.

BIBLE EXPERIENCE

28

LEVEL 1: CONNECT

WHAT: drama
WHY: to be sure that we are accepted by God
WITH: magazine page 182, flip chart or large sheet of paper, marker pens

1 Ask a couple of young people to perform or read through the sketch on page 182. If boys are reading or performing, change the names as appropriate.

2 Discuss with the group:

- Who's right – Katie or Emma?

- Can Emma make it as a star with just positive thinking or does she need some talent?

- Is she likely to be accepted on to the show?

- For what other situations in life do you need to have the right talent or qualifications before you can be accepted?

3 Read or tell the story of the faith of the Canaanite woman from Matthew 15:21–28, explaining some of the history from Bible background. Why might the woman have been rejected or ignored by Jesus?

4 Encourage the group to think for a moment about reasons why people might not feel accepted by God. Invite suggestions and write them on a flip chart or large sheet of paper. Then rip the sheet up in front of everyone, or invite them to do it. None of these reasons excludes people from being accepted by God. Everyone is accepted by him, if they come to Jesus and want to know and trust him.

LEVEL 2: INTERFACE

WHAT: newspaper stories
WHY: to be sure that we are accepted by God
WITH: stories from newspapers and magazines, flip chart or whiteboard, marker pens, Bibles

1 Before the session, look for stories in newspapers or magazines that show people being rejected or made to feel unacceptable – for example, asylum seekers being turned away, footballers being penalised for their behaviour, pupils not getting into the school of their choice.

2 Show these to the group. In pairs, invite the young people to discuss which of these are appropriate reasons for not being accepted and which are bad reasons. Together, come up with a list from these stories of some of the bad reasons people are excluded from things, and any other examples that people think of. Draw the figure of a person on the flip chart or whiteboard and write the reasons across it.

3 Read to the group (or encourage a good reader to read) Matthew 15:21–28. Discuss with the group:

- Why might the woman have been rejected by Jesus? (You may need to fill in some of the background information from Bible background.)

- How many of these reasons are similar to those you discussed earlier?

Jesus cuts through the barriers of race, religion and gender, and treats the woman as if she were a Jew, showing that God accepts everyone who turns to him through trusting and following Jesus.

4 Go through the words that you wrote on the figure, emphasising that none of these things can stop us being accepted by God.

LEVEL 3: SWITCH ON

WHAT: Bible study
WHY: to be sure that we are accepted by God
WITH: Bibles

1 Read Matthew 15:21–28 to the group. In the form of a debate, discuss the woman's approach and Jesus' response. Have one person arguing that Jesus was rude and the other arguing that he wasn't. The rest of the group can join in the debate on either side.

- For what reasons could the woman have been rejected by Jesus?

- What do you think about his initial response to her (vs 23,26)?

2 Challenge the group to think of different tones of voice that Jesus could have used to say, 'I was sent only to the lost sheep of Israel' – angrily, apologetically, provocatively, and so on. Invite the young people to try out the conversation saying this phrase in different ways that alter the tone of the conversation. We can't know exactly how Jesus said this phrase. You may want to add at some point that the phrase 'dogs' means a pet dog and so isn't being used in the sense it could be today. From what you know of his character, how do you think he said it and what do you think he meant by it?

3 Divide the young people into three groups and ask each group to look up one of these Bible passages: John 4:1–10; Luke 7:1–10; Acts 10:1–35. Invite them to report back to the group on the barrier(s) that Jesus or Peter overcomes in the story.

4 Challenge the groups to list barriers that stop people being accepted by others in our society today. God does not allow any of these to stop him accepting us. We are all accepted by God through turning to Jesus in faith and trust.

RESPOND

 MUSICAL

WHAT: singing
WHY: to worship God for his acceptance of us
WITH: song 'I'm Accepted, I'm Forgiven'

1 Start by inviting the group to talk about anything that makes them feel they are unacceptable to God. They may find it easier to talk in more general terms about 'other people'. If they feel their wrongdoing makes them unacceptable, remind them of what you have been covering in this series – God is always ready to forgive us our sin and make us clean again. Encourage everyone to pray in silence, and to give these barriers and feelings of unworthiness to God.

2 Then sing the song together. Start by singing, 'We're accepted, we're forgiven…' Then sing, 'You're accepted, you're forgiven…' And finally invite everyone to own this for themselves by singing, 'I'm accepted, I'm forgiven…'

3 You could finish with some thanksgiving songs, such as:

- 'Thank You for Saving Me'
- 'Thank You Jesus'

 PRACTICAL

WHAT: artwork
WHY: to encourage others that they are accepted by God
WITH: blank postcards or pieces of card, art materials, collage materials

1 Talk with the young people about how sure they are that God accepts them. If you did the scale exercise at the start, you could return to it and see if their views on the final statement have changed. Talk about what makes us feel unacceptable and unworthy of God's love. Remind them that lots of people tend to feel they are unacceptable to God and it's good to encourage each other that we are acceptable.

2 Ask everyone to think of one person who could do with some encouragement. Suggest that they make a card for that person to remind them that God accepts and loves them exactly as they are. While they are making their cards for others, they are also taking in the message of acceptance for themselves. The cards could have a Bible verse on them such as Acts 10:34.

3 Spend a few minutes praying that the cards will be well received, and that those who made them and those who receive them will be sure that God accepts them.

4 Encourage the young people to take their cards away and deliver them.

 CREATIVE

WHAT: prayer
WHY: to affirm the young people's acceptance in God's eyes
WITH: large hoop or backless picture frame, strips of patterned cloth or ribbon that can be tied across the hoop or frame – one for each person

1 You may like to do this activity with some worship music playing in the background. Lead a time of reflection, inviting the young people to think about every part of their lives – the things they are proud of, the things they regret, the friendships and relationships they have, their hopes for the future, their gifts and talents, the parts of themselves they wish they could change, and so on.

2 As they think about these things, invite each person to choose a strip of cloth that represents who they are.

3 Remind people that God accepts them just as they are in every part of their lives; there is no way they can be unacceptable to him, no matter what they do. Even when we sin, God hates what we have done wrong but he still loves and accepts us.

4 Pass round the hoop or picture frame and encourage the young people to tie their cloth across it, weaving it in and out of the pieces that are already there. This represents the fact that every part of their lives is acceptable to God and will be woven by him into the work of his kingdom if they trust and follow Jesus. End by praying that the young people will have an increasing certainty of their acceptability in God's sight.

MORE ON THIS THEME:

If you want to do a short series with your group, other sessions that work well with this one are:

I HATE YOU!

Bible bit
Matthew 15:21–28

So what is it that makes us acceptable to God? Is it the way we look? The place we come from? Our accent or the way we speak? The colour of our skin? The list could go on...

The woman in the passage was not the 'right' race according to the Jews, but Jesus, after stating this to her, showed that when it comes to being accepted by God, faith cuts through every barrier. It is faith that makes us acceptable, as we shall see.

Can you link up in pairs these groups who, traditionally, have not got on with each other? For each pair, think about where their dislike of each other takes place. What can you find out about what caused it and what people are doing to try to put things right?

TUTSIS
ALLIES
ARSENAL
PROTESTANTS
BLACKS
HOBBITS
GREEKS
DEMON
JEW
TRENDY
ISRAELIS

Answers on page 319.

CATHOLICS
HUTUS
PALESTINIANS
SPURS
ANGEL
SAMARITAN
ORCS
GOTH
TROJANS
NAZIS
WHITES

NO MATTER WHAT

Two girls are talking.
One is practising a dance routine, badly.

Katie: Emma, what are you doing?

Emma: I'm practising my routine.

Katie: Your routine for what?

Emma: Well, they're recruiting for the new *Pop Academy* reality TV show and I just know that this time I'm going to be a star.

Katie: Emma, what are you talking about? You've auditioned for the last nine series and haven't got through. And besides, those shows are the last way that anyone is going to become a star these days – the person who wins the show always disappears out of sight as quick as your Martin when it's time for him to buy a round of drinks in the pub.

Emma: *(Stops and looks indignant.)* Katie, don't be so negative. I need to think positively if I'm going to win. And don't be rude about my Martin! You were being rude, weren't you? Or was that a compliment to say that he's fast?

Katie: Yes, I was being rude. And it's going to take more than positive thinking for you to win *Pop Academy*.

Emma: I thought you were my friend. You should be encouraging me!

Katie: I am your friend and I do want to encourage you, but I also think you need to be realistic. Much as I love you, I just don't think you've got what it takes to win *Pop Academy*.

Emma: Like what haven't I got then?

Katie: Well, for a start, you can't dance. That routine is hopelessly out of time to the music and you're just not supple enough.

Emma: Durr – that's why they give you lessons on the show to make you better.

Katie: Yes, but they're looking for a bit of talent to start with. And you can't sing either. Well, you can sing one note, very well, but even Kylie wouldn't be a star if she could only sing one note.

Emma: Well, I'm practising. I can go up and down a bit now – look… *(Takes a deep breath but Katie butts in before she can start singing.)*

Katie: And, I don't know quite how to put this, but you need to be able to sing and dance at the same time.

Emma: And you think I can't?

Katie: No… well, yes, but you get really out of breath.

Emma: So basically, you're saying that I can't dance and I can't sing.

Katie: Well, I wouldn't have put it quite as bluntly as that, but yes, that is what I'm saying.

Emma: That's the trouble with you, Katie Cartwright. You let a few little obstacles get in the way of you achieving your dreams. I'll invite you to the launch of my first album – see you then!

Fill the card in if you want to be accepted by God, and ask one of your church leaders to tell you more about being accepted.

The following is accepted by God no matter what:

Name

Address

Date of birth

Short description

ID CARD

29

BEFORE AND AFTER

BENJAMIN IS RICH. REALLY RICH. HE DOESN'T HAVE TO WORK AND, INSTEAD, HE IS ABLE TO SPEND ALL HIS TIME IN THE SYNAGOGUE LEARNING ABOUT GOD FROM THE RABBIS AND TEACHERS THERE. ONE DAY, HE HEARS ABOUT A RABBI WHO IS TRAVELLING AROUND AND TEACHING SOMETHING VERY DIFFERENT.

BENJAMIN AFTER...

I wish I'd never gone. What an idiot. I should have left it well alone, but now I've spoilt it. Jesus said I could have eternal life, but that I had to leave everything behind. All my money, all my stuff. How could I do that?

I can't give up everything to follow Jesus! What if he stops travelling and teaching? What happens if he sends everyone away? I'll have nothing to fall back on. As if it wasn't enough that he told me to give up everything, as I walked away I heard him say that it was really hard for rich people to enter the kingdom of God. Well, that's that. I'm not giving up my money. Not for some promise of forgiveness. You can't live on promises, can you?

BENJAMIN BEFORE...

I heard something interesting in the synagogue this morning. I mean it's always interesting, but this was something different. One of the teachers said that a man was on his way. They called him a rabbi, but the way they spoke about him made it sound like he was strange, unusual, that he had something new to say.

When I asked the rabbis and teachers about him, they didn't really know what to say. So, I've decided to go and find this man. I want to ask him a question, something that's been bugging me for months. I want to know how to have eternal life. I follow all the rules, but I hear this man – Jesus, I think he's called – has been talking about living in the kingdom of heaven. What is that? I've got to know how to get this eternal life for myself!

READ MARK 10:17–31.

30

Bible: Luke 4:16–30; Isaiah 61:1–3a

THE REAL BIBLE CODE

THE AIM: To see how the Old Testament points towards Jesus

The aim unpacked

Through the centuries people have tried to find secret codes within the biblical text. Jesus showed that the future could be foreseen from the Old Testament, yet when he showed the people that he was the one who would fulfil what had been predicted hundreds of years earlier, the authorities were none too happy. Challenge your group to open their minds and look at Jesus in a new way.

WAY IN

 **theGRID MAGAZINE**

WHAT: puzzle
WHY: to think about looking for hidden meanings
WITH: magazine page 191

1 Invite everyone to look at page 191.

2 Explain that in the silly article about swans in the breakfast cereal there is a secret message. See if anyone can crack the code without further clues (unlikely).

3 Tell them that after the first letter 'G' there are ten unnecessary letters before the next letter of the message, and so on.

4 The completed message reads, 'Good day to you. We do hope you enjoy this session. It's about Jesus in the Old Testament.'

 **SCENE SETTER**

WHAT: competition
WHY: to check up on background knowledge of the Old Testament
WITH: prepared cards (see below)

1 This activity will not be suitable for a group with little or no Bible experience.

2 Write the name of each Old Testament book on a separate piece of card. Then write the following headings, each on a separate larger piece of paper: 'Law'; 'History'; 'Wisdom'; 'Major prophets'; 'Minor prophets'. Place the headings on the floor in the right order.

3 Shuffle the rest of the cards and challenge the young people to try and place each of the Old Testament books in the right order under the appropriate heading. When they have finished, tell them how many they have got right under each heading and give them a chance to make changes, if necessary. Repeat this stage until they have finished or are bored.

4 The correct order of the Old Testament books is: Law (Genesis–Deuteronomy); History (Joshua–Esther); Wisdom (Job–Lamentations); Major prophets (Isaiah–Daniel); Minor prophets (Hosea–Malachi).

5 Explain that the Old Testament can seem quite dry and remote, but in this session we are going to look at how it all points to Jesus.

 **THEMED GAME**

WHAT: game
WHY: to introduce the concept of pointing towards something

1 This game is best played in a large room or hall, although with marked boundaries you could play it outdoors.

2 Everyone stands against one of the walls, except for the person who is 'It'. They must stand in the middle of the playing area.

3 This person points to a wall and everyone must run to this wall or boundary. The person who is 'It' must try to tag players before they reach the wall. No one can be tagged if they are touching a wall. Anyone tagged becomes 'It' as well.

4 All the people who are 'It' must huddle in the middle and agree which wall to point to next. The winner is the last person to be caught.

5 If appropriate, link to the session by explaining that you will be looking at something that points very clearly to something else.

BIBLE EXPERIENCE

 LEVEL 1: CONNECT

WHAT: scroll making
WHY: to see how the Old Testament points towards Jesus
WITH: Bibles, card or thick paper, glue or staples, small canes or sticks

1 This activity is ideal for younger groups. Print a copy of Isaiah 61:1–3a from *The Message* onto thin card for each young person.

2 Hand out Bibles. Ask everyone to find where the Old Testament finishes and the New Testament starts. Briefly explain that the Old Testament was written in the centuries before Jesus (BC) and the New Testament was written after his death and resurrection (AD). Look together at a Bible sideways and see that there is almost three times as much Old Testament material as New Testament.

3 Give out the copies of the Isaiah passage. Explain that Isaiah lived about 600 years before Jesus but said things about him; he was a prophet. Luke was a guy who recorded the events of Jesus' life. Ask the young people to follow the text as you read Luke 4:16–22. Ask:

- What was remarkable about what Jesus did?
- What differences are there between Isaiah and Luke?
- What similarities?

The differences are drawn from elsewhere in Isaiah. Jesus, holding the scroll of Isaiah, says, 'While you heard these words just now, they were coming true!'

4 Make the point that the Old Testament pointed to Jesus, and he took this key Bible passage as his mission statement – a description of what he was about to do. Jesus didn't fulfil only this passage but all the Old Testament thoughts and prophecies. As it is such an important passage, everyone can make their own scroll and take it home.

5 Invite the young people to glue or staple the canes to the top and bottom of the page and then roll the scroll up.

6 End by asking a confident volunteer to read the Isaiah verses again, this time unrolling their scroll as Jesus would have done.

 LEVEL 2: INTERFACE

WHAT: Bible study
WHY: to see how the Old Testament points towards Jesus
WITH: magazine page 192, Bibles

1 Divide the group into pairs and distribute copies of page 192. Refer the young people to the article called 'The last stand'. Ask them to read it and then explain to each other what actually happened.

2 Explain that, in the centuries before Jesus, readers of the Old Testament struggled to understand what it all meant. Isaiah spoke these words a long time before Jesus was alive. They understood the words but found it hard to grasp the big picture. Now ask a volunteer to read Isaiah 61:1–3a. These Bible verses summarise the behaviour of a true prophet of God (someone who tells the people what God is saying).

3 Ask the group, 'So how would you feel if someone came out and read those Bible verses and then said, "It's me; I'm the one who does these things"?'

4 Back in their pairs, invite the young people to imagine they are the crowd that has just heard Jesus say this very thing. What would be their reaction? There are clues in Luke 4:22,28.

5 Run a short debate in character about how Jesus should be treated. Have the young people play the parts of his family, his sympathisers (he doesn't have any disciples until Luke 5) and the religious leaders. Then debate the issues that arise from Jesus' words.

6 Explain that Jesus' life and actions following this event demonstrated that he did fulfil this and other Old Testament prophecies about the Messiah. (The Messiah was 'God's chosen one'. There are many references in the Old Testament to the Messiah, who was going to save God's people.) If your group members are keen, they could glance ahead in Luke's Gospel to find examples of Jesus doing what he announced in Luke 4:18,19.

 **LEVEL 3: SWITCH ON**

WHAT: Bible study
WHY: to see how the Old Testament points towards Jesus
WITH: different Bible versions

1 Divide the group into pairs and ask them to do a 'Compare and contrast' exercise between Isaiah 61:1–3a and Luke 4:18,19. Ask them to make a list of the similarities and differences between the two passages.

2 To explain how some of the differences may have arisen, read the passage from several different translations of the Bible. The meaning will remain the same but some of the words will change.

3 Ask the young people, in their pairs, to work through Luke's Gospel for a few minutes looking for and noting examples under the following headings:

- Freedom for those treated unfairly
- Sight for the blind
- Announcing good news
- Freedom for captives (think 'oppressed')
- Good news for the poor

Ask some of the pairs to start at different points in the Gospel to make sure it is completely covered.

4 Invite them to give feedback after a few minutes. Conclude by making the point that Jesus didn't just say he was the fulfilment of Old Testament prophecy – he demonstrated it in his actions too.

189

RESPOND

 MUSICAL

WHAT: sampling
WHY: to worship God for his ongoing message
WITH: music which uses samples and copies of the originals (see below), playback equipment, musical instruments (optional)

1 Many tracks today use samples of older tunes. Give an example of this, listening first to the original and then to the newer version. Use ones that are long-lasting, such as:

- the James Bond theme for *You Only Live Twice* used by Robbie Williams on 'Millennium'
- Chic's 'Good Times' that became The Sugarhill Gang's 'Rapper's Delight'
- More examples can be found at www.whosampled.com.

2 Say that, just as the new song builds on the old song and becomes more than the original, the New Testament builds on the Old Testament. The Old Testament contains the 'tune' and Jesus in the New Testament fulfils the 'melody' and creates a complete 'song'.

3 Encourage the young people to get into small groups and create their own worship song, using the words from Isaiah as inspiration and building on 'samples' from other worship songs or popular music they like. They could recreate them with musical instruments or by singing the sounds *a cappella*-style.

4 Explain that the message in today's passage was prophesied in Isaiah, initiated with Jesus and can now be lived out by his church.

5 Conclude by praying together that your group will continue to live out the message of Jesus. You could do this silently or out loud, depending what your group feels comfortable with.

 PRACTICAL

WHAT: research
WHY: to put Jesus' claim into practice
WITH: internet access

1 If you have access to the internet during your session, use an online search engine to research some organisations that work with prisoners, the blind or the poor. Alternatively, do this before the session, either by yourself or by asking group members in advance to do the research and bring it with them.

2 Choose one of the organisations and talk about who they are and what they do. It's probably wise to check them out first to make sure they are reputable. Write to them or email them, asking in what ways a small (and probably not very wealthy) youth group could get involved.

3 Choose one idea to put into practice when you receive a reply. Use the receipt of the reply as an opportunity to remind the group of what Jesus said he had come to do: a claim that had been written hundreds of years before.

 CREATIVE

WHAT: posters
WHY: to display Jesus' claim
WITH: Bibles, craft materials, newspapers

1 Invite the young people to create posters of Jesus' claim from Isaiah 61:1–3a.

2 Hand out newspapers and blank paper to create the posters. You could cut letters out of newspapers and create the words with these. The resulting scroll would look a little like a ransom note, which might make for an interesting discussion. Did Jesus pay a ransom to free the captives?

3 Encourage the young people to decorate their posters in whatever way they want in order to make them as visually striking as Jesus' words would have been to the original hearers.

4 Finish with prayer, thanking God that his prophets heard his words and passed them on to his people, and that we are able to recognise Jesus for who he is.

MORE ON THIS THEME:

If you want to do a short series with your group, other sessions that work well with this one are:

THE REAL BIBLE CODE

There is a secret message in this short story. The letters of the message are evenly spaced apart with the same number of letters between each one. The first letter of the secret message is G.

Bible bit
Luke 4:16–30;
Isaiah 61:1–3a

The theme of many fantasy books and films (especially bad ones) is that one day someone special will come and save the day. Often these stories will have some mystical wise person telling the main character that they are that prophesied person, because they have no knowledge of it themselves. But in this bit of the Bible, Jesus is saying that he is this person – he is claiming to be the one about whom Isaiah spoke more than 400 years ago – but Jesus' audience isn't too sure.

'Gosh, I've had to do some very odd things. My day began in a daze and yet partly normal. You need food though. I had cornflakes. Do you eat such? Do. My food included a small swan-like bird. Especially odd, and clear not only to me, oh, but to all my other family perfectly. The only person you'd expect not to have a grumble would be a right twit. Nobody gets a juicy swan as one's nosh.

So I yomped along to the town's shops and went into the nice supermarket saying, "Why ever put a small swan in our last shopping?" I imagined my money back, but no.

"That's so brilliant," said the woman. "Sensible action, and have won a big prize. Not only a prize but also a free trip to a cool jumbo cereal event. You can satisfy your unusual, half-soaked, very sick urges and no longer fret or fear that hazardous breakfasts are out there. Will there be a bad swan in this top cereal or exciting box, soon or ever? I think not."

And a big cheque amounting to heaps of money now is mine. So thanks.'

Answer on page 319

THE LAST STAND

(with acknowledgement to Miles Kington for his original idea)

THE STAND-UP COULDN'T MAKE IT
SO HE SENT A STAND-IN.
THE MANAGEMENT DIDN'T LIKE THE STAND-IN
AS THE STAND-UP WAS OUTSTANDING
AND HAD A LONG-STANDING APPOINTMENT;
SO THERE WAS A BIT OF A STAND-OFF.

EVENTUALLY THE STAND-IN
AGREED TO STAND DOWN
AND WENT AND SAT IN THE STANDS,
FEELING LIKE HE'D BEEN STOOD UP.
WHEN THE ORIGINAL STAND-UP STOOD ON STAGE
EVERYONE IN THE STANDS STOOD AND APPLAUDED.
HE SET A HIGH STANDARD AND NOBODY
WOULD HAVE STOOD FOR LESS.

UNDERSTAND?

TRIVIA

The Old Testament is very long, but only people who haven't really studied it say it is boring.

The Old Testament book most quoted in the New Testament is Isaiah.

The Old Testament book of Esther doesn't mention God at all.

The Old Testament chapter most quoted in the New Testament is Psalm 118.

31

OBSTACLES

There was a man who couldn't walk and who wanted to see Jesus and get better. Below are some of the obstacles he faced that would prevent him from achieving his goal. Can you think of any others (not just practical obstacles but also emotional ones – for example, how do you think he would have been feeling)? Read Luke 5:17–26 to see how his obstacles were overcome and write the solution down under each one.

OBSTACLE 1
Jesus is in another part of the village and I can't walk to him because I'm disabled.
Solution

OBSTACLE 2
Jesus is in a crowded house and I can't get in there.
Solution

OBSTACLE 3
I want my legs to be better, but my condition is incurable.
Solution

OBSTACLE 4
Solution

OBSTACLE 5
Solution

OBSTACLE 6
Solution

'But in all these troubles we have complete victory through God, who has shown his love for us. Yes, I am sure that nothing can separate us from God's love – not death, life, angels, or ruling spirits. I am sure that nothing now, nothing in the future, no powers, nothing above us or nothing below us – nothing in the whole created world – will ever be able to separate us from the love God has shown us in Christ Jesus our Lord.'
Romans 8:37–39 (ERV)

32

EXTRAVAGANT WORSHIP

THE AIM: To celebrate that we can be forgiven

The aim unpacked

Many people see the church as a 'club for the converted', not a 'home for sinners', yet none of us has become perfect, and we continue to sin. However, Jesus forgives those who come to him in faith and ask for it. As for those who are yet to know God's forgiveness, it's up to us to show them the joy that it brings.

WAY IN

 **theGRID MAGAZINE**

WHAT: **problem situations**
WHY: **to consider what it means to forgive**
WITH: **magazine page 201**

1 Divide the young people into pairs or threes. Encourage them to read 'So what should I do?' from page 201 and discuss the questions at the bottom of the page.

2 Invite feedback from the groups. In particular, discuss what it means to forgive someone. Say that sometimes it can seem as if forgiveness is saying that the wrong that was done or the hurt we have suffered doesn't matter. In fact, forgiveness is making the decision not to make someone pay for what they have done; it's deciding not to take revenge; it's letting go of hurt and bitterness; it's being open to having the relationship restored.

3 Discuss how people should relate to those who have hurt them. Point out that forgiving someone doesn't mean we have to be a doormat to be walked over. If someone keeps deliberately hurting us, we can forgive them, but we can also think about putting some distance in the relationship until they show signs of genuine change.

 **SCENE SETTER**

WHAT: **forgiveness-o-meter**
WHY: **to explore what it means to forgive**
WITH: **the numbers '1' to '10' on ten separate sheets of paper**

1 Stick the numbers on the floor or a wall to make a scale from one to ten.

2 Read out the scenarios below. For each one, ask the young people to stand on the scale at a point that represents how much pain is caused (1 = less, 10 = more). Ask them to move to a point which represents how easy it would be to forgive the person who committed that action. Invite a few people to explain their decisions.

- Your friend says he can't go to the cinema with you because he's going out with his parents, but later you discover he went bowling with other friends.
- Your new bike is nicked from outside a shop.
- A young man is beaten up in a racist attack.
- A girl is framed for shoplifting by her 'friends'.

3 Discuss: Is it harder to forgive someone if they have caused more pain? What does unforgiveness do to you? If you stay angry and vengeful, how does it affect you?

4 Make sure the group understands what it means to forgive – to let go of the need for revenge and be open to restoring the friendship.

 **THEMED GAME**

WHAT: **stuck in the mud**
WHY: **to think about how sin and not being forgiven weighs us down**
WITH: **two or three full rucksacks**

1 Stuff the rucksacks with bulky items such as clothes and blankets. They need to be awkward to carry rather than too heavy.

2 Invite the group to play stuck in the mud. One person is 'It'. When 'It' touches someone, that person has to stand still – they are stuck in the mud – until another player comes and crawls through their legs to release them. Give the rucksacks to a few young people to carry on their backs as they play the game. Swap the person who is 'It' and the people wearing the rucksacks every so often.

3 Introduce the theme of the session – to celebrate that we can be forgiven. Point out that the game is a mirror of how sin can make us stuck in our relationship with God – we need him to come and release us (by forgiving us). But the people who were weighed down by the rucksacks were doubly burdened. Ask how it felt to play once the rucksacks were taken off. (If appropriate, make the connection that the rucksacks could represent our unforgiveness towards other people.)

BIBLE EXPERIENCE

 LEVEL 1: CONNECT

WHAT: drama
WHY: to realise what it means to be forgiven
WITH: resource pages 203 and 204 Bible

1 Ask three people to act or read out the sketch on resource pages 203 and 204. It shows two people winning prizes of holidays: one is really happy and the other isn't.

2 Divide the young people into small groups and ask each group to discuss the following questions:

- Why was Jane so excited? Why was Wayne so unimpressed?
- Would you be more like Jane or Wayne if you won a holiday?
- Invite the groups to feed back their answers to everyone.

3 Read or tell the story from Luke 7:36–50 – the story of the 'sinful' woman anointing Jesus' feet with perfume. Back in their small groups, ask the young people to discuss:

- How did Simon and the woman respond differently to Jesus?
- Why did they respond differently?
- What's the connection with the sketch?

4 Point out that forgiveness is something to be celebrated, but first we need to ask for God's forgiveness and receive it. If we think we're doing OK, we probably won't think we need much forgiveness from God. If we are aware of all the ways we have let God down – as the woman was aware – then we'll really appreciate the forgiveness that God has given us and we'll really have something to celebrate.

 LEVEL 2: INTERFACE

WHAT: ranking exercise
WHY: to understand what sin is and why we need forgiveness
WITH: magazine page 202, Bibles

1 Look at the list on page 202 of different things we can do wrong, from 'serious' things, such as murder and adultery, to more commonplace wrongs, such as lying or cheating. Together, think of some more things to add until you have at least 15.

2 Challenge the group to rank these wrongdoings in order of seriousness in the eyes of the law – 1 being the most serious and 15 being the least serious. Some placings will depend on context – for instance, you don't get into trouble with the police over lying to your mate, but you would if you lied in court.

3 Next invite the young people to rank them according to the harm they cause to other people, discussing their reasons why.

4 Finally, ask them to discuss and rank them according to their seriousness in God's eyes. Talk about what sin is – turning away from God, shown in actions such as these. Allow some discussion and then suggest reading a Bible story to help.

5 Read together Luke 7:36–50. Invite the group to discuss these questions in pairs, then feed back their answers:

- Who did Simon consider to be the greater sinner – himself or the woman?
- What do you think Jesus thought about their sin?
- Why did the woman pour perfume on Jesus' feet?

6 Explain that God doesn't 'grade' sin. Anything that causes someone to turn away from God makes him sad. Simon's arrogance and self-righteousness was more of a barrier between him and God than the woman's sin was between her and God, because he didn't acknowledge it and ask for forgiveness. Once we understand the ways we have sinned and have asked for forgiveness, then we really have something to celebrate!

 LEVEL 3: SWITCH ON

WHAT: Bible study
WHY: to understand what sin is and why we need forgiveness
WITH: Bibles

1 Ask a confident volunteer to read Luke 15:1–7 to the group.

2 Discuss together the following questions. If necessary, draw out the points listed, but try to let the young people come up with answers for themselves.

- Who is Jesus referring to as the 'lost sheep'? The Pharisees referred to the people Jesus spent time with as 'sinners', so this implies that the 'lost sheep' are non-Christians rather than Christians who have fallen away. However, God's heart is to have all his children safe and in his presence.
- Why did Jesus use the example of sheep? His audience would have been familiar with sheep and shepherds and what it meant to lose a sheep (a valuable object).
- What similarities are there between sheep and humans? Sheep all look the same from a distance; they can be stupid; they follow each other blindly; they are helpless without the shepherd.
- Does this parable mean that God doesn't care about the 99 sheep? God wants everyone to love him. He cares for each of us as if we were the one lost sheep.
- What does this parable tell us about Jesus' mission? Jesus came to save those who are lost.
- In what ways are we sometimes like the Pharisees in the story (v 2)? We can look down on those who aren't Christians or who have fallen away. We can sometimes take our salvation for granted and forget that we were once 'lost', or we can think that we are OK and don't need saving.

3 Give everyone a few minutes to reflect on their attitude towards 'lost-sheep'-type people or towards what God has done for us and ask him for forgiveness if necessary. Finish with a prayer.

RESPOND

 MUSICAL

WHAT: listening to a music track
WHY: to celebrate that we can be forgiven
WITH: whiteboard and pens, board erasers, 'Celebration' by Kool and the Gang, playback equipment

1 This activity gives the young people a chance to celebrate the fact that they are or can be forgiven. Give board erasers to a couple of people and pens to the others.

2 Invite everyone to think for a moment about all the things we do wrong that separate us from God and spoil our relationship with him. Explain that while you play the track, you want them to write those things on the board. Then the people with the erasers are going to rub them out because God will forgive us for those things if we ask him. Play the track 'Celebration' while they do this. Ask them to swap the erasers and pens every so often so everyone has a chance to do both parts of the activity.

3 Invite the young people to pray, or you lead them in prayer, thanking God for his forgiveness.

4 If you don't have a whiteboard, you could use a flip chart and, instead of rubbing out the 'sin', invite a young person to tear off the page and rip it into small pieces.

5 Other songs you could listen to or sing are:

- 'Thank You for Saving Me' by Martin Smith
- 'I'm Accepted, I'm Forgiven' by Rob Hayward

 PRACTICAL

WHAT: making posters
WHY: to celebrate that we can be forgiven
WITH: large sheets of thick paper, art materials such as paint, glue, old magazines to cut up

1 Divide your young people into small groups, if necessary. Invite them to design posters or adverts that focus on the joy of forgiveness. Encourage them to think of slogans that capture the theme of celebrating the fact that we can be forgiven, and to think of striking images to go with them. Explain that these posters will be displayed (if possible) in places where people from outside your church can see them, so they shouldn't make the language or images too 'religious'. The aim is to spread some of the joy that we can feel about being forgiven rather than to tell everyone that they are miserable sinners and are all going to hell, which is the attitude that people often expect from the church.

2 When they have finished, invite the groups to show their posters to each other. Then discuss where they could be put up around the community – on the church notice board, in church members' front windows or in any public places where they have permission. Even if they don't stay up for very long, they could make a difference to the people who see them.

3 Ask people to put up the posters on their way home, if possible. (You may have to obtain permission to do this first.)

 CREATIVE

WHAT: metaphors
WHY: to celebrate that we are forgiven
WITH: Bible

1 Read Psalm 103:12 to the group. It's a great image of what God has done with our sin – moved it as far from us as the east is from the west – in other words, as far away as is possible.

2 Divide the young people into small groups to create metaphors or similes of their own that describe what forgiveness is all about. They may want to think about distance as a starting point, as in the verse from the psalm, or cleansing/washing, or a fresh start, unburdening, lightening the load, or being set free. They could start their metaphors/ similes with the words, 'God has forgiven your sin, just like...', if that's helpful.

3 Invite the group to spend a few moments in quiet prayer thinking of the things for which they want to ask God's forgiveness. Then read out the verse from the psalm again as a cue for everyone to read out their metaphors in turn. Then read 1 John 1:9 to assure the young people that their sins are forgiven.

MORE ON THIS THEME:

If you want to do a short series with your group, other sessions that work well with this one are:

**Bible bit
Luke 7:36–50**

It's easy to fall into a 'state of forgiveness' when we're involved in organised church. It can sometimes seem like a 'club for the converted', not a 'home for sinners' – but none of us is perfect yet, and we will continue to mess up.

However, Jesus can forgive us, and has forgiven those who have come to him in faith and asked for it. So because we are forgiven, we should celebrate that fact! We need to jolt ourselves out of any self-satisfaction, like Simon in this passage, and show others the joy that forgiveness brings.

SO WHAT SHOULD I DO?

NATHAN

My younger brother went into my room at the weekend. Offence number 1 – he's not allowed in there without asking me. Then he 'borrowed' my new tablet. Offence number 2 – he's been told before not to take things out of my room, and I certainly would never have lent it to him. Then – offence number 3, the worst of the lot – he managed to spill soft drink over it so that the case is ruined and the screen is all sticky. He's very sorry, of course, now that he's ruined my tablet and Mum is telling him to apologise…

What I want to know is, what's a suitable punishment to give him so that he realises the error of his ways and doesn't do it again? Do you think beating him to a pulp is too extreme?

MADDIE

I spent ages looking for the perfect top to wear to my friend's party this weekend and I finally found it – a white top with beads and embroidery on it. I managed to get chocolate on it so I put it in the wash. But now my mum has washed it with my brother's red rugby socks so it's gone a horrible pink colour, and I'm sure it's shrunk too! Mum says she's sorry, and that I should just wear it because it looks fine like that and no one will know it was meant to be white. But I know, and I'm really upset. I'm not speaking to Mum at the moment and she's really upset too. My dad says I should forgive her, but she's ruined my whole weekend! I went back to the shop and they've got one more of the same top which I've asked them to reserve for me. I can't afford it, but I think my mum should buy it for me. Don't you think that's reasonable?

EMMA

I'm never going to trust anyone again as long as I live! I told my best friend, Chloe, a secret which she promised not to tell anyone else. Now I've found out she told that awful gossip, Lauren! I thought she hated Lauren anyway… She says she's sorry and she wants to be friends again, but I feel like I never want to speak to her again. My mum says I should just forgive her, but that feels like I'm saying to her that what she did doesn't matter, when it really does matter to me. Strange thing is, I do really miss her because we were really good friends. I want her to know how much she hurt me, but can we be friends again?

THINK ABOUT…

Who is in the wrong? How has the person been hurt? How would you answer their question? What would it mean for them to forgive the person who has hurt them?

SUPER-SERIOUS OR SORT-OF-OK?

Rank these wrongdoings in order of seriousness – 1 being the most serious and 15 being the least serious.

TOBY

I'm gutted. My girlfriend, Natasha, and I went to John's party at the weekend and we were having a great time – at least, I thought we were. I went to the loo and then got talking to a couple of my mates about football, so I guess I was away from her for about half an hour. Then I went to find her and caught her snogging Darren Jones! I couldn't believe my eyes. We had a big row at the party and I went home. But now she keeps ringing me up and saying she's sorry and that she wants to get back together. I feel really used, although I do still like her loads. But if we get back together, how do I know she won't just do it again? What should I do?

Sin = turning away from God

God doesn't 'grade' sin. Anything that causes someone to turn away from God makes him sad. Once we understand the ways we have sinned and have asked for forgiveness, then we really have something to celebrate!

HOW SERIOUS ARE THESE WRONGDOINGS...

	...in the eyes of the law?	...according to the harm they cause other people?	...in God's eyes?
Murder			
Adultery			
Vandalism			
Stealing			
Drug dealing			
Lying			
Cheating			

You're a winner!

Two characters, **Wayne** and **Jane**, are waiting to hear if they have won a raffle. The Caller is dishing out the prizes.

Jane: I'm so excited.

Wayne: Hmmmm...

Jane: I just can't wait. I bet I don't win anything. Or if I do, I bet I win that china dog that looks like it's swallowed a wasp. Who'd want that in their house? It's hideous.

Wayne: *(Trying to be cool.)* Yeah, I know.

Jane: Ooh, look they're calling out the numbers. Mine are 220 to 224, pink tickets. What have you got?

Wayne: Mind your own business. *(Keeping his tickets hidden in his hand.)*

Jane: Phew, there goes the china dog. The first prizes to be called out are never that exciting, are they? What I'd most like to win is that top prize, the holiday. Apparently there are two of them – a whole fortnight in the Algarve, sounds fantastic.

Wayne: Shh, I can't hear the numbers.

Jane: *(Speaking a little more quietly.)* Sorry, I'm just on tenterhooks, me. Well, we haven't won the whisky or the carriage clock...

Wayne: ... or the dried flower arrangement, thank goodness. I wouldn't mind the tickets to the Premiership match...

Jane: Well, you need 447 green for those – no? Bad luck.

Wayne: This is getting boring now. I'm not going to win anything. Maybe I'll go home.

Jane: Oh, no. You have to stay to the end, just in case. Anyway there's only three more prizes, and then the two holidays.

Wayne: *(Menacingly.)* Well, shut up then so we can hear the numbers.

Jane: OK! *(Clutches her tickets tight, closes her eyes and crosses her fingers.)*

Caller: 389, pink, for the meal in the restaurant.

Wayne and Jane: *(together)* No.

Caller: 901, green, for the trip to the theatre.

Wayne and Jane: *(together)* No.

Caller: 225, blue, for the all-expenses-paid trip to Alton Towers.

Jane: Oh, so close...

Caller: And now for our top two prizes kindly donated by Tripps Totally Tropical Travel Treats – two identical holidays to the Algarve – an all-inclusive trip to the sun to be taken in the last two weeks of June, and you get to take a friend. And the first winner is... 145, pink!

Wayne: *(Not impressed.)* That's me – I've won. Oh, I've never really fancied the Algarve...

Jane: *(Excited for him.)* Lucky you – congratulations!

Caller: And the second winner is 223, pink!

Jane: *(Screams in delight.)* That's me! I don't believe it. I've won! How fantastic! I don't believe it. Things like this never happen to me. I just can't believe it – I've won! That's so amazing! I've won!

Wayne: *(Ignoring her.)* And the last two weeks in June? I was going to go and stay in Cornwall for a surfing break with my brother for a week then. I'll have to cancel that now. Anyway, I don't know if I can get another whole two weeks off because of my holiday in the States in October.

Jane: *(Nearly in tears, she is so excited and happy.)* I wasn't going to be able to afford a holiday this year. I thought I'd end up sunbathing in my back garden. This is so amazing; it's like a dream come true. I know nothing about the Algarve but I'm sure it'll be great. And I can take my friend Sue – she'll love it.

Wayne: Maybe I can persuade the bloke who won the Premiership tickets to swap. Let me go and see.

Jane: *(Stares after him.)* Some people just don't know when they've got something to be grateful for! Hey, I'm a winner! *(Jumping up and down in excitement.)*

THE BETTER THING

THE AIM: To make spending quality time with God a priority

The aim unpacked

Jesus continues to turn things upside down today, challenging us that our standing with God is not dependent on the things we do in his service but in time spent building our relationship with him (which will naturally overflow into action). In today's session, we are going to explore how we can make spending quality time with God a priority, why it's important and how we might do it in practice.

WAY IN

 **theGRID MAGAZINE**

WHAT: discussion
WHY: to consider how to prepare for important company
WITH: magazine page 208

1 Encourage the young people to read the article from page 208 entitled 'Newsflash!'

2 Ask the group to use the article to answer the following questions:

- What did the people of the town do to plan for the Queen's visit?
- How do you think the boy felt when she agreed to come?

3 Ask the group to imagine that day. What would happen? How would they behave if the Queen were to visit them? If you have an active group, give them some time to plan a short role play or to write a follow-up article describing the Queen's visit from the boy's point of view.

4 If appropriate, explain that today's Bible passage tells us about a party with a very important guest.

 **SCENE SETTER**

WHAT: comic strip diary
WHY: to think about how the young people spend their time

1 Start by asking the group, 'What is your favourite part of the day and why?' They are likely to say a part of the day when they have free time, such as when they get home from school.

2 Give everyone pens and paper and ask them to create a comic strip entitled 'A typical day in the life of me'. Stick people will do! Challenge them to condense it into 12 scenes – one for every two hours of the day.

3 As the young people do this, discuss with them how they spend their time. A large part is probably sleeping and school, but what about the rest of their time? If you have time and it's appropriate, ask, 'Where does God fit in?'

4 Put a time limit on this activity – if necessary, they can sketch out their ideas and bring the finished article next week for show and tell!

 **THEMED GAME**

WHAT: feast!
WHY: to enjoy sharing quality time together
WITH: party food (required), knife, fork, gloves, scarf, hat, plate, large chocolate bar, dice (all optional)

1 Ask everyone in advance to bring something for a little feast, or provide a small selection of party food. Be aware of dietary requirements and/or allergies.

2 Enjoy chatting and eating together! You could play a food-related game – for example, the chocolate game. Seat the young people in a circle with the chocolate bar on a plate and the knife, fork, gloves, scarf and hat nearby. Take turns to roll the dice. When somebody rolls a six, they sit in the middle of the circle, put on the garments and then begin to chop up the chocolate bar with the knife and fork. No hands! They can eat whatever they can cut and pick up with the knife and fork. While they are doing this, the rest of the group continues to roll the dice. If someone else rolls a six, they interrupt the player in the middle who takes off all the garments and the new person puts them on. And so on! Stop when time is up, or when all the chocolate is gone!

BIBLE EXPERIENCE

 LEVEL 2: INTERFACE

 LEVEL 3: SWITCH ON

LEVEL 1: CONNECT

WHAT: activity and discussion
WHY: to make spending quality time with God a priority
WITH: Bibles, magazine page 209

1 Introduce the Bible passage by explaining that it is about a party with a very important guest. (This links particularly well with *Way in 'theGRID* magazine'.) The hosts were two women who were both very excited about the visit of this VIP, but they reacted to his arrival in very different ways.

2 Read Luke 10:38–42 together. Bring the story alive as much as possible. If your young people are willing, appoint three people to act out the parts of Martha, Mary and Jesus as you read. This will help the group to engage with the passage.

3 Give out copies of page 209 and use the chart to trace the emotions through the story.

4 Discuss the emotions of the characters and use the circles to draw the expressions of the three different characters as you read each bitesize Bible bit again. Ask the young people:

- Are there any changes as the story goes on?
- Why might this be?
- Which character do you relate to most?

5 Finish with a fun challenge. Close the Bibles and challenge the young people to retell the story in 30 seconds, using only the pictures they've drawn and seeing how much they can remember.

LEVEL 2: INTERFACE

WHAT: discussion and activity
WHY: to make spending quality time with God a priority
WITH: Bibles, magazine page 209

1 Start by asking the young people about their weekend. While they are speaking, start fidgeting, biting your nails, sorting out Bibles, etc – something to make it clear that you're not listening!

2 Ask those who were speaking to explain how they felt about your behaviour. Ask more generally how the young people feel when they are not listened to. Does anyone have any funny stories on this theme?

3 Give everyone a Bible and read Luke 10:38–42 together.

4 Use the chart on page 209 to trace the emotions through the story.

5 Read the passage again and use the circles to draw the facial expressions and emotions of each character as you discuss them (note that for Jesus, a and c are the same!). What do their feelings reveal?

6 Ask the young people to consider how they feel about God. Do they identify more with Martha or with Mary? Who would they like to be like?

LEVEL 3: SWITCH ON

WHAT: Bible study
WHY: to make spending quality time with God a priority
WITH: large sheets of paper, Bibles (different versions if possible), sticky notes (in different colours), background music (optional), small prize (optional)

1 Divide the group into pairs or small groups as appropriate and give out Bibles or copies of the passage – a different translation to each group. (You could use www.biblegateway.com to print several different versions.) Give them five minutes to read and summarise the passage in the form of a tweet (only 280 characters allowed!) – they can use their phones to help them do this if they have them.

2 Ask the group to share their summaries – you could give a prize for the best one!

3 Give out two different-coloured sticky notes to each of the young people – one colour for Jesus and one for us. Ask them to write on the sticky notes what this passage tells us about Jesus and what it might teach us about ourselves. Encourage them to use their Bibles to do this, looking for key words and phrases to help them find answers. Stick the sticky notes in two different parts of the room. You could play music quietly in the background while they do this, so no one feels uncomfortable about taking time to think. Encourage everyone to write something down, no matter how simple or obvious. You may like to prepare a couple of answers of your own so nobody has to be the first to post!

4 Spend time as a group looking at each of the suggestions. What does this passage teach us about Jesus? What does it teach us about ourselves? How are the two connected?

5 Conclude by emphasising that Mary got it right – spending time with Jesus is the better thing. This should be our priority. Is it easy to do though?

RESPOND

 MUSICAL

WHAT: worship words
WHY: to explore what God is like and how we should respond
WITH: worship songs with printed lyrics, playback equipment

1 Choose some worship songs that your young people know well. Print out the lyrics.

2 Sing or listen to the songs together. Give out copies of the lyrics and encourage the young people to look at them carefully as they listen or sing, even if they know the songs off by heart.

3 Give out pens and invite the young people to underline words and phrases in the songs about God and words or phrases about our response to him (perhaps with different colours).

4 Read out all the things from the songs that are about God. You have just proclaimed all these truths about him – this is fantastic worship! How does noticing all these things about God make you feel about him? How could or should we respond?

5 Next read out all the bits about our response to God. Do they match your ideas? Some of them may seem a little bit crazy (for example, 'I fall down on my knees'). Invite the young people to think about these things and discuss what they actually mean.

6 Challenge the young people to consider the words carefully next time they are singing in church. Sometimes we make big commitments in our sung worship without even realising it! These are great things to promise because God wants us to make spending time with him a priority, so now it's up to us to actually do it!

7 Sing a song to close, if time allows, worshipping God wholeheartedly!

 PRACTICAL

WHAT: week planner
WHY: to plan how to make spending time with God a priority this week
WITH: resource page 210

1 Give out copies of resource page 210 and pens.

2 Explain that Martha and Mary show us two different ways to respond to Jesus. Martha loved Jesus but was so caught up in doing stuff for him that she forgot to spend time listening to him. One way to make sure we spend time with God is to plan our time!

3 Ask everybody to fill in the diary page with the plans they have for next week (school, youth group, regular sports or clubs, special occasions, etc).

4 Encourage the young people by pointing out that some time with God is better than no time, so even a small slot is a good start! It could be five minutes every day, 20 minutes twice a week or an hour once a week (or more). It will be different for everyone. And the more time they spend with God, the more time they'll want to spend with God!

5 Invite the group to write in specific slots when they will spend time with God.

6 It is probably a good idea to suggest things that people can do with these slots. They could pray, read their Bible, sing, dance, write to God – be creative! Next week you can all share what you have learned.

7 Finish by praying that God will help you all stick to your plans and that he will show you how much he loves it when we make spending time with him a priority.

 CREATIVE

WHAT: 'Better thing' bookmarks
WHY: to remind us how to spend time with God
WITH: coloured paper or card, craft materials

1 Start by sharing ideas of what we might do to spend time with God. Try to think of some really unusual or crazy ideas – for example, shouting a psalm (although not at night-time, of course!) or making a collage of creation and using it to worship God. Come up with as many ideas as possible before moving on to the next stage.

2 Give everybody a piece of bookmark-shaped card and access to the craft materials.

3 Explain that you are each going to create a 'Better thing' bookmark. Jesus said that Mary had chosen the 'better thing' because she chose to sit and listen to Jesus while her sister stressed about the house. This bookmark will be a reminder of how you can choose the 'better thing' – putting God first and making it a priority to spend time with him.

4 Ask each young person to choose at least five ideas from the initial list that they like and might be willing to try. Encourage them to be as creative as possible while they copy these ideas onto the bookmark and decorate it with sequins, stickers, ribbon or whatever craft materials are available.

5 Tell the young people to keep this bookmark in their Bible and to use it to help them spend time with God on their own. Make sure you allow time in the next session to share the things they have done.

MORE ON THIS THEME:

If you want to do a short series with your group, other sessions that work well with this one are:

30	The real Bible code	Luke 4:16–30; Isaiah 61:1–3a
31	No waiting list	Luke 5:17–26
32	Extravagant worship	Luke 7:36–50

Bible bit
Luke 10:38–42

It's really easy to get busy with stuff. Sometimes we are so concerned with doing stuff for Jesus that we forget to actually spend time with him! Jesus said that Mary chose 'the better thing'. Listening to Jesus' words would stay with her for ever, but Martha's tidy house and tasty supper would soon be gone. Jesus wants us to cherish what lasts for ever, and so we should make spending quality time with him a priority. So next time you're rushing off to youth group or music practice before speaking to God that day, take five and say hello. The world can wait!

NEWSFLASH!

QUEEN VISITS BOY'S TOWN!

No one was more surprised than George when he received a reply to his letter saying that the Queen would be paying a special royal visit. Other local people, including the Mayor, had written to the royal palace before to ask her to come, but with no luck until now!

The Queen went on a trip to Romford in East London for the first time to see a boy who had written her a letter. Fourteen-year-old George invited Her Majesty after she had been unable to attend the town's Golden Jubilee celebrations that were being held in her honour.

After wandering round Romford market and learning some of the local Cockney rhyming slang, the 'Big Baked Bean' stopped off at the local school. There she was treated to a special royal performance of music, drama and dance, she perused the art gallery and met some of the students, including George himself!

Photograph of the Queen: de:Benutzer:Mr.Clemens

IT'S AN EMOTIONAL
ROLLERCOASTER!

Draw expressions on the faces to show how the characters' emotions change while you read Luke 10:38–42.

THIS IS HOW I FEEL…

MARTHA **MARY** **JESUS**

A) … ABOUT JESUS

B) … ABOUT THE JOBS TO BE DONE!

C) … ABOUT MYSELF

RESOURCE PAGE

USE WITH SESSION 33 RESPOND 'PRACTICAL'

Monday	Friday ....
Tuesday	Saturday ....
Wednesday	Sunday ....
Thursday	

Photocopiable resource © Scripture Union 2018

BACK TROUBLE

THE AIM: To discover that Jesus heals even when other people don't like it

The aim unpacked

In this session we find Jesus teaching in a synagogue. While he's teaching, he heals a woman who has been crippled for 18 years! Unsurprisingly, the woman's response is to praise God. But the leader of the synagogue is furious because Jesus healed this woman on the Sabbath day and the synagogue leader classes this as work! He tells people that they should only turn up for healing on a workday.

WAY IN

 theGRID MAGAZINE

WHAT: quiz
WHY: to start thinking about 'Sabbath'
WITH: magazine page 214

1 Hand out copies of page 214 and invite the young people to look at the 'Sunday rest' activity. Ask: Which of these might you normally do on a Sunday?

2 Discuss with your group whether they think any of these activities should be classed as 'work'.

3 God gave the Jewish people a rule about not working on the Sabbath (which for them was actually a Saturday). God said that everyone needs to have a rest from work at least one day a week. Ask the young people to think about and respond to these questions:

- What do you think about this idea?

- Do any of the activities you like doing on a Sunday involve other people having to work?

- How do you think they might feel about this?

 SCENE SETTER

WHAT: game
WHY: to think about freedom
WITH: two poles, piece of string

1 Explain to the young people that they are trying to escape from prison! They have successfully evaded the guards and are confronted with their last hurdle – an electric fence. Set up the two poles with a piece of string between them high enough that none of the group can simply step over. Explain that this is the last obstacle between them and freedom.

2 Their challenge is to work out how to get the entire team safely across the fence without touching it. Only one person may cross at a time, and once over the fence they may not come back to help – only those on the 'inside' may assist.

3 If you don't have enough space to physically do this exercise, perhaps discuss as a group how they would work together to get free from various traps or situations. Introduce the rest of the session by talking about how Jesus freed a woman from an illness.

 THEMED GAME

WHAT: obstacle course
WHY: to think about being bent over double
WITH: equipment for creating a simple obstacle course, two beanbags

1 Before the young people arrive, set up a simple (and safe) obstacle course.

2 Divide the group into two teams and challenge each team to complete the course in the fastest time. However, there is a catch! They must do it bent over double, with a beanbag balanced on their back. If the beanbag falls off they must stop and put it back on before continuing.

3 Either set up two identical courses and do this activity as a head-to-head race, or set up one course and time both teams to see who completes it in the shortest time.

BIBLE EXPERIENCE

 **LEVEL 1: CONNECT**

WHAT: drama
WHY: to discover that Jesus heals even when other people don't like it
WITH: Bible, props

1 Divide the young people into groups of about four each and ask them to read Luke 13:10–17.

2 Ask them to imagine they are reporters and have to create a short segment about this incident for the evening news. As part of their report they need to interview the following people:

- The woman who was healed
- The synagogue leader
- An onlooker

3 Once the young people have had time to prepare their reports, ask each group to act theirs out to everyone else.

4 Then ask the young people what they thought of the synagogue leader's reaction. What would they have said to him if they had been there? Conclude by discussing what they think should be learned from this incident.

 LEVEL 2: INTERFACE

WHAT: Bible exploration
WHY: to understand that Jesus' actions made him unpopular
WITH: Bibles, selection of celebrity magazines

1 Discuss these questions with your group:

- Have you ever done something that made you unpopular?
- What did you do, and why?
- Who did it make you unpopular with?

2 Give out the magazines. In groups of three or four, challenge the young people to choose a celebrity and discuss what that celebrity might have to do to make themselves unpopular with their fans (for example, a top footballer to score an own goal).

3 Everyone likes to be popular – and we all have expectations of other people. When people stop behaving in the way we expect them to, they often become less popular. Ask the young people to discuss whether they think this is fair, and why.

4 Read, or ask a confident reader to read, Luke 13:10–17 to the group.

5 Discuss together the following questions:

- What do you think the people expected from Jesus?
- What do you think the synagogue leader expected?
- How did he feel when Jesus didn't behave in what he considered to be the 'right' way?
- Do you think what Jesus did was right or wrong? Why?

6 Encourage the young people to share examples of when they have acted in a way that was different from what people expected, and to consider whether these were good or bad experiences.

7 Discuss how we can determine when it's right to go against what others expect from us. Try to keep this focused on specifics rather than being too general.

 LEVEL 3: SWITCH ON

WHAT: Bible study
WHY: to discover that Jesus heals even when other people don't like it
WITH: Bibles

1 Read Luke 13:10–13 together and talk about what Jesus did. He didn't overlook the woman, but called her over. Then he healed her. Chat about the words Jesus used: 'You are free.'

2 Discuss these two questions with the young people:

- How do we 'see' others who are different from us?
- What can we learn from Jesus' example in this story?

3 Read Luke 13:14 and ask the young people what they think about the anger expressed by the leader of the synagogue:

- Why did the synagogue leader get so angry?
- Do you think his anger was justified?

4 Point out to the group that the religious leaders often became annoyed with Jesus because he kept messing up their comfortable routine. They were so upset by this that they appeared to be unable to see the big picture and how amazing it was that Jesus had just healed someone who had been suffering for 18 years!

5 Encourage the young people to think about the routines of their lives. Stress that there is nothing wrong with routine, but sometimes there are more important things at stake. Discuss some daily routines and think about what things might interrupt them. For example, missing a TV show to visit a grandparent in hospital.

6 Ask a young person to read Luke 13:15–17. Discuss the following questions:

- How does Jesus respond to the criticism?
- How different would this situation have been if Jesus had responded by 'undoing' the healing? What would you think of Jesus then?
- How do you respond when people criticise your faith? Do you stand firm or back down? Why? How can we support each other?

RESPOND

 MUSICAL

WHAT: reflection
WHY: to reflect on how God identifies with the sick and disabled
WITH: 'Out of the Depths' by Sinead O'Connor, playback equipment, big cushions or beanbags (optional)

1 The track 'Out of the Depths' by Sinead O'Connor is available online or on the album *Theology*.

2 Create a comfortable environment for relaxed listening. Low lighting with beanbags or big cushions would be ideal.

3 Introduce the track by explaining that throughout the Gospels we see evidence that Jesus particularly identified with the people that society valued the least – the sick, the poor and the disabled. Encourage the young people to listen to the lyrics carefully and to use the time to reflect on their own relationship with God.

 PRACTICAL

WHAT: planning for action
WHY: to put into practice what has been learned
WITH: internet access, guest speaker (both optional)

1 Say that in this session we have seen how Jesus made an impact on the life of a disabled woman by healing her. But how can we, following Jesus' example, make an impact on the lives of those who are sick or disabled in our own towns and cities?

2 Divide the young people into small groups and ask them to think about people or groups in your area who are sick or disabled – for example, church members, family and friends, a local children's hospital or retirement home.

3 Challenge the groups to choose one of these groups and to think about what their needs might be. Find out what you can about them using the internet, local newspapers and information sources. (Do some work in advance on this and, if possible, invite someone from a local group to discuss the issues with the young people.)

4 Then challenge them to think about what they could do, as a group, to show God's love to this group of people. It could be something simple like donating toys or games to a children's ward, or something more long term, like volunteering to help with the gardening at a local retirement home on a regular basis. Encourage the young people to make a plan and to do everything they can to make the ideas discussed during this session a reality.

 CREATIVE

WHAT: prayer
WHY: to think about how we respond to God
WITH: blank postcards

1 Ask a young person to read out Luke 13:10–13.

2 Ask your group:
- What was the first thing the woman did after she was healed?
- Why do you think she thanked God when it was Jesus who healed her?

3 Discuss with the group:
- What is our first reaction when something good happens to us? Do we ever remember to thank God?
- Do you think we should thank God? Why (not)?
- Why do people sometimes forget to thank God?

4 Give each person a blank postcard and explain that we are going to spend some time thanking God for the good things in our lives. Ask them to think of three good things in their lives which they would like to thank God for. Encourage each person to write a few short sentences on their postcard, thanking God for these things.

5 When everyone has written on their cards, gather round in a circle. Ask each person to pass their card to the right. Then take it in turns to read out what is written on the cards and spend some time thanking God.

MORE ON THIS THEME:

If you want to do a short series with your group, other sessions that work well with this one are:

Bible bit
Luke 13:10–17

Jesus heals a woman who has been crippled for 18 years! Unsurprisingly, the woman's response is to praise God. You would have thought everyone would have been happy, but not so! The leader of the synagogue is furious! Why? Well, it's because Jesus healed this woman on the Sabbath day and the synagogue leader classes this as work! He tells people that they should only turn up for healing on a workday. Crazy?!

What do you like to do on a typical Sunday? Watch TV? Go out with your friends? Go to church?

SUNDAY REST

Have a look at the pictures below and tick the ones you like to do on Sundays. Jot down why you like to do these activities along with who you usually do them with.

GOING TO CHURCH

PLAYING SPORT

MEETING FRIENDS

SHOPPING

DOING HOMEWORK

WATCHING TV

?

Many people have to go to work on Sundays – nurses, doctors, shop workers, to name just a few. But in the Old Testament, God told his people, the Jews, that for one day a week no one should do any work. Why do you think God might have made this rule? Do you think it is a good idea?

ONE OUT OF TEN

THE AIM: To be thankful that God heals people through his Son, Jesus

The aim unpacked

Jesus healed ten people from a dreaded skin disease. Despite the amazing thing Jesus did for these ten people, only one – yes that's right, only one – bothered to come back to thank him! Shocking! As we look at this story, we will have the opportunity to think about all the amazing things God has done, and still does, for us. Do we thank him as often as we should?

WAY IN

 **theGRID MAGAZINE**

WHAT: list making
WHY: to practise being thankful
WITH: magazine page 219

1 Hand out copies of page 219. Invite the young people to complete the 'Reasons to be thankful' activity, either individually or in pairs.

2 Spend some time discussing the answers with the group. Are there any themes in the lists? Which things were people thankful for most?

3 For some fun, you might like to try practising saying 'thank you' in different languages, using page 219 for reference, or asking members of your group.

 **SCENE SETTER**

WHAT: good news activity
WHY: to think about how different people respond in different ways

1 Ask the young people to imagine they have just received a phone call to say they have won a competition and are now a millionaire! Give everyone a piece of paper and a pen and ask them to make a list of the first five things they would do after receiving the call.

2 Invite the young people to compare their lists, in pairs, and to think about the similarities and differences.

3 Conclude by making the point that people respond in different ways to good news.

 **THEMED GAME**

WHAT: blindfold game
WHY: to learn about being dependent on others
WITH: bowls of ice cream, spoons, blindfolds, sheets or bin liners to cover clothing, scarf (optional)

1 Divide the young people into pairs. Either have everyone playing at once, or take it in turns so the rest of the group can watch the fun.

2 Ask two players to sit opposite each other and blindfold them both. Ask one player to put their hands behind their back – you may want to actually tie them there with a scarf! Cover their clothes with an old sheet or a bin liner – this might get messy! Give the other person a bowl of ice cream and a spoon. The challenge is for this player to feed the ice cream to the other. (Be aware of food allergies and observe proper hygiene.)

3 After the game, discuss with the group how it feels to be dependent on someone else for something you would normally do yourself. Explain that in this session we'll be looking at a group of people who suffered from leprosy. They would have had to depend on each other a great deal.

BIBLE EXPERIENCE

 LEVEL 1: CONNECT

WHAT: drama
WHY: to be thankful that God heals people through his Son, Jesus
WITH: Bibles, props

1 Divide the young people into groups and ask each group to prepare a short drama sketch based on the following scenario: It's Christmas Day and three children are opening presents. However, only one of the children says thank you. Encourage the young people to explore within their sketches why two of the children didn't say thank you and how the giver of the presents felt. Once the groups have had enough time to prepare their sketches, offer them the opportunity to present them to everyone else.

2 Ask a volunteer to read aloud, or read yourself, Luke 17:11–19.

3 Use some of the following questions to discuss this story:

- Why do you think nine of the men didn't go back?

- What do you think about this?

- How do you think Jesus felt about this?

- What can we learn from this story?

- Why do you think it's important that we say thank you to God and to other people?

 LEVEL 2: INTERFACE

WHAT: creative writing
WHY: to be thankful that God heals people through his Son, Jesus
WITH: Bibles, magazine page 218

1 Hand out copies of page 218 and ask the young people to read the two diary entries. Encourage them to discuss with one another what it might feel like to have leprosy today and what it must have felt like in Jesus' day.

2 Read aloud, or ask a young person to read, Luke 17:11–19.

3 Divide the young people into ten groups. If your group has fewer than ten people, divide into five groups. Ask one group to imagine that they are the one man who went back to thank Jesus, and the rest to imagine that they are one of those who was healed but did not go back. Ask each group to write a short statement explaining what they did after they were healed. Encourage them to consider how they felt, where they went, what they did, who they told and what made them go back and thank Jesus, or not.

4 When all the statements have been written, ask each group to read theirs out. Finish with the statement from the person who went back to thank Jesus.

5 Encourage any discussion that this activity creates. Ask the group whether or not they are surprised that nine of the men didn't go back to thank Jesus. Challenge them to consider how they respond when good things happen to them. Are they quick to thank people?

 LEVEL 3: SWITCH ON

WHAT: discussion
WHY: to be thankful that God heals people through his Son, Jesus
WITH: Bibles, two large sheets of paper or whiteboard

1 On a large sheet of paper or whiteboard, ask the young people to write down as many different ways as possible that we can say thank you to people. For example, write them a letter, give them a box of chocolates, send them some flowers, send them an email or a text message.

2 Discuss with the group how it makes them feel when someone says thank you to them. Also discuss how it makes them feel when people do not say thank you to them.

3 Ask a volunteer to read Luke 17:11–19 to the group and then discuss the following questions:

- Are you surprised that only one out of ten people came back to thank Jesus? Why?

- Are you surprised that it was a Samaritan who came to say thank you? Why (not)? What can we learn from this?

4 On another large sheet of paper or the whiteboard, make a list of some of the things we should be thankful to God for. Do we always thank God for the things he does? If not, why not? How do you think God wants us to thank him for all the amazing things he does (and has done) for us?

RESPOND

 MUSICAL

WHAT: reflection
WHY: to reflect on our dependence on God
WITH: 'When the Tears Fall' by Tim Hughes, playback equipment, beanbags and cushions (optional)

1 Create a peaceful and comfortable environment in your meeting area. You could use soft lighting, beanbags and cushions. Invite the young people each to find a space and relax.

2 Say that it's amazing how God heals people. Perhaps we know people personally who have been miraculously healed by God. However, the reality is that God doesn't seem to heal everyone. We all probably know people who have prayed and prayed for healing yet are still sick. This can be a very sensitive issue.

3 Play the song 'When the Tears Fall' by Tim Hughes and encourage the young people to reflect on the fact that although we don't know all the answers, God is so much bigger than the problem, and we should cling to him.

4 Provide an opportunity for the young people to chat to leaders about any issues this may have raised.

 PRACTICAL

WHAT: thank-you letters
WHY: to thank people for the things they do for us
WITH: envelopes, card and craft materials (optional)

1 Give out paper and pens. Ask everyone to think back over the last week or so and make a list of ten things they have to be thankful for.

2 Once they have done this, encourage them to read through their lists and mark the things they haven't said thank you for.

3 Encourage everyone to write a thank-you letter for one of the items on their list. This letter could be to a parent, youth leader or God. If time and resources allow, you might want to be more creative and make thank-you cards.

 CREATIVE

WHAT: drawing prayer
WHY: to pray about the issue of leprosy today
WITH: resource page 220, art materials, information about The Leprosy Mission (optional)

1 Explain that many people suffer from leprosy today. While it may not be exactly the same disease or hold the same stigma or prognosis as it did in Bible times, they still need healing, and we can pray for them. You might like to have some information available about what modern-day leprosy is and how it can be treated.

2 Remind the young people that prayer does not always have to be about speaking. There are many different ways we can communicate with God. Invite your group to explore the idea of prayerful drawing by giving everyone a copy of The Leprosy Mission Prayer from page 220 and asking them to illustrate a phrase or a sentence from it.

3 Allow time for everyone to complete their drawings, then gather the group together and read the prayer aloud as you look at the artwork.

MORE ON THIS THEME:

If you want to do a short series with your group, other sessions that work well with this one are:

34   *Back trouble*   *Luke 13:10–17*

LEPROSY: THEN AND NOW

Bible bit
Luke 17:11–19

'You're so ungrateful!' Be honest – how often has this accusation been levelled at you? Jesus healed ten people from a dreaded skin disease, called leprosy in some Bible versions. Despite this amazing event, only one person – yes that's right, only one – bothered to come back to thank him! Shocking! How can you thank God more often for the amazing things he's done in your life?!

DIARY OF A LEPROSY SUFFERER – TODAY

My name is Rukmini and I live in East India with my son, who is 17 years old. I was diagnosed with leprosy when numb patches started to appear on my skin. I was afraid that I would give the disease to my boy, but the leprosy clinic told me how to stop this from happening. They gave me a drug treatment which I have been taking for five months. Soon the disease will be gone, and I will be well again. As the disease was recognised early I have not lost much feeling, and I will continue to be able to use my hands and feet as normal. I am so grateful.

DIARY OF A LEPROSY SUFFERER – IN JESUS' TIME

My name is not important. I have been cast out from my family ever since God afflicted me with this terrible disease. I live with the other leprosy sufferers, outside the town. We scavenge for food and water. Even if we had money we wouldn't be allowed to approach the market to buy anything. We must not cut our hair, and we have to dress in worn-out rags. If we go near anyone, we must shout out, 'Unclean!' as we go, so that no one accidentally comes near and touches us. If they did, they would become unclean too. I will die here, without seeing my family again – they are too afraid to visit me. No one can help me. Each day I feel a little less, my fingers grow numb and soon I will not be able to feed myself. Then I will have to rely on the other people who have leprosy, those who can still use their hands, to help me. I do not understand what I have done to deserve this life.

FACT BOX

Different versions of the Bible describe the sick men's condition differently. In the ancient world, the term 'leprosy' was used for a range of skin disorders, and may not be the same thing as what we know as Hansen's disease today. In Bible times, a person with a skin disease would not have been able to attend worship and would have been denied all social contact. Touching such a person would make someone ritually impure too, but that did not bother Jesus. The requirement to be examined by the priest comes from Leviticus chapters 13 and 14.

Read Luke 17:11–19 to find out what happened when Jesus met some people like this. How did he change their lives?

YES – WHY?

NO – WHY NOT?

Would you have gone back to say thank you? Ask your friends and get some of their votes too.

THANK YOU!

Have a go at saying 'thank you' in these languages!

Chinese (Cantonese)
do jeh
(daw-dyeh)

Russian
spasibo
(spah-see-boh)

Hebrew
toda
(toh-dah)

French
merci
(mehr-see)

Swedish
tack
(tahkk)

Spanish
gracias
(gra-see-us)

Italian
grazie
(gra-see)

German
danke
(dahn-kah)

Swahili
asante
(ah-sahn-the)

Polish
dziekuje
(dsyen-koo-yeh)

REASONS TO BE THANKFUL

What do you have to be thankful for?
Can you think of ten things?
Write them here.

1
2
3
4
5
6
7
8
9
10

The Leprosy Mission Prayer

Almighty Father, the giver of life and health, look mercifully on those who suffer from leprosy. Stretch out your hand to touch and heal them as Jesus did during his earthly life. Grant wisdom and insight to those who are seeking the prevention and cure of the disease; give skill and sympathy to those who minister to the patients; reunite the separated with their families and friends; and inspire your people with the task set before The Leprosy Mission, that it may never lack either the staff or the means to carry on its healing work, in accordance with your will, and to the glory of your holy name.

We ask this for the sake of Jesus Christ, your Son, our Lord. Amen

The Leprosy Mission Prayer

Almighty Father, the giver of life and health, look mercifully on those who suffer from leprosy. Stretch out your hand to touch and heal them as Jesus did during his earthly life. Grant wisdom and insight to those who are seeking the prevention and cure of the disease; give skill and sympathy to those who minister to the patients; reunite the separated with their families and friends; and inspire your people with the task set before The Leprosy Mission, that it may never lack either the staff or the means to carry on its healing work, in accordance with your will, and to the glory of your holy name.

We ask this for the sake of Jesus Christ, your Son, our Lord. Amen

Training programme

	Breakfast	Morning	Lunch	Afternoon	Dinner	Evening
Monday						
Tuesday						
Wednesday						
Thursday						
Friday						
Saturday						
Sunday						

My goal is:

I will need these things to help me:

I will need to change/give up these things to prepare:

Other notes:

37
TOOLED UP

THE AIM: To recognise that God prepares us for the battles ahead in the Christian life

The aim unpacked

In this session, Paul uses the stunning visual illustration of the armour of God. It is all too easy to see the Christian life as a boring, generally low-impact state of being governed by rules of 'don't do this' and 'don't do that'. However, from the illustration that Paul gives us, it is clear that a Christian life should be anything but that.

WAY IN

 **theGRID MAGAZINE**

WHAT: discussion
WHY: to introduce the theme of preparation
WITH: magazine page 229

1 Hand out copies of page 229.

2 Ask each young person to select their top ten holiday essentials from the items shown, in order to be well prepared for a holiday or journey.

3 After a couple of minutes, find out what everyone's top three items are and see if there are any similarities.

4 If appropriate, explain that in this session we'll be looking at preparing ourselves for something else.

 **SCENE SETTER**

WHAT: sticky note game
WHY: to explore the theme of being equipped for activity

1 Give each young person a sticky note and a pen.

2 Ask each young person to think of an activity and write it on their sticky note – for example, horse-riding, going to the library, travelling in space, making a film. Collect all the sticky notes, muddle them up and stick one to the back of each young person.

3 Challenge them to discover what activity is on their back. Say that they must not look at their own sticky note; they must only ask 'yes' or 'no' questions about what they would need for the activity. For example, 'Would I need a riding hat? A library card?' They can only ask one question to each person.

4 The winner is the first person to come to you knowing the activity that is written on their sticky note.

 **THEMED GAME**

WHAT: newspaper battle
WHY: to explore the ideas of 'attack' and 'defence'
WITH: old newspapers or magazines, rubbish bags, whistle or bell (or very loud voice), volleyball net or chairs

1 Divide your room in half, with a volleyball net or a line of chairs. Divide the young people into two teams and give each team the same number of newspapers or magazines.

2 Allocate a side of the net/chairs to each team and invite them to prepare their paper by screwing it into balls.

3 Explain that the object of the game is to throw as much paper as possible over to the other team's side. The paper must be thrown over the net or chairs, not pushed under. The winning team is the team with the least amount of paper on their side after, say, three minutes (or more if they seem to be enjoying themselves). It can be helpful to have two adults at the net to stop foul play.

4 Ask the young people to pick up all the paper afterwards. Ask the group if they think they might have improved the result with any extra equipment, and can they think what?

5 Ask whether they felt the game was about defending their half of the 'court' or attacking the other side.

BIBLE EXPERIENCE

 LEVEL 1: CONNECT

WHAT: quiz and reflection
WHY: to recognise that God prepares us for the battles ahead in the Christian life
WITH: Bibles, bag of props containing a shoe, hat, belt, shield, toy sword, breastplate (eg waistcoat, flak jacket) or images of these items

1 Ask the young people if they have ever forgotten something really important when they have gone out for the day, to school or on holiday. Suggest that they tell the person next to them what they forgot and what happened as a result.

2 Say that packing the right stuff for where you are going is important. Give out Bibles. Ask for a couple of volunteers to read aloud Ephesians 6:10–18, and encourage the young people to follow the text as it is read.

3 Bring out the bag of props (or pictures). Ask for a volunteer to pick something out of the bag and challenge everyone to find where that item of armour is mentioned in the passage. Ask: Why do you think that item might be important? Repeat until all the items have been discussed.

4 Explain that through God we can have all these things to help us live our lives, especially when it's tough, but also when things are going well. To live to the fullest as Christians we need to make sure we are prepared. The armour of God is a great illustration of how we should prepare ourselves.

 LEVEL 2: INTERFACE

WHAT: freeze-frame drama
WHY: to recognise that God prepares us for the battles ahead in the Christian life
WITH: magazine page 230, Bibles, bag of props containing a shoe, hat, belt, shield or umbrella, toy sword, breastplate (eg paper plate)

1 Divide the young people into pairs or threes. Give each small group a copy of page 230 and ask them to find the 'God's armour' activity.

2 Either: Read Ephesians 6:10–18 out loud to the group. Encourage them to listen out for the items of armour and to fill in the tag for each one on the page. Go through the answers. Or: Give everyone a Bible and ask them to turn to Ephesians 6:10–18. Ask the groups to find the verse in which each item is mentioned and fill in the corresponding tag on page 230. Encourage them to discuss what they think this armour is for, then take feedback in the main group.

3 Give each pair or three a prop from the list above. Ask them to think of a situation in which they might use this as they live their Christian life. (This could be interesting as it will give you some insight into what they think living as a Christian is like.)

4 Invite each pair or three to create a freeze-frame (a still image of a situation using people and props), and ask everyone else to guess what the situation is.

5 Explain that we need to be prepared if we are to get the best out of any situation. It's the same in our Christian life. We can also see, from the items that Paul says we need, that being a Christian is not an easy journey but a battle.

 LEVEL 3: SWITCH ON

WHAT: discussion
WHY: to recognise that God prepares us for the battles ahead in the Christian life
WITH: Bibles

1 Ask for a couple of volunteers to read out Ephesians 6:10–18 and encourage everyone to follow the text as it's read aloud.

2 Ask some of these questions:

- Does anything surprise you in this passage?
- What is the armour of God?
- What do you use the armour for?
- Why is it important to use the full armour of God?
- How do you fight wearing this armour?
- Why is it crucial to stand?
- What are the differences between this kind of armour and regular military armour?

3 Divide the group into pairs or threes and ask them to discuss which pieces of armour they think they have and which ones they'd like upgraded.

4 Encourage the groups to pray for each other to receive these gifts from God.

BIBLE EXPERIENCE

RESPOND

 MUSICAL

WHAT: Bible reflection and songs
WHY: to explore the theme of relying on God
WITH: Bibles, reflective music, playback equipment, musicians (optional), background music

1 Hand out Bibles. Play some reflective music. Read aloud Psalm 40:1–3 slowly and encourage the young people to follow it in their Bibles.

2 Ask them to look carefully at the words of the psalm and share anything that they find surprising or that is good news in these verses.

3 Either listen to or sing a couple of these songs:

- 'Awake, Awake, O Zion (Our God reigns)' by Nathan Fellingham
- 'Give Thanks (Forever)' by Chris Tomlin
- 'How Lovely on the Mountains (Our God reigns)' by Leonard E Smith
- 'When I Was Lost (There is a new song)' by Kate and Miles Simmonds

 PRACTICAL

WHAT: prayer
WHY: to think about what armour the young people do or don't have
WITH: resource page 231

1 Give each young person a copy of resource page 231 and a pencil or pen.

2 Invite them to write or draw in the open suitcase the items of armour they think they don't have.

3 Invite everyone to get into pairs or threes and suggest that they pray for one another and for situations where they feel they might need a better shield, belt, etc.

4 Encourage the young people to keep their pictures in a special place as a reminder, and to continue to pray for each other.

 CREATIVE

WHAT: foot art
WHY: to emphasise that Jesus brings a gospel of peace
WITH: trays of paint, roll of paper (eg lining paper), temporary tattoos (optional), henna (optional), resource page 232

1 Explain that one of the themes in this session's Bible passage is walking. Suggest that the young people do one of the following, depending on your resources.

- Give out copies of resource page 232. Encourage the young people to make the feet into 'feet fitted with the readiness that comes from the gospel of peace' (Ephesians 6:15, NIV). Invite them to think about what it might mean to have 'the readiness that comes from the gospel of peace'.

- Prepare shallow trays of paint and spread a long length of paper on the floor. Invite the young people to remove their footwear and create footprints on the paper. Encourage some to write, 'Walking the gospel of peace' in the middle. Don't pressure anyone who is uncomfortable taking their footwear off; they can write the words instead.

- If possible, have some temporary tattoos or henna available. Encourage the young people to decorate their own or each other's feet with designs symbolising 'peace'. Make sure anyone with sensitive skin doesn't have anything put on their feet but encourage them to paint other people's. Also make sure they know how long the tattoos or henna will last and check in advance whether their school or parents will allow them to have these.

- Give out copies of resource page 232. Encourage each young person to cut out the foot and write how they might 'walk peacefully' on it.

MORE ON THIS THEME:

If you want to do a short series with your group, other sessions that work well with this one are:

TOP 10
HOLIDAY ESSENTIALS

You're preparing to go on a loooong journey to somewhere fabulous – what would you pack? Pick your top ten items, and then compare your answers with a friend!

Bible bit
Ephesians 6:10–18

Being a Christian isn't about sitting still in church, listening attentively to your group leader and being the most boring kid in your class at school. Being a Christian means preparation; it means having the right equipment; it means being ready for battle! 'Eh! What are you talking about? The most action we see at our church is when a baby starts crying.'
Well, if you don't believe me, take a look at what Paul says in this reading.

Complete works of Shakespeare

Music to listen to

Bag

String

School uniform

Swimwear

Teddy bear

Deodorant

Sunscreen

Homework

TV

Bible

Football

Sunglasses

Teabags

Clothes

Portable dining table

Pegs

37

GOD'S ARMOUR

Read Ephesians 6:10–18 and fill in the tags. Which is your favourite piece of God's protection? Can you think of a situation in your Christian life when you might need to use it?

ITEM:

AS IN VERSE:

REQUIRED FOR

ITEM:

AS IN VERSE:

REQUIRED FOR

ITEM:

AS IN VERSE:

REQUIRED FOR

ITEM:

AS IN VERSE:

REQUIRED FOR

ITEM:

AS IN VERSE:

REQUIRED FOR

ITEM:

AS IN VERSE:

REQUIRED FOR

USE WITH SESSION 37 RESPOND 'CREATIVE'

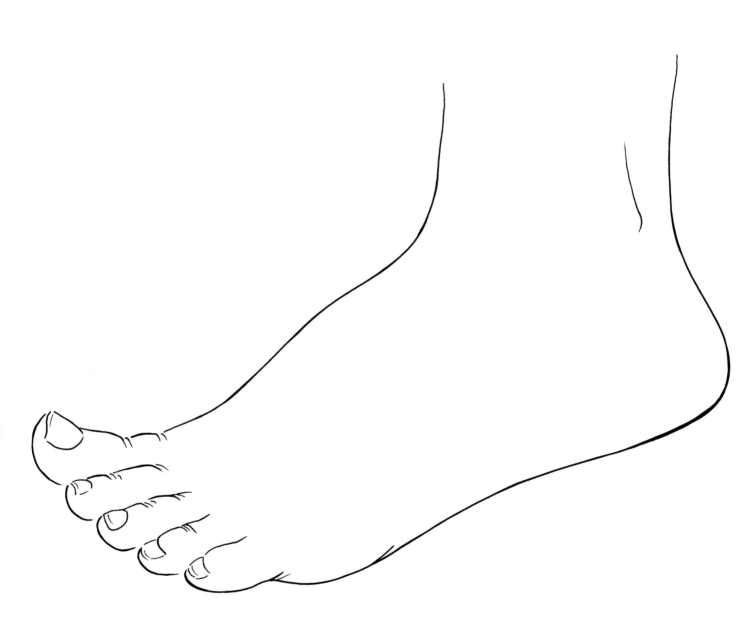

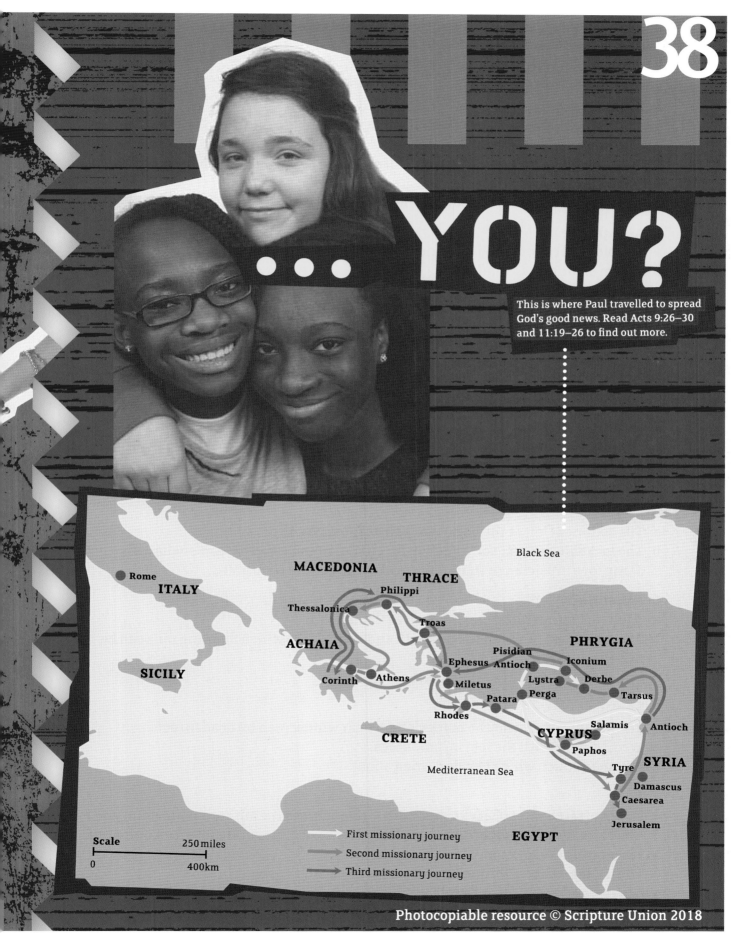

38

...YOU?

This is where Paul travelled to spread God's good news. Read Acts 9:26–30 and 11:19–26 to find out more.

Rome
ITALY
MACEDONIA
THRACE
Philippi
Thessalonica
Troas
Black Sea
ACHAIA
Ephesus
Pisidian
Antioch
PHRYGIA
Iconium
Corinth
Athens
Miletus
Lystra
Derbe
Patara
Perga
Tarsus
SICILY
Rhodes
CYPRUS
Salamis
Antioch
CRETE
Paphos
SYRIA
Tyre
Damascus
Mediterranean Sea
Caesarea
Jerusalem
EGYPT

Scale
0   250 miles
     400km

⟶ First missionary journey
⟶ Second missionary journey
⟶ Third missionary journey

RESOURCE PAGE

1 Blottesque

a A painting characterised by blots, heavily laid on. The resulting picture will have a very 'rough and ready' appearance.

b A cleaner, an employee of an ink factory who is given the task of mopping the floor and wiping down surfaces.

c Very, very drunk after consuming Bols Bleau liqueur.

2 Alliaphage

a A geological time-period just prior to the Jurassic age.

b A form of jungle camouflage.

c A garlic eater.

3 Abecedarian

a Something completely devoid of sophistication, from an ancient word based on the first four letters ABCD, meaning arranged in alphabetical order.

b A person from the ancient Scottish town of Abecedare.

c A person who has lived to the age of 110.

4 Doctress

a To make less stable, from the ancient term for removing supports or tresses.

b A female physician or doctor.

c A small tree with alleged healing properties.

5 Jiggs

a The sediment left at the bottom of a cup of ground coffee.

b The lockable dungeon on a galleon for crew members who have misbehaved.

c Slang for a musician in Hampton Court at the time of Henry VIII.

6 Ribaudoir

a A teller of rather filthy stories, such as Chaucer.

b The small area between the tow path and a canal into which mooring pins can be driven.

c The second vestry in a French cathedral.

7 Lectica

a The technical term for the marks left on a car windscreen by dead insects.

b Writing done with the feet by amputees.

c A Roman couch which can be carried about.

8 Peen

a The central chapter of a text book which summarises the author's main point and is therefore the most important chapter to revise when preparing for an examination.

b The gravel at the bottom of a goldfish tank.

c The wedge-shaped, thinner end of a hammer head.

EVERYONE SAYS YES

THE AIM: To explore God's plan to spread the good news

The aim unpacked

Today's Bible passage shows the followers of Jesus working together to solve issues. Encourage the young people to think about their faith in relation to other faiths, or to those with no faith at all. The first Christians worked together to further God's plan. How can you encourage your group to do the same?

WAY IN

 **theGRID MAGAZINE**

WHAT: personality test
WHY: to think about different people's strengths and weaknesses
WITH: magazine page 242

1 Hand out copies of page 242 and ask the young people to look at the Winnie the Pooh personality types.

2 Suggest that they work out who in the group best fits which personality type. It is important to stress that no one type is better or worse than any other, and that all the types have both strengths and weaknesses.

3 Challenge the young people to decide which personality type they would give the following tasks to and why:

- plan a party
- sing a song
- paint a picture
- resolve an argument

4 Say that we are all different, and we all have different gifts to offer each other. It is important to recognise both our own strengths and those of others if we are all to work together effectively and get along happily!

 SCENE SETTER

WHAT: matching
WHY: to encourage working together
WITH: resource pages 243 and 244 copied and cut into sections

1 This activity can be done with individuals, pairs or small groups, depending on the size of your group.

2 Mix up the sections of resource pages 243 and 244, and hand a section to each group or pair. Challenge them to put the story in order. To do this they will need to talk to other people and find out which sections they have.

3 Once the young people are happy with their story, invite them to read out the sections one at a time. Check them against Acts 15:1–35 in a Bible to see if they have put it together correctly!

 THEMED GAME

WHAT: mini-golf
WHY: to experience working together as a team
WITH: plastic cups, golf clubs or hockey sticks, ping-pong balls, objects to create obstacles, such as beanbags, boxes, cardboard tubes, chairs, ropes

1 Divide the young people into teams and challenge each team to design a 'hole' of a mini-golf course. The holes themselves should be formed by the plastic cups (on their sides) with some obstacles to make it harder to get the ball into the hole.

2 When all the holes are completed, play a round of the course, with each team starting at a different hole. Each team member takes it in turn to putt.

3 If you wish, invite the young people to comment on their favourite holes or designs that they think were particularly good.

BIBLE EXPERIENCE

 LEVEL 1: CONNECT

WHAT: role play
WHY: to explore God's plan to spread the good news
WITH: Bibles

1 Read Acts 15:1–35 aloud to the young people, or ask a confident young person to read it.

2 In groups, give the young people ten minutes to create their own modern-day drama or role play based on the passage. If they are struggling for ideas, suggest these as possible settings to get them started:

- A new boy starts at your school. He wants to hang out with you and your mates, and although you are keen for him to join in, your mates are not so sure... How do you convince them?

- You have new neighbours, and their daughter is your age and interested in jazz dance, like you. You'd love to get to know her, but your friends would think her dress sense was so uncool. What do you do?

- Your friend's brother wants to join the football team. You know he's an excellent striker, but his attitude to training is very different, and the rest of the team might need some convincing. Should you encourage him to join the team?

3 Invite the groups to present their dramas or role plays.

4 Chat through the following questions with the young people:

- Why did you end the dramas or role plays the way you did?

- Did you manage to convince the others to let the person join your crowd? If so, how?

- Was that the right thing to do, and why?

- What does this say about God's plan to spread the good news?

- How do their dramas reflect God's plan to spread the good news, as shown in the passage? (How are the dramas the same, and how are they different?)

 LEVEL 2: INTERFACE

WHAT: discussion
WHY: to explore God's plan to spread the good news
WITH: Bibles

1 Read Acts 15:1,2 to the young people. Ask them who was potentially being excluded from the kingdom of God by what the men from Judea were teaching.

2 Think about your own church. Are there some people who would find it difficult to fit in there? What things do you think might make it difficult for someone to come to church?

3 Read Acts 15:6–11 to the young people.

Ask:

- What was the solution to this issue?

- Why did the apostles reach the decisions not to exclude the Gentiles and not to require them to be circumcised? (You might want to refer them to Peter's dream in Acts 10.)

4 Ask the young people to think about what barriers there might be to joining a church today:

- Are there any special rules which have to be observed if you join a church today?

- What are they?

- Do you think they help or hinder people?

- What do you think you could do, as a group or as individuals, to help create a community where all people are welcomed in the name of Jesus?

 LEVEL 3: SWITCH ON

WHAT: Bible study
WHY: to explore God's plan to spread the good news
WITH: Bibles

1 Ask for a volunteer to read Acts 15:1–20 to everyone.

2 Divide the young people into small groups and ask them to discuss these questions:

- How many people were involved in the decision-making process described in this passage?

- What factors are described which influenced those discussing the decision?

- How might the outcome have been different if one individual or one group had been responsible for making the decision?

3 Say that although there were key spokespeople in this debate (Saul, Barnabas, the Pharisees and Peter), no one person was responsible for making a decision. Instead, the group heard the evidence from Saul and Barnabas that God was reaching out to the Gentiles (the Jews believed that God was only interested in saving the Jews) and were challenged by it to alter the way they thought.

4 Hand out paper and pens. Encourage the young people to spend some time reflecting on how they usually approach decision making, using the following questions:

- Do I try to find out God's will before I make decisions in my life?

- Do I seek the advice of others when I am unsure of what to do?

- Am I ready to listen to friends when they have difficult decisions to make?

- Do I give good advice when asked?

- Am I willing to rely on others for guidance in my life and faith, or do I prefer to go it alone?

5 Say that learning to share our spiritual journey with others can be a great way to grow, but it requires courage and openness. Suggest that over the next few days the young people could reflect on what they can learn from the example of the early Christians in this passage.

RESPOND

39

 MUSICAL

WHAT: singing
WHY: to worship God
WITH: copies of the words and music to the hymn 'Just as I Am' by Charlotte Elliot

1 You may wish to introduce the hymn with this brief bit of history. An elderly man asked Charlotte Elliott if she were a Christian; she felt insulted, and told him to mind his own affairs. But after the man left, she could not get the question off her mind, so she went to ask the man how to find Christ. He told her to come just as she was. She did, and wrote the beautiful song, 'Just as I Am'.

2 Lead a time of worship, singing the hymn and some other songs, praising God for his saving work.

 PRACTICAL

WHAT: illustration
WHY: to think about how we can make a difference when we work together
WITH: old-fashioned kitchen scales with pan and weights, large beads with holes, luggage tags

1 This activity is designed to help us think about how lots of people taking small actions can have a big result. You could focus on different issues, but we suggest the issue of fair trade. Prepare by writing on each luggage tag an action that can be taken to help promote fair trade. (This can be done with your group or prepared beforehand.) Some examples:

- Buy a fair trade chocolate bar
- Ask your school shop to stock fair trade products
- Find out where and how clothes are made before buying them
- Use the internet to find fair trade trainers

Some can be duplicated, but try and have a variety for people to choose from. Tie each tag to a large bead.

2 Explain how small actions can make a difference to big problems. Place a weight on the scales and explain that it represents the burden of unfair trade in the world – the millions who live in poverty because they are not paid a fair wage for their work.

3 Invite each person to look through the tags and choose a pledge they would like to commit to. Ask them to untie and keep the tag as a reminder of what they have agreed to do, and to place the bead on the scales. As more beads are added, the scales will begin to tip. Point out that when many individuals choose to take action, they can make a difference and contribute to God's plan.

 CREATIVE

WHAT: creative prayer
WHY: to pray for other people, including those with different beliefs
WITH: quiet music, playback equipment

1 Have some appropriate quiet music playing in the background. Ask the young people to think carefully of a few people in their lives for whom they would like to pray specifically over the next week. They might include people who have a different faith or no faith at all.

2 Ask them to write down the names of these people on a sheet of paper, together with one or two 'facts' about each person (likes/dislikes, hobbies and interests, for example). As they write, encourage them to pray for each person, asking God for the courage to speak God's word to these people, and to help each person to hear him.

3 Finish with the following prayer: 'Lord, help us to be open to you and your leading. Help us to be faithful to you. Show us the people you want us to speak to and influence. Amen.'

4 Ask the young people to take their paper home and to continue praying for the people they have written down.

MORE ON THIS THEME:

If you want to do a short series with your group, other sessions that work well with this one are:

WINNIE THE POOH PERSONALITY TEST

Bible bit
Acts 15:1–35

We're all different, thankfully! God has created each one of us to be unique, and he did that for a reason. We each have a different skill that we can use to work together to spread the good news about Jesus! What's yours?

The characters in *Winnie the Pooh* all have very different personalities. Which animal are you most like? Read the descriptions below and try to identify yourself and your friends.

RABBIT
TYPE 1

Rabbit is the organiser amongst the animals of the Hundred Acre Wood: 'Now,' said Rabbit, 'this is a Search and I've Organised it.'

Rabbit is:
- hard working
- efficient
- responsible
- keen to improve himself and others
- honest
- good at following rules
- practical

KANGA
TYPE 2

Although Kanga is mum to Roo, she is motherly towards all the other animals too.

Kanga is:
- caring
- supportive
- compassionate
- thoughtful
- keen to look after the needs of others

ROO
TYPE 3

Roo is very energetic, and loves to show off: 'Look at me jumping!' squeaked Roo, and fell in another mouse-hole.

Roo is:
- enthusiastic
- energetic
- a performer
- adventurous
- keen to learn

EEYORE
TYPE 4

Eeyore is very aware of the dark side of life but can also be very caring.

Eeyore is:
- creative
- imaginative
- romantic
- depressive
- sensitive
- emotional

OWL
TYPE 5

Owl is a classic teacher. He loves knowledge and likes to share it with others.

Owl is:
- curious
- independent
- solitary
- interested in learning
- keen on routine

PIGLET
TYPE 6

Piglet is the best type of friend you could ask for – loyal and committed to those he loves.

Piglet is:
- loyal to his friends
- committed
- a good team member
- keen to belong
- curious
- interested in others

TIGGER
TYPE 7

Tigger is an eternal optimist – when faced with a question he doesn't know the answer to he will always imagine the best.

Tigger is:
- energetic
- enthusiastic
- optimistic
- adventurous
- a risk taker
- playful

CHRISTOPHER ROBIN
TYPE 8

Christopher Robin is the leader of all the animals and directs their activities.

Christopher Robin is:
- a leader
- strong
- decisive
- fair
- a risk taker
- protective

POOH
TYPE 9

Pooh is a peacemaker – always trying to help everyone else get along. He himself finds it easy to be friends with everyone, and does not have an inflated opinion of himself.

Pooh is:
- easy-going
- humble
- cooperative
- respectful
- accepting

Acts 15:1–35 (NCV)

Then some people came to Antioch from Judea and began teaching the non-Jewish believers: 'You cannot be saved if you are not circumcised as Moses taught us.' Paul and Barnabas were against this teaching and argued with them about it. So the church decided to send Paul, Barnabas and some others to Jerusalem where they could talk more about this with the apostles and elders.

The church helped them leave on the trip, and they went through the countries of Phoenicia and Samaria, telling all about how those who were not Jewish had turned to God. This made all the believers very happy.

When they arrived in Jerusalem, they were welcomed by the apostles, the elders, and the church. Paul, Barnabas and the others told about everything God had done with them. But some of the believers who belonged to the Pharisee group came forwards and said, 'The non-Jewish believers must be circumcised. They must be told to obey the law of Moses.'

The apostles and the elders gathered to consider this problem. After a long debate, Peter stood up and said to them, 'Brothers, you know that in the early days God chose me from among you to preach the Good News to those who are not Jewish. They heard the Good News from me, and they believed. God, who knows the thoughts of everyone, accepted them. He showed this to us by giving them the Holy Spirit, just as he did to us.

To God, those people are not different from us. When they believed, he made their hearts pure. So now why are you testing God by putting a heavy load around the necks of the non-Jewish believers? It is a load that neither we nor our ancestors were able to carry. But we believe that we and they too will be saved by the grace of the Lord Jesus.'

Then the whole group became quiet. They listened to Paul and Barnabas tell about all the miracles and signs that God did through them among the non-Jewish people.

After they finished speaking, James said, 'Brothers, listen to me. Simon has told us how God showed his love for the non-Jewish people. For the first time he is accepting from among them a people to be his own. The words of the prophets agree with this too:

"After these things I will return. The kingdom of David is like a fallen tent. But I will rebuild its ruins, and I will set it up. Then those people who are left alive may ask the Lord for help, and the other nations that belong to me, says the Lord, who will make it happen. And these things have been known for a long time." (Amos 9:11–12)

'So I think we should not bother the non-Jewish people who are turning to God. Instead, we should write a letter to them telling them these things: stay away from food that has been offered to idols (which makes it unclean), any kind of sexual sin, eating animals that have been strangled, and blood. They should do these things, because for a long time in every city the law of Moses has been taught. And it is still read in the synagogue every Sabbath day.'

The apostles, the elders and the whole church decided to send some of their men with Paul and Barnabas to Antioch. They chose Judas Barsabbas and Silas, who were respected by the believers. They sent the following letter with them: 'From the apostles and elders, your brothers. To all the non-Jewish believers in Antioch, Syria, and Cilicia: Greetings! We have heard that some of our group have come to you and said things that trouble and upset you. But we did not tell them to do this. We have all agreed to choose some messengers and send them to you with our dear friends Barnabas and Paul — people who have given their lives to serve our Lord Jesus Christ. So we are sending Judas and Silas, who will tell you the same things. It has pleased the Holy Spirit that you should not have a heavy load to carry, and we agree. You need to do only these things: stay away from any food that has been offered to idols, any animals that have been strangled, blood and any kind of sexual sin. If you stay away from these things, you will do well. Goodbye.'

So they left Jerusalem and went to Antioch where they gathered the church and gave them the letter. When they read it, they were very happy because of the encouraging message. Judas and Silas, who were also prophets, said many things to encourage the believers and make them stronger. After some time Judas and Silas were sent off in peace by the believers, and they went back to those who had sent them.

But Paul and Barnabas stayed in Antioch and, along with many others, preached the Good News and taught the people the message of the Lord.

WHO IS WITH ME?

Bible bit
Revelation 1

After the resurrection, Jesus ascended into heaven, where he is now. But Jesus is also with us, isn't he? How does that work? Jesus wasn't just some historical man who stopped being relevant thousands of years ago. He is still alive, in his full glory in heaven, and he is still at work. We have his Word which continues to teach and inspire us, and we have the Holy Spirit to help us live a life that gives glory to God.

41

AT CHURCH...
AT HOME...
WHEN I PRAY...
IN FUN TIMES...
WHEN THINGS
GO WRONG...
AT WORK...
IN MY DOUBTS...
AT SCHOOL...
WHEN I AM
FEELING LOST...
IN WORRYING TIMES...
WHEN I AM OUT
WITH MY FRIENDS...
WHEN I READ
THE BIBLE...

TELL ME ABOUT YOU VIS

THE CHARACTERS:

Bernard Brainsworthy is a psychiatrist for the rich and famous of ancient Greece; he loves tapping his note-taking pencil on his clipboard.

John is an elderly disciple, a follower of Jesus, and is widely believed to have written one of the Gospels.

THE SCENE:

Bernard has been visiting John on the island prison of Patmos for a number of years. Today John is telling Bernard of the vision he recently had. The very philosophical Bernard is finding it all a bit hard to understand…

Bernard: So John, please go over that again.

John: Well, it's like I said. There I was having a good pray…

Bernard: Pray? Oh yes – that's where you believe you're talking to your God. Do carry on.

John: I was having a good pray when suddenly I heard a loud voice behind me.

Bernard: Now, that was the voice that was a trumpet?

John: No, not a trumpet, but it sounded like a trumpet. It was so loud and powerful – like an announcement, a herald, like that bit in *Shrek 2* where Shrek and Fiona are invited to Far Far Away.

Bernard: *Shrek 2*?

John: Never mind, that would take too long to explain. Anyway, this voice told me to write down everything I saw and send it to seven churches.

Bernard: Any particular seven churches?

John: Well, yes and no.

Bernard: Now, now, don't be evasive!

John: I'm not! You see, there are seven churches that are mentioned in particular, but…

Bernard: Go on… *(Hastily making notes on his clipboard.)*

BERNARD BRAINSWORTHY

John: But... well, it has something to do with the number seven...

Bernard: What? It's your lucky number, the final number in your weekly Grecian Lotto draw?

John: No, the number seven signifies something. It's not just a number – it also means being complete.

Bernard: Rriiigghhhttt... *(Looking and sounding very sceptical.)*

John: So although it was supposed to be sent to seven specific churches, it could also mean that it is to be sent to all the churches.

Bernard: *(Becoming confused.)* So this vision was to be written and sent to either seven churches or all the churches?

John: Well, no. Initially the seven churches that I was told about...

Bernard: And who was it talking to you again? A giant walking trumpet?

(He chuckles at his own joke.) *(John doesn't find it funny and looks at Bernard as though he is a little pathetic.)*

John: No, not a trumpet – seven lampstands!

(Bernard almost falls off his couch and John has a good chuckle at confusing him.)

Bernard: Sorry?

John: Well, when I turned around, the first thing I saw was seven lampstands, and they were golden – a bit like your tan, although that's a bit more bronzy.

Bernard: Ah, the number seven again! Does that mean they represented all the lamps in the world? Does that mean you saw a very bright light?

John: No, I saw seven golden lampstands, and they are ... well, I'll tell you about that in a minute.

Bernard: OK. Why don't we take a five-minute break and then we'll get back to what you saw among the lampstands?

JOHN

Jesus said …

'Do not be afraid. I am the First and the Last. I am the One who lives; I was dead, but look, I am alive for ever and ever!'

Revelation 1:17,18

Jesus said …

'Do not be afraid. I am the First and the Last. I am the One who lives; I was dead, but look, I am alive for ever and ever!'

Revelation 1:17,18

Jesus said …

'Do not be afraid. I am the First and the Last. I am the One who lives; I was dead, but look, I am alive for ever and ever!'

Revelation 1:17,18

Jesus said …

'Do not be afraid. I am the First and the Last. I am the One who lives; I was dead, but look, I am alive for ever and ever!'

Revelation 1:17,18

Jesus said …

'Do not be afraid. I am the First and the Last. I am the One who lives; I was dead, but look, I am alive for ever and ever!'

Revelation 1:17,18

Jesus said …

'Do not be afraid. I am the First and the Last. I am the One who lives; I was dead, but look, I am alive for ever and ever!'

Revelation 1:17,18

Bible: Exodus 15

MAJESTIC AND HOLY

THE AIM: To remember all the amazing things God has done

The aim unpacked

The people of Israel are singing a song of worship to God after their triumphant escape from Egypt. The song talks about the character of God, his strength and his awesome power, and celebrates their victory. Then it is back to reality with a bump. All the amazing things God has done for the people are forgotten as they travel around the desert searching for water. Are we as quick to forget God's awesomeness?

WAY IN

theGRID MAGAZINE

WHAT: celebrations
WHY: to think about the amazing things that we celebrate

1 Challenge the young people to make a list of all the different things we celebrate.

2 After a few minutes ask if there is anything that they want to share with the whole group, perhaps something that they think others may not have considered.

3 Then ask the young people to offer some suggestions for how we celebrate. What do we do? In what ways do we share our joy and excitement with others?

4 Explain that this chapter of Exodus has celebration at the heart of it and remembering all the amazing things God has done is definitely a cause to celebrate.

SCENE SETTER

WHAT: song
WHY: to think about how God is awesome
WITH: a copy of the song 'Everything Is Awesome' from *The Lego Movie*

1 Say that 'awesome' is a word that is common and overused today. Play the song.

2 Ask the young people to suggest things that we describe as awesome today.

3 Ask the question: 'Do you really believe that everything is awesome?'

4 Explain that the definition of 'awesome' is impressive, excellent, or extremely good.

5 Ask the young people to suggest ways in which God is awesome and note them down.

6 Close by turning these comments into prayers of thankfulness and gratitude.

THEMED GAME

WHAT: game
WHY: to help us to remember

1 Ask everyone to sit in a circle.

2 When everyone is ready, ask someone to start by saying 'I went to the shop and I bought a...'

3 The next person to take their turn has to say what the previous person said and add their own item. This continues around the circle. Whoever forgets the exact sequence is out of the game, until you have a winner.

4 If you want to make this game even more difficult, apply stipulations. For example, all items mentioned must be blue. Or edible. Or beginning with the letter 'r'. Or blue, edible and beginning with the letter 'r'!

5 Although this is a bit of a silly game, remind the young people that remembering the things that God has done for us is not only a key element of our praise of him, but also helps us to remain positive and encouraged.

BIBLE EXPERIENCE

LEVEL 1: CONNECT

WHAT: party
WHY: to think about all the reasons we have to celebrate because of the incredible things God has done
WITH: flip chart, pen

1 Explain to the young people that we are going to be thinking about all the amazing things that God has done and that is a cause of great celebration.

2 Ask the young people to come up with a list of all the things they can that people celebrate. Write them on the flip chart.

3 Read together Exodus 15:1–11 and ask them the following questions:

- How does the idea of God as a warrior fit with your understanding of God?

- This song of gratitude acts as a strong reminder of what God has done. How can we remember the work of God in our lives?

- This section ends with the question: 'Is there anyone who is like God?' What do you think?

4 Now read together Exodus 15:12–18 and ask the following questions:

- Do you believe that God offers unfailing love (v 13)? Why?

- This section of the text continues to express gratitude to God and says that the Lord reigns for ever and ever. What do you think that means?

- How do you think you might relate this to your own experience of God? Is there anything God has done in your life, or the life of people you know, that has led you to praise him in such a way?

5 Return to your list of things that people celebrate. Ask the young people to think about how you might celebrate these things, for example you might celebrate a birthday with presents or by going out for a meal.

6 Explain that in celebration of all that God has done for the people of Israel they write songs, share truth and experience, encouragement and joy, and worship God through this. Ask: How would you celebrate the miraculous work of God in your life?

LEVEL 2: INTERFACE

WHAT: Bible study
WHY: to remember all the amazing things God has done
WITH: Bibles, flip chart, marker pens

1 Read Exodus 15 together as a group, perhaps with different members of the group reading it.

2 The first part of the chapter is about remembering all the amazing things God has done for the people of Israel, culminating in his parting of the sea in order that Moses and the people could cross in safety. There is plenty for the people to celebrate. Invite the young people to share on the flip chart paper the amazing things that God has done and that they wish to praise and thank him for.

3 When all the young people have had sufficient time to contribute, remove the paper and remind them that very quickly after they had worshipped God, the people of Israel were complaining to God about their situation. They had forgotten all that God had done. It is as if they had torn up the paper (tear up the flip chart paper). Ask the following questions:

- Do you find it surprising that the people of Israel forget the work of God so quickly?

- Do you forget the work of God in your life? What can you do to try and avoid this?

4 Take another piece of flip chart paper and invite the young people to write again those amazing things that God has done.

5 Finish with a time of prayer where you encourage the young people to speak out those things that they have written in praise to God.

LEVEL 3: SWITCH ON

WHAT: discussion
WHY: to think more carefully about all the amazing things God has done and how majestic and holy he is
WITH: Bibles, resource page 262

1 Split the young people into four equally sized groups.

2 Give each group a copy of resource page 262 and one of the following sections of the reading: 1–11; 12–18; 19–21; 22–27. Ask each group to work through the questions together.

3 Bring the groups back together and spend some time hearing from one another.

4 Explain that this chapter serves as a reminder to Christians that it is all too easy to forget the saving works of God in our lives as we move on to the next problem. It is significant that God reasserts his position and authority at the end of the chapter, although it may come as a surprise that he needs to.

RESPOND

 MUSICAL

WHAT: worship
WHY: to sing some songs in praise of God and all the things he has done for us
WITH: worship songs, musical accompaniment or playback equipment

1 Ask the young people these questions:

- How would you describe your relationship with God at the moment?

- Can you call to mind one thing that God has done for you?

2 Explain that there is always a reason to praise God, even if we have to think for a little while to remember one!

3 Close by singing one or more of these songs as a praise of God and all he is doing in your lives:

- 'How Great Is Our God' by Chris Tomlin

- 'Here I am to Worship' by Tim Hughes '10,000 Reasons' by Matt Redman

- 'Shackles' by Mary Mary

- 'Guide Me, O Thou Great Redeemer'

 PRACTICAL

WHAT: letters
WHY: to act as a reminder of all the amazing things God has done
WITH: paper, pens, envelopes, stamps

1 Give out pens, paper and envelopes.

2 Ask the young people to each find a space on their own and to write a letter to themselves including several things that they have either heard God has done from the Bible, or in the stories of others, or from their own experience.

3 When they have written their letters, ask them to place them in the envelopes and address them to themselves. Post the letters to the young people in a week or so.

 CREATIVE

WHAT: responding to God
WHY: to see that the way we respond to God and his work in our lives is personal to us
WITH: a choice of materials, eg paper, pens, paint, clay

1 Give the young people the chance to respond creatively to the amazing work of God in their life. For example, they could respond by:

- choreographing a dance

- making up a mime or sketch

- creating a painting

- writing a poem

- making something from clay

2 Bring the young people back together and encourage them to share what they have done with the rest of the group if they are prepared to do so.

3 Conclude by saying a prayer thanking God that not only is he worthy of our praise, but that he created us with a diverse range of gifts and talents that we are able to use in our praise of him.

MORE ON THIS THEME:

If you want to do a short series with your group, other sessions that work well with this one are:

What do we learn about the people of Israel from these verses?

What do we learn about God from these verses?

Are there any images that particularly stand out to you?

Is there anything we can learn from these verses that would be helpful for us today?

Is there anything in this section of the passage that you do not understand?

If you could summarise this section in just three words, what would you use?

43

ONLY THE LONELY

THE AIM: To remember that we are part of a large Christian community, wherever we are

The aim unpacked

Paul gives valuable advice to the community of Christians in Philippi. As we read his words almost 2,000 years later, we can relate to the loneliness that he feels because of his imprisonment. Despite our busy modern world, where communication is easier and quicker than ever before, many of us still feel alone. Paul points out that even though he is alone, he is still part of the Christian community.

WAY IN

 **theGRID MAGAZINE**

WHAT: discussion starter
WHY: to think about the different aspects of loneliness
WITH: magazine page 266

1 Give out copies of page 266 and pens. Ask the young people to read the article introducing the theme of loneliness, and to complete the activity on their own.

2 Bring the group together and invite them to take it in turns to share their favourite and least favourite words. Discuss any areas of disagreement.

3 Find out how many young people prefer solitude compared to how many prefer to have people around them. Reassure them that both preferences are OK!

 **SCENE SETTER**

WHAT: loneliness activity
WHY: to think about loneliness
WITH: displayed pictures cut out of newspapers

1 Before the session, find some pictures of faces (from newspapers or magazines) and glue them to white backing sheets. Write, 'I think this person is lonely because ...' below each picture. Display these around the room.

2 Allow the young people to wander round the room and to jot down why they think the people in the pictures might be lonely.

3 Share the reasons in a large group.

4 Say that it is not easy to work out why someone is lonely just by looking at them. Some people with many acquaintances might be lonely; not everyone who is alone is lonely.

 **THEMED GAME**

WHAT: numbers game
WHY: to think about how it feels to be left out

1 Ask the young people to spread out around the room. Call out numbers and encourage them to form groups made up of that number of people. Anyone who can't find a group is eliminated from the game.

2 Afterwards, invite the young people to discuss these questions in twos or threes:

How did you feel when you couldn't join a group in the game?

• How happy are you on your own?

• Do you prefer being alone or with others?

• Can you be lonely in a crowd? Why is this?

3 If you don't have a big enough group to make this game work, encourage your young people to consider what they would do if they were stranded, all alone, on a desert island. Ask them to tell the group what three items they would want to have with them and talk about how they would spend their time. Then discuss the questions above.

BIBLE EXPERIENCE

LEVEL 1: CONNECT

WHAT: discussion
WHY: to remember that we are part of a large Christian community, wherever we are
WITH: flip chart or whiteboard, marker pens

1 Invite the young people to call out all the community groups that they belong to. Include family, neighbourhoods, sports clubs, societies, school and church groups. You could display the results as a giant Venn diagram (the one with the overlapping circles).

2 Read Philippians 1:1–4 to the group. Say that Paul, who was the first person to persuade the church to tell non-Jews about Jesus, was in jail (without much company apart from the guards), and he wrote to everyone in the church that was based in the old city of Philippi.

3 In pairs, invite the young people to share stories of times when they have been troubled or upset and someone came along to encourage them. What happened? How did things work out? Ask if anyone would like to share their story with the whole group. Consider encouraging them to write some of their stories down for your group or to place in the church newsletter.

4 Now read the rest of Philippians 1 to the young people. Afterwards, ask them why they think Paul sounded so happy.

5 Just as Paul and the church in Philippi were in contact with each other, today's Christian groups can stay in touch. Discover some of the ways we can do this in *Respond* 'Practical'.

6 Remind the young people that even though they are all part of different communities (refer to your diagram from earlier), they are all part of one community in Christ.

LEVEL 2: INTERFACE

WHAT: making lists
WHY: to remember that we are part of a large Christian community, wherever we are
WITH: magazine page 267, lyrics to 'My Favourite Things' from *The Sound of Music*

1 Before the session get a copy of the lyrics of 'My Favourite Things' from *The Sound of Music*, or look together at page 267.

2 Show the song lyrics to the group and ask, 'How many of these things would make you happy if you were sad?'

3 Hand out copies of page 267 and invite the group to fill in their top ten favourite things, on their own. They could even put their lists to the tune of 'My Favourite Things'. If you want to, spend five minutes creating a group list and put it to music.

4 In smaller groups, invite the young people to read Philippians 1 and list Paul's reasons for having confidence in God and in the Philippians. Share their results. Did they find:

- partnership with them and their help (v 5)
- God's workmanship (v 6)
- God's grace (v 7)
- God's purposes (v 12)
- the gospel (vs 17,18)
- being prayed for (v 19)
- the Holy Spirit (v 19)
- their single-mindedness (v 27)
- being saved (v 28)

5 Remind the group that this confidence can also be ours, because we serve and worship the same God as Paul and the Philippian Christians worshipped. Would the young people find these things encouraging to remember if they were feeling down? If you have time, to aid memory, why not try putting this list to the 'My Favourite Things' tune and learning it together?

LEVEL 3: SWITCH ON

WHAT: Bible study
WHY: to remember that we are part of a large Christian community, wherever we are
WITH: CD or MP3 of 'So Lonely' by The Police and copies of lyrics, playback equipment, concordances, Bible dictionaries and atlases

1 Play 'So lonely' by The Police (from the album *Outlandos D'Amour*) to the group and display the lyrics.

2 Discuss, briefly, why the lyricist seems to be lonely. (A relationship breakdown.)

3 Invite the young people to read Philippians 1 in pairs, and then to look through the passage for all the encouragement they can find in it.

4 Make the point that Paul was alone but he was listing for his readers the reasons to be encouraged. To help them understand the background to this passage, encourage the young people to look through the dictionaries and concordances to find out as much as possible about Philippi and the believers there. Find out about Lydia and her conversion and the trouble that Paul had had there. (Point them to Acts 16.)

5 Invite them to read through Philippians 1 again, individually. Explain that although Paul was alone in jail he was not alone in spirit; other Christians were with him in prayer and praise.

RESPOND

 MUSICAL

WHAT: singing
WHY: to emphasise harmony and cooperation
WITH: pianist, keyboard player or singers, sheet music

1 Before the session, find out whether any of the young people can play the piano or keyboard and read music. If the response is negative, invite someone who can to join the group for the session. Give them the music beforehand and explain what you want them to do.

2 In the session, ask the musician to play just the melody line of the song. Then ask them to play each of the other lines (such as the chords or the bassline) by themselves. Finally, invite them to play all the lines together. Alternatively, you could do this with some singers singing various parts of a vocal line (such as soprano, tenor, alto).

3 Ask them a few brief questions about how harmony works.

4 Choose some well-known songs to sing with just your voices. Start with someone singing solo – it would make the point well if someone with a poor voice would dare to do it. Add the other voices, in harmony, so the original voice is either drowned or complemented.

5 Explain that the Christian community should work in harmony. We are all distinct but part of a larger group. Pray in a large group, thanking God that we are all part of one big community.

 PRACTICAL

WHAT: being part of the community
WHY: to be part of a Christian community between meetings

1 Explain to the group that although Paul was alone in prison, he still knew that he was part of the wider Christian community. One way he did this was by writing letters to the believers he had visited.

2 Ask the group to think of ways in which they can stay in contact with each other between meetings, to avoid feeling lonely or isolated.

3 Share ideas and see if there are any that you could put into practice. Some things the young people might come up with are:

- To keep in touch using mobile phones – or landlines if some young people do not have mobile phones. Emphasise that the idea is to create community, not exclude people.

- To create a list of group members in a prayer chain. If someone has a prayer request, they communicate it to the first person on the list – usually the leader – who then calls the next person and so on.

4 Alternatively, you could make a list of practical things the group can do to welcome and help lonely people. Perhaps you could produce a group slogan or motto which describes your attitude towards newcomers – for example, 'You're only a stranger here once.'

5 Remember to obtain parental permission in advance if you or any other leaders are likely to be contacting the young people individually by phone, email or text message.

 CREATIVE

WHAT: prayer
WHY: to combat loneliness by praying against it
WITH: quiet music

1 Start by asking the young people, 'What is the first thing in the Bible that God said was "not good"?' Ask them to look up Genesis 2:18 where God says, 'It is not good for the man to be alone.' Explain that when they hear this verse in the next few moments they should move closer together, repeating the verse as they do so.

2 Think about and write down as many things that you can think of together which might make someone lonely – for example, being housebound or elderly, or bereavement, or having difficulty making friends.

3 Play some quiet music and invite the young people to spend time praying quietly and individually for people who are lonely, especially any that they know personally. After a few moments say the verse and gather together.

4 Pray out loud together, thanking God that he is with those Christians who are lonely.

MORE ON THIS THEME:

If you want to do a short series with your group, other sessions that work well with this one are:

ISOLATION
CASTAWAY
LOST
ABSENT
TRAPPED
CALM
MISSING
QUIET
TRANQUIL
JAIL
HOME
SOLITUDE
PEACE
SECLUSION
ADRIFT
BEDROOM
LONELINESS
SERENE
PRIVACY
RETREAT

Draw a cloud around your favourite word. Scribble out three words you really don't like. Read Philippians 1 and draw stars next to the ones you think Paul felt like, or add some of your own words on the same theme.

**Bible bit
Philippians 1**

Do you love being with people, talking and hanging out? What happens when they leave? Are you devastated that there's no one to talk to or thankful that you're on your own?
Paul was in prison, alone. But he was still part of the Christian community and wrote letters to encourage them.

SIGN LANGUAGE

Loneliness. The old poet Wordsworth (well, he lived a long time ago) 'wandered lonely as a cloud'. Obviously he hadn't been in our part of England much. We have loads of them! I wonder if he'd ever wandered lonely in a crowd; like doing his Christmas shopping in a huge crush of people, none of whom he recognised...

Loneliness is really complicated. Some people genuinely prefer their own company to being with others. They don't dislike people but after spending a while in company they need to be alone – to go back into their cave/study/bedroom, or whatever.

Others are wired differently. They get enthused and motivated by others and they go crazy if they spend too much time on their own.

THESE ARE A FEW OF MY FAVOURITE THINGS

An old song but a classic! It's a list of the singer's favourite things that they remember to make them happy when they are sad.

'MY FAVOURITE THINGS'

From *The Sound of Music*

Raindrops on roses and whiskers on kittens,
Bright copper kettles and warm woollen mittens,
Brown paper packages tied up with strings,
These are a few of my favourite things…

When the dog bites, when the bee stings,
When I'm feeling sad,
I simply remember my favourite things
And then I don't feel so bad.

Why not create your own list of favourite things? Perhaps you could even put it to the tune!

Read Philippians 1 to find out some of the things that encouraged Paul when he was in prison. Write down what you find and the verse numbers for each thing. Can you fit these to the tune?!

YOUR TOP TEN

1
2
3
4
5
6
7
8
9
10

PAUL'S TOP TEN

VERSE NO.

1
2
3
4
5
6
7
8
9
10

44
HUMILITY

THE AIM: To serve others, using Jesus' example of humility as our guide

The aim unpacked

In this session about belonging to the Christian community, we explore what it means to be humble – perhaps one of the hardest aspects of Christian living. Being humble is about serving others, putting others first and ourselves second. This is at the heart of the Christian message. Paul illustrates humility with the example of Jesus Christ, who is our model for loving and serving.

WAY IN

 theGRID MAGAZINE

WHAT: quiz
WHY: to think about our own humility (or lack of it)
WITH: magazine page 271, dictionaries

1 Hand out copies of the quiz from page 271.

2 Emphasise that it is not very scientific, but it simply introduces the idea of humility. Talk about the results. Who chose the most Ds? Does everyone agree with the scoring system and comments?

3 Suggest that the young people get into pairs and think about what the word 'humble' means. Challenge them to create a dictionary-type definition. Discuss their definitions and look up the correct definition in a dictionary.

 SCENE SETTER

WHAT: life skills cards
WHY: to think about the meaning and value of humility
WITH: copies of the cards from resource page 273 (a set for each young person)

1 Before the session, cut out the cards and divide them into sets. Each card displays a life skill and a value in points. Place the cards in piles on a table so that everyone can walk around the table and see them all.

2 Tell the group that they can have above average ability in a number of life skills. They have 100 points to 'spend' on the cards on the table.

3 Invite them to look at the cards and talk about the different attributes. Be ready to explain what some of the characteristics mean.

4 When everyone has made their choices, talk about their decisions. What sacrifices were necessary to obtain the more valuable cards? Does everyone agree with the values placed on the attributes? Did anyone take humility? Why? Why was humility so expensive? In this game, humility is the most expensive card. In life, humility can also cost a great amount because it often means putting others first, which can be very hard to do.

 THEMED GAME

WHAT: relay race
WHY: to experience putting pride aside
WITH: two sets of dressing-up clothes, two digital cameras (or mobile phones with cameras), a laptop or PC and projector (both optional)

1 Divide the young people into teams of about four. Place the dressing-up clothes in two piles at one end of the meeting room. If you have more than two teams, choose two to go first.

2 Team members must take it in turns to run to the end of the room, put on all the clothes and run back to the team to pose for a photograph. Then they should run back and take off the clothes ready for the next person. The first team to have photos of every team member in the clothes is the winner.

3 If you have a computer and projector available, you could display the photos later in the session. Alternatively, you could do it at the next session and hold a caption competition! Please ensure that this activity is carried out in compliance with your group's safeguarding policy concerning photographs.

4 Make the point that sometimes we care far too much about what other people think we look like. Being humble often involves doing things that cause other people to think, 'Why are they doing that?!'

BIBLE EXPERIENCE

44

 ## LEVEL 1: CONNECT

WHAT: film clip
WHY: to serve others using Jesus' example of humility as our guide
WITH: a copy of the film *Groundhog Day* (rated PG), playback equipment

1 MIntroduce the film clip by explaining that Bill Murray plays a character called Phil Connors, a weather forecaster who is forced to live the same day over and over again. He develops tremendous knowledge of and insight into the people he meets. In this clip he tries to convince his producer Rita (Andie MacDowell) of his predicament.

2 Play this clip of Phil and Rita seated at a restaurant table and the waitress coming to take their order. (Start at 1:03:25; end at 1:06:50 as they leave the restaurant.)

3 Then ask these questions:

- How does Phil try to convince Rita that he is a god?
- If you were a god, how would you convince someone?

4 Read, or ask a young person to read, Philippians 2:6–11 to the group. Ask:

- Do you believe that Jesus is God?
- What would convince you?
- What convinced Paul to write this to the Philippians?

5 Explain that eventually Connors uses his powers for the good of the community. Only then does he manage to escape – when he learns something about himself. What does that tell us about humility? You could show a second clip to illustrate this (the hospital scene followed by the scene outside in the cold). Start the film at 1:16:55 ('Are you the one who brought the old man in?') and end it at 1:18:35 (when Connors realises that the man has died in the cold).

6 Ask:

- What were Connors' limitations?
- What limitations did Jesus face in the Bible passage?
- What would it mean for us to be humble?

 ## LEVEL 2: INTERFACE

WHAT: drama and Bible study
WHY: to serve others using Jesus' example of humility as our guide
WITH: magazine page 272, flip chart

1 Ask for a volunteer who is good at mime. Ask another two people to read the list of dos and don'ts from 'A day of do and don't' on page 272, taking alternate lines. The first person should try to act out each of the different things as they read!

2 Ask everyone to read Philippians 2 and to make a list of the different dos and don'ts that are mentioned in the passage on two separate sheets of flip chart paper. Ask:

- What would a person who followed all the dos and don'ts in the passage, and got them right, be like?
- Which is the hardest 'do' action? And the hardest 'don't' action? Give reasons for each.

3 Invite the young people to work in small groups to produce a short drama sketch based on the list.

4 Gather the group together and watch the sketches. Then spend some time discussing:

- What would it take, this week, for you to demonstrate humility?
- What would you have to do, or not do?

5 Read verses 5–11 again slowly, perhaps using verse 5 as a memory verse.

 ## LEVEL 3: SWITCH ON

WHAT: Bible study
WHY: to serve others using Jesus' example of humility as our guide
WITH: very large sheet of paper (or roll of wallpaper), marker pens, masking tape

1 Ask the young people to read the whole chapter of Philippians 2, perhaps giving sections to different readers. Appropriate breaks would be: verses 1–5; verses 6–11; verses 12–18; verses 19–24; verses 25–30.

2 Divide into three groups (or multiples of three if necessary) and ask each group to look at the example of Jesus, Timothy or Epaphroditus from the Bible passage. What can we learn from their examples? What could we put into practice ourselves and what is unique to those individuals? Obtain feedback from the groups about their answers.

3 Ask for a volunteer to lie down on a sheet of paper and draw around them. Display the outline and write 'Portrait of a humble person' above it.

4 Ask the group to suggest attributes of a humble person and write them on the appropriate body parts. If they are stuck, suggest things like, feet that go the extra mile; willing hands to help; a mind that thinks of others.

5 Ask for a second volunteer. Make their outline on the floor with masking tape (think murder-mystery style). Finish the activity by asking: 'If you died tomorrow would you be remembered as a humble person?' Keep silent for a moment to allow the question to have an impact. (Remember to be sensitive to your group, though.)

RESPOND

 MUSICAL

WHAT: song
WHY: words and music for 'From Heaven You Came' by Graham Kendrick, playback equipment or musician(s)
WITH: to think about the humility of Jesus

1 Play or sing together Graham Kendrick's hymn 'From Heaven You Came', pausing after each verse.

2 Display the words and then pray, giving thanks for every example of humility, line by line after each verse and chorus.

3 If they meant what they sang, invite individuals to share how they might change their behaviour this week. How might they put such service and humility into practice?

 PRACTICAL

WHAT: rotas
WHY: to serve others
WITH: blank paper for rotas, a list of tasks to be done in your church

1 Before the session, talk to the people who prepare rotas for activities such as welcoming people into the church, providing refreshments, collecting hymn books and washing up.

2 Suggest to the young people that, in the light of this session's teaching, you would like to give them some opportunities to serve people.

3 Display the rotas and give the young people the opportunity to sign up. Encourage the leaders to get involved too.

4 Read out, without any pressure, the list of opportunities there are within the wider church and explain to the young people what to do and who to contact if they would like to help.

5 Set up some kind of system for reminding people at each session what they have agreed to do. Finish with prayer, asking God for opportunities to serve his church and the local community.

 CREATIVE

WHAT: prayer
WHY: to ask God to help with humility
WITH: washing line, pegs, soluble ink pens, bowl of water

1 Fix up the washing line across the meeting area. Read, or ask a young person to read, Luke 18:9–14, the story Jesus told of the Pharisee and the tax collector.

2 Explain that one aspect of humility is confession – a willingness to turn your back on past arrogance and selfishness. The Pharisee may well have been right about the good things he did, but his problem was that he thought he was better than others.

3 Give out pens, paper and pegs (make sure the pens contain water-soluble ink). Invite everyone to be silent and to think about areas of their lives where they may not have been as humble as they could have been. Ask everyone to write down a few words to describe or represent their sin.

4 Peg the pieces of paper to the washing line and remain silent.

5 Take the pieces of paper down off the washing line and plunge them into the bowl of water to represent washing the sins clean away – get it?

6 Give everyone back a sheet of blank paper as a visual aid.

MORE ON THIS THEME:

If you want to do a short series with your group, other sessions that work well with this one are:

SO... HOW HUMBLE ARE YOU?

1

You dream that you've just scored a simple tap-in from 10 cm out after a great team move.
Do you...
a) throw your shirt over your head and run to the crowd, arms aloft?
b) cartwheel off towards the corner flag?
c) grab the ball and run back to the halfway line; only three more to equalise?
d) point to your teammate who gave you the killer pass?

2

You've just beaten your best friend in a long drawn-out shoot-'em-up computer game.
Do you...
a) taunt them?
b) buy them a T-shirt with the word 'loser' on it?
c) suggest you play the best of seven to give them a chance to win?
d) chat through the game over a pizza?

3

You're at home and you notice that there's some washing up that needs to be done.
Do you...
a) get your brother or sister to do it, but take the credit when your parents come home?
b) do it but make sure everyone sees you doing it?
c) quietly wash up, not wanting any praise for helping?
d) wash up and then start cleaning the toilet?

4

The teacher asks for a volunteer to go across to another building to get something she's forgotten. It's freezing outside.
Do you...
a) outstare the teacher?
b) look at your socks?
c) volunteer at once, without flinching?
d) prod your neighbour so that they put their hand up?

5

Your youth group needs someone to play the lead role in the Christmas presentation.
Do you...
a) go and ask the leader if you can do it?
b) talk to your friends and try to persuade them to nominate you?
c) wait for a chance to show them what you can do?
d) promote somebody else?

Bible bit
Philippians 2

The world says that if you want to succeed you have to put yourself first, even trample on others if necessary. God wants us to live differently. Being humble is about serving others, putting others first and ourselves second; it is at the heart of what it means to be a Christian. Paul illustrates humility with the example of Jesus Christ, who is our model for loving and serving.

Mainly A

World domination is only a battle away.

Mainly B

You really want other people to notice you.

Mainly C

You are probably a bit better at most things than you think you are. Things may not always work out but you'll be surprised at what God can do.

Mainly D

You are a good friend to have – good at things but not afraid to let someone else have the limelight. That's humility.

DEFINITION: HUMBLE

The Concise Oxford Dictionary says that humble means 'to have or show a low estimate of one's own importance'.

This definition is helpful but it doesn't say completely what we mean by being humble. We are not unimportant – God thinks we are extremely important. We are important in our Christian community too. We should show a low estimate of our own importance and have a high regard for the importance of others. This means putting others first. The best example of this is in Philippians 2:5–11. Jesus was important but he showed humility. He put others first, including you and me.

How would you define humble?

Who is the most humble person you know?

HELPING OTHERS

Write down the names of five people you could help this week and how you intend to help them.

1
2
3
4
5

How can you ensure that you are humble as you do these things?

A DAY OF DO AND DON'T

DO get up – it's late.

DON'T rush your food; chew it.

DON'T leave your stereo on all night.

DON'T run in the corridor.

DO wipe your shoes before you come in.

DO eat fruit and vegetables – they're good for you.

DON'T push – there are others in the queue, you know.

DO turn the TV off during supper.

DO hurry up – you'll miss the bus.

DO go to bed – it's late.

DO leave your homework on my desk, please.

DON'T eat too many biscuits – they'll spoil your tea.

DON'T give me excuses – you had plenty of time to do it.

READ PHILIPPIANS 2 AND MAKE A LIST OF THE DIFFERENT DOS AND DON'TS THAT ARE MENTIONED IN THE PASSAGE.

DO

DON'T

Draw a circle around the hardest 'do' action.
Draw an arrow to the hardest 'don't' action.
What would a person who followed all the dos and don'ts in the passage, and got them right, be like?

Humble 100 points	Good with numbers 5 points	Quick-witted 5 points
Strong fashion sense 5 points	Good at cooking 20 points	Good memory 15 points
Sporty 10 points	Healthy 50 points	Good-looking 25 points
Good musician 10 points	Wealthy 35 points	Good at listening 50 points
Good at craft 10 points	Physically strong 10 points	Loyal 30 points
Good at writing 10 points	Good at problem solving 25 points	Prayerful 20 points
Good at organising 15 points	A quick learner 20 points	Helpful 25 points

45
DREAMS

THE AIM: To question how God uses dreams as a method of communication

The aim unpacked

In this session, we find out how God communicates through dreams. The Bible details many instances where dreams are used to communicate a message and they often reveal the future or a truth, as in today's main passage. However, Christians today believe that all truth was revealed in Jesus, therefore there would be no new revelations that add to the message of the Bible.

WAY IN

 **theGRID MAGAZINE**

WHAT: communicating (differently!)
WHY: to think about different ways to communicate
WITH: magazine pages 277 and 278, flags (or sheets of paper attached to sticks)

1 Give out copies of pages 277 and 278 and ask the young people to look at the different ways of communicating. Ask which ones the young people would choose to use.

2 Encourage the young people to have a go at semaphore. Divide them into pairs and ask them to communicate a message from one to the other using semaphore.

3 You could either give everyone a message to communicate or let them think of something themselves. You could give out prizes for the pair who can communicate the quickest, most accurately, or with the most style!

4 Chat about how easy or difficult it was to communicate using flags. What are the easiest methods of communication?

 **SCENE SETTER**

WHAT: discussion
WHY: to think about dreams
WITH: prize (optional)

1 Gather the young people together and ask them to try and think of the weirdest dream they've ever had (which they feel able to tell the rest of the group).

2 Share dreams together, but don't put pressure on anyone to share a dream if they don't want to.

3 If you wish, you could vote for the weirdest dream and award a prize.

4 Discuss together what the purpose of dreams is. Explain that a dream is the experience of envisioned images, sounds or other sensations during sleep. The events that take place in dreams are often impossible or unlikely to occur in physical reality and are usually outside the control of the dreamer. Dreamers may experience strong emotions while dreaming. The discipline of dream research is called oneirology. During a typical lifespan, a human spends a total of about six years dreaming.

 **THEMED GAME**

WHAT: consequences game
WHY: to think about dreams

1 Give out pens and paper to each young person. Explain that you are going to play a game of consequences, but are going to write a dream sequence, writing one line each and folding the paper over as you pass it on to the next person.

2 Play the game, using these guidelines to write each section:

- The setting of the dream
- First main character
- Second main character
- Action of first main character
- Action of second main character
- Something that was just about to happen when I woke up

3 Pass them on once more and then invite people to read out the 'dreams'. Decide which would be the best dream and which one would be the most disturbing!

BIBLE EXPERIENCE

 LEVEL 1: CONNECT

WHAT: Bible exploration
WHY: to question how God uses dreams as a method of communication
WITH: Bibles, paper and pens

1 Give out the paper and pens and ask the young people to draw six circles or faces. Ask the young people to fill in the first two faces: how they would feel after waking up from a good dream, and how they would feel after waking up from a bad one. Ask for feedback from the group and enjoy looking at some of the expressions on the faces! (Be sensitive when discussing bad dreams, though, as some people suffer with disturbed sleep.)

2 Read Matthew 1:18–25 together. Ask the group to go through the story again on their own, filling in faces three to six:

- Face three: how did Joseph feel when he heard that Mary was pregnant (and it wasn't his baby)?
- Face four: how did Joseph feel immediately after he woke up from his dream?
- Face five: how did Joseph feel when he had had time to think about what the angel had said?
- Face six: how did Joseph feel when Jesus was born?

3 Look at the expressions the young people have drawn and see whether there are any differences between them.

4 Ask how different the story would have been if God hadn't sent the angel in a dream to Joseph, and challenge the group to think about how it might have ended. Think about how important the dream was in order for Joseph to know what to do. Things would have been very different if he had not believed the dream but had looked elsewhere for his guidance!

LEVEL 2: INTERFACE

WHAT: biblical comparison
WHY: to question how God uses dreams as a method of communication
WITH: Bibles, copies of magazine page 278

1 Explain that you are going to look at the dreams of two people called Joseph from the Bible: one from the New Testament and one from the Old.

2 Read Matthew 1:18–25. Ask the young people to describe the dream that Joseph had:

- How easy was it for Joseph to know what this dream was about?
- What might stop Joseph from following what God was saying in the dream?

3 Ask the young people to fill in the New Testament Joseph side of the chart on page 278. Chat together about how the dream was fairly straightforward for Joseph to understand, but the message God gave him must have been hard to follow: it would have been a disgrace for Mary to have become pregnant outside of marriage, and Joseph knew that the baby was not his.

4 Then read aloud Genesis 37:1–11 and ask the young people to describe the dreams that Joseph had:

- How easy was it for Joseph to know what these dreams were about?
- What might stop Joseph from following what God was saying in the dreams?

Challenge the young people to consider why God might want to use dreams in different ways to communicate with people. Help them to fill in the Old Testament Joseph side of the chart from page 278. The Old Testament Joseph's dreams needed interpreting; the meanings were not obvious. If the group know the rest of Joseph's story, why do they think God used dreams with hidden meanings? Joseph's talent for interpreting dreams got him into, and then out of, a lot of trouble, and God used the dreams to give him glory!

5 Discuss whether the group thinks God uses dreams to communicate today.

LEVEL 3: SWITCH ON

WHAT: Bible study
WHY: to question how God uses dreams as a method of communication
WITH: copies of resource page 279

1 Split the group into pairs and give each pair a copy of resource page 279. Ask the pairs to look up the Bible verses on the sheet and answer the questions for each one. Start each pair off on a different passage so that every reference is covered, even if each pair doesn't manage to examine them all.

2 After a certain amount of time, or when the pairs have examined all the passages, bring the group together and discuss their answers. What do the young people make of each dream?

3 Together, look at the differences between each dream. Are there any differences in the types of dreams that the group can identify?

4 Discuss whether any of our dreams have some kind of divine meaning. Does the group think that God uses dreams to talk to us today? What does the group think of the ways some people use books to try and interpret dreams?

RESPOND

 MUSICAL

WHAT: creating a musical dreamscape
WHY: to think about using dreams as a means of communication
WITH: various musical instruments such as keyboard, percussion, wind instruments

1 If you have musicians in your group, encourage them to bring their musical instruments with them to the session. Also have available a variety of simple percussion instruments and encourage any good singers to use their voices as instruments too.

2 Explain to the group that you are going to create a piece of music together to try to reflect dreams and how God might use them to communicate with us. Come up with some ideas of what a musical dreamscape might sound like. Bring in some of the ideas from the Bible passages you have studied – for example, sounds for an angel, fiery chariots or the sun, moon and stars.

3 Think carefully together about how you will finish the piece. How were the dreams from the Bible finished off? How will your piece finish?

4 Practise the piece. When you have finished, talk about what the group now thinks about God using dreams to communicate with his people.

 PRACTICAL

WHAT: survey
WHY: to encourage others to question how God uses dreams as a method of communication
WITH: flip chart or whiteboard, marker pens

1 Explain to the young people that they are going to find out what other people in the church think about God using dreams. Split the group into pairs or threes and ask them to think of some questions that they could ask the whole church in order to find out their thoughts on God's use of dreams.

2 After a while, bring the group back together and ask for feedback. Write the ideas on the flip chart or whiteboard. Ask the group to decide on the best five questions to ask.

3 Together, create a questionnaire with these questions and reproduce the survey so that the young people can ask the other people in the church.

4 Arrange for a time, maybe immediately after a service, for the group to carry out their survey.

5 In the next session, collate all the results and try to draw some conclusions from the responses. What is their opinion of how God uses dreams? From the biblical evidence the young people have looked at, what can they say about people's opinions?

 CREATIVE

WHAT: making a diary
WHY: to think about God communicating through dreams
WITH: stapler or hole punch, string

1 Talk about how God used dreams to talk to people in the Bible. Ask the young people if they think God can talk to them in the same way.

2 Encourage the young people to make a diary in which to write their dreams. Give out paper and felt-tip pens and ask them to make a front cover for their diary by folding a sheet of paper in half.

3 Fold some more sheets of paper and put them inside. Fix them together either using the stapler or by punching holes in the sheets and tying them together with the string.

4 Invite the group to keep a record of any dreams they have during the next few weeks.

5 Remember to revisit this activity next time you meet, so that you can all look back at the dreams and prayerfully consider whether God has been speaking through any dreams the young people may have had.

MORE ON THIS THEME:

If you want to do a short series with your group, other sessions that work well with this one are:

46	*Stars in their eyes*	*Matthew 2*
47	*Jesus is born*	*Luke 2:1–21*
48	*God in the flesh*	*Luke 2:1–21*
49	*Jesus will come again*	*Revelation 22:12–21*

International maritime signal flags

These are flags used by ships to communicate with each other. There is a whole alphabet of flags, and some of them have special meanings too: the 'J' flag also means that you are on fire and carrying dangerous cargo; the 'O' flag means you have a man overboard and the 'L' flag means you're in quarantine.

Semaphore

This uses flags held in different positions to make up letters. It was used to communicate across distances, but it wasn't very private and was limited by what the weather was like!

Morse code

Morse code uses sound, electric pulses or light to communicate. Letters are made up of short or long sounds/pulses/flashes (called either dots and dashes or dits and dahs) and pauses. 'A' is made of a dot and a dash, 'Z' is two dashes followed by two dots. It was invented in the 1840s.

IN CODE

Can you pass a message to one of your mates? Use this alphabet to communicate!

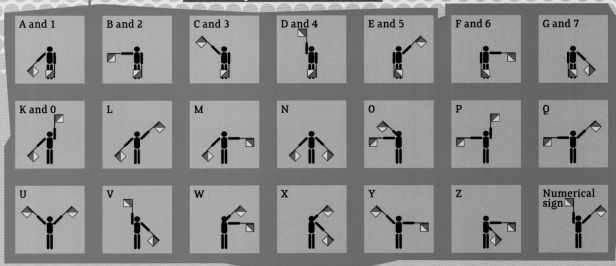

A and 1 · B and 2 · C and 3 · D and 4 · E and 5 · F and 6 · G and 7
K and 0 · L · M · N · O · P · Q
U · V · W · X · Y · Z · Numerical sign

Your young fiancée tells you she is going to have a baby and it is God's. You…

a) say, 'Thank you, but no thanks; my mum warned me about girls like you.'
b) accept that that is the way of the world these days.
c) dream about how you're going to get revenge on both her and the guy who got her into that fix.

The answer is none of the above! When God gets involved in your dreams you know it.

JOSEPH THE DREAMER?

Both the Old Testament and the New Testament have a Joseph who has dreams, but how does God use the dreams of both Josephs? Examine Genesis 37:1–11 and Matthew 1:18–25 and fill in both sides of this chart!

	Old Testament (Genesis 37:1–11)	New Testament (Matthew 1:18–25)
How easy was it for Joseph to know what his dream was about?		
What would stop Joseph from following what God was saying in the dream?		

 H and 8

 I and 9

 J

 R

 S

 T

 Annul sign

Error

Numerical means: 'I'm signing numbers not letters'
Annul means: 'Start again'

Genesis 37:1–11

Describe the dream:

How easy is it to understand?

Why does God give the dream to the dreamer?

What does the dream mean?

Daniel 7

Describe the dream:

How easy is it to understand?

Why does God give the dream to the dreamer?

What does the dream mean?

Matthew 1:18–25

Describe the dream:

How easy is it to understand?

Why does God give the dream to the dreamer?

What does the dream mean?

Acts 10

Describe the dream:

How easy is it to understand?

Why does God give the dream to the dreamer?

What does the dream mean?

Acts 16:6–10

Describe the dream:

How easy is it to understand?

Why does God give the dream to the dreamer?

What does the dream mean?

46
STARS IN THEIR EYES

Bible: Matthew 2

THE AIM: To discover that God comes to all people

The aim unpacked

In this session we'll explore what we can learn from Jesus' second set of visitors – the wise men. This is a great illustration of the fact that Jesus comes to all people. However, not everyone was happy. The latter half of this session's passage is rather gruesome as we look at how Herod undertook drastic measures to try to eliminate Jesus. Although it manifests itself very differently today, many people still do what they can to get rid of Jesus.

WAY IN

 **theGRID MAGAZINE**

WHAT: quiz
WHY: to think about birthplaces
WITH: magazine page 283, small prize

1 Give out copies of magazine page 283. Invite the young people to complete the quiz about birthplaces, perhaps working with a partner.

2 After a few minutes go through the answers and present a prize to the winner(s).

3 Conclude this activity by making the point that birthplace is no barrier to becoming a celebrity. In this session we will discover that the people who visited Jesus came from many different backgrounds and places. Your background is no barrier to getting to know Jesus. And remember, we saw in the last session how Jesus had a very unusual birthplace!

 **SCENE SETTER**

WHAT: discussion
WHY: to think about visitors

1 You may like to begin this activity by asking the young people to share their favourite 'Knock, knock' joke.

2 Invite everyone to talk to a partner for a few minutes about visitors. Ask, 'Who has visited your house recently and why?'

3 Invite the pairs to share the results and to try to put people into categories – friends, family, people doing work in the house, etc. Also try to establish who has had the most bizarre or random visitor in the last few weeks!

4 End by making the point that in this session we'll be thinking about the people who came to visit Jesus after he was born.

 **THEMED GAME**

WHAT: guessing game
WHY: to think about who can bring gifts to Jesus
WITH: small pieces of paper

1 Ask each individual to think of someone they know well and to write down on a small piece of paper a gift they would like to give to that person if they could afford to. It can be hugely valuable or cheap, sentimental or practical. They should not write the name of the recipient on the paper.

2 Collect in the papers and read them out one by one, asking the group to try to work out who each gift might be from, and who it might be for (best friend, parent, grandparent, sister, brother, pet dog, etc).

3 Now work through the list again and think about which gift would be appropriate for which member of the group. Everyone in the group must 'receive' one gift, and only one, and no one may get the gift they thought of themselves. Which gift is appropriate for whom?

4 Explain that the people who visited Jesus after his birth brought different gifts for different reasons because Jesus comes to everyone, whoever they are.

280

 ## LEVEL 1: CONNECT

WHAT: collage
WHY: to discover that God comes to all people
WITH: old magazines, backing paper, map or atlas

1 Provide a selection of magazines and invite the young people to cut out faces from as many different ethnic backgrounds as possible. Then ask them to make a collage of these faces.

2 As they do this, discuss as a group what the statement 'Jesus comes to all people' means to them.

3 Read Matthew 2 and ask the young people to make a note of all the different places that are mentioned and the journeys made. Identify these places and journeys on a map or atlas and help the young people to grasp the length of the journeys involved, particularly as the travellers didn't have the means of transport we have today!

4 Ask a few volunteers to tell the rest of the group about the longest journey they have ever made.

5 Encourage the young people to think about the journey that was made by the wise men. They travelled a long way! Ask:

- Why do you think they were prepared to do this?

- What sort of sacrifices might they have had to make in order to undertake this journey?

Ask the group to consider what they are prepared to do to 'meet with Jesus', and what are some of the sacrifices they might have to make.

6 Conclude by explaining that the good news of the gospel is not that we have to make a long journey to Jesus, but that Jesus made a long journey to us – he came from heaven to live among us. And he made it possible for all people to know him personally.

 ## LEVEL 2: INTERFACE

WHAT: character investigation
WHY: to discover that God comes to all people
WITH: magazine page 284

1 Explain to your young people that they have been appointed as detectives to investigate the events surrounding the wise men's visit to Jesus. Dodgy goings-on are suspected and they've been called in to investigate the various characters involved.

2 Divide the young people into at least four groups and distribute copies of page 284. Ask them to look at the 'No. 1 detective agency' activity. Allocate one of the following to each group: Herod; Mary and Joseph; wise men; chief priests and teachers of the Law.

3 Read Matthew 2 and encourage the young people to listen out for information on their character(s).

4 Give everyone a few minutes to collate their notes and prepare a summary of their findings. Gather the group together to share the results of the investigation. As a group, decide who you would want to interview further, either as a witness or as a suspect.

5 Talk about how Jesus came for all people. This is seen throughout his life by the way he engaged with people from all different backgrounds – Jews and foreigners, men and women, rich and poor, healthy and sick. In fact, his birth provides us with a clear picture of this as well. Both local shepherds and wise men from afar came to visit him. Shepherds in those days were very poor, uneducated and rough people, whereas the wise men were highly educated and, from the gifts they brought to Jesus, we can tell that they weren't short of money.

6 Conclude by discussing these questions:

- If Jesus came for all people, why do you think some people were so keen to stop him?

- Why do you think so many people celebrate Christmas without really remembering Jesus?

- Why do so many people want Jesus out of the picture today?

 ## LEVEL 3: SWITCH ON

WHAT: quiz and Bible study
WHY: to discover that God comes to all people
WITH: magazine page 284, Bibles, Bible reference books or internet access

1 Hand out copies of page 284 and give everyone a few minutes to complete the 'Wise men quiz'.

2 Read, or ask a young person to read, Matthew 2:1–11.

3 Give everyone the opportunity to change any of their answers, but ask them to keep a record of which ones they change. Then read out the answers: 1 d, 2 c, 3 b, 4 a, 5 c, 6 c, 7 d, 8 b, 9 d.

4 Collect in the scores and say that often our understanding is based on tradition rather than what it actually says in the Bible. Find out who had the highest score. Explain that these wise men were a very different group of visitors to the shepherds. (You may want to reread, or at least summarise, Luke 2:8–20 at this point.)

5 Divide the young people into two groups. Ask one group to do some research about shepherds and the other group to do some research on wise men. Either gather together a selection of books, or ideally provide access to the internet.

6 Bring everyone together and invite the groups to feed back. Explain that the examples of these two very different groups of people show us that Jesus comes to all people, regardless of their background. To reinforce this further you might like to read Galatians 3:28 (gender) and 1 Timothy 4:12 (age).

RESPOND

 MUSICAL

WHAT: world music
WHY: to celebrate that God comes to all people
WITH: song lyrics, variety of instruments (if possible)

1 Try to get hold of a variety of instruments from around the world, along with a well-known song with verses in different languages. You can find plenty on the internet. ('We Are Marching in the Light of God' would work well.)

2 Teach the song to the group. Give as many people as possible an instrument and encourage everyone to celebrate the fact that God comes to all people.

3 You may also like to read Psalm 72:1–19 to the group.

 PRACTICAL

WHAT: plan to communicate Jesus
WHY: to make it known that Jesus comes to all people
WITH: large sheet of paper, flip chart or whiteboard

1 Say that in this session we've explored the idea that Jesus comes to all people. The church, sometimes known as 'the body of Christ', is Jesus' representative here on earth. Ask the young people, 'What can the church do to demonstrate that Jesus comes to all people?' This might well spark some discussion, especially if the young people in your group don't think your church is welcoming to all people.

2 Encourage the group to discuss in threes or fours what the church, and you as a group, could do to communicate that Jesus comes to all people. Gather the group together and write down all the ideas on a large sheet of paper, flip chart or whiteboard.

3 Choose one of the ideas and begin to plan it. Make a list of jobs that would need doing in order to make it happen. Then create a timeline and allocate the jobs to different young people.

4 Make sure you revisit and refine this plan over the coming weeks to make sure it's not forgotten.

 CREATIVE

WHAT: prayer collage
WHY: to pray that all people would discover God
WITH: magazines, newspapers, paper, large sheets of paper

1 Divide the young people into small groups, give out the materials and ask them to produce a collage that represents 'all people'. Encourage them to include different nationalities, ages and groups of people.

2 Ask everyone to think about how they can reveal God to all the different people they know.

3 Conclude by encouraging everyone to write or say a short prayer asking that the people they've been thinking about in this activity would discover God.

MORE ON THIS THEME:

If you want to do a short series with your group, other sessions that work well with this one are:

45	*Dreams*	*Matthew 1:18–25*
47	*Jesus is born*	*Luke 2:1–21*
48	*God in the flesh*	*Luke 2:1–21*
49	*Jesus will come again*	*Revelation 22:12–21*

PLACE OF BIRTH

Match the stars with their places of birth!

Lynwood, USA	1	A — Natalie Portman, Actress
Paris, France	2	B — John Barrowman, Actor/Musical performer
Jerusalem, Israel	3	C — Victoria Beckham, Singer/Fashion designer
Honolulu, Hawaii	4	D — Venus Williams, Tennis star
Glasgow, Scotland	5	E — John Sentamu, Archbishop of York
Kampala, Uganda	6	F — Thierry Henry, Footballer
Kentucky, USA	7	G — Anthony 'Ant' McPartlin, TV presenter
Colchester, England	8	H — Barack Obama, Former President of the USA
Harlow, England	9	I — Dermot O'Leary, TV presenter
Newcastle-upon-Tyne, England	10	J — Johnny Depp, Actor

**Bible bit
Matthew 2**

Jesus was visited by both shepherds and wise men. This is quite significant. Shepherds in those days were very poor, uneducated and rough people, whereas the wise men were highly educated and, from the gifts they brought to Jesus, we can tell that they weren't short of money. This is a great illustration that Jesus came for all people. We see this throughout his life: he comes to men and women, rich and poor, healthy and sick, Jews and foreigners.

However, despite this, not everyone was happy. The second half of this passage is rather gruesome as we read about King Herod's drastic measures to try to eliminate Jesus. Although it reveals itself very differently today, many people still do what they can to 'get rid' of Jesus.

Answers on page 319

WISE MEN QUIZ

How much do you know about the Christmas story? Complete the quiz, then check out your answers by reading Matthew 2.

1
About those visitors to Jesus... where did they come from?
a) East Ham
b) China
c) East of Eden
d) The east

2
Where did they go first?
a) Burger King
b) Bethlehem
c) Jerusalem
d) Nazareth

3
Who called them in for a chat?
a) The local police officer
b) The king
c) The chief priest
d) Jesus' father

4
What was this person's name?
a) Herod
b) Herodias
c) Pilate
d) Henry

5
Where did the local experts say the Christ was to be born?
a) Jerusalem
b) Nazareth
c) Bethlehem
d) Samaria

6
And where were the visitors sent?
a) Jerusalem
b) Nazareth
c) Bethlehem
d) Samaria

7
How many of these visitors were there?
a) Three
b) Two
c) Four
d) We aren't told

8
Did they visit Jesus in:
a) a manger?
b) a house?
c) a pub?
d) a hotel?

9
Which of these gifts did they not bring?
a) Myrrh
b) Incense
c) Gold
d) Silver

NO.1 DETECTIVE AGENCY

You have been appointed as a detective to investigate suspicions of dodgy goings-on in the events surrounding the wise men's visit to a baby called Jesus. Who would you want to interview further, either as a witness or a suspect?

Read Matthew 2 and write some information on each character.

SUSPECT: HEROD

Emotional state:

Possible motivation:

Suspicious activities:

Summary:

SUSPECT: WISE MEN

Emotional state:

Possible motivation:

Suspicious activities:

Summary:

SUSPECT: MARY AND JOSEPH

Emotional state:

Possible motivation:

Suspicious activities:

Summary:

SUSPECT: CHIEF PRIESTS AND TEACHERS OF THE LAW

Emotional state:

Possible motivation:

Suspicious activities:

Summary:

Jesus came for all people. Both rough local shepherds and rich, foreign wise men saw that he was special and wanted to visit him themselves. So why do you think some people were so keen to stop him?

JESUS IS BORN

THE AIM: To see that God is faithful by sending Jesus

The aim unpacked

This session gets to the heart of the Christmas narrative – the birth of God's anointed, the Christ. We examine how God, who has promised the Messiah to his people, is faithful through the birth of Jesus. It is easy to miss the real meaning of Christmas amongst all the glitz and consumerism. Let's remind ourselves that God loved us and sent his Son to save us.

WAY IN

 **theGRID MAGAZINE**

WHAT: choosing and discussion
WHY: to explore what Christmas is all about
WITH: magazine pages 288 and 289

1 Give out copies of pages 288 and 289, and ask the young people to look at 'What is Christmas about for you?' Allow a few minutes for the group to look at the list. (Be aware that Christmas might not be a happy time for some, so make sure you deal with that sensitively.)

2 Split the group into pairs or threes and encourage them to share which words on the list they relate to, and why. Is there anything else they would have chosen? Do they feel differently about Christmas now than they did when they were younger?

3 As a whole group, think about how the 'world' perceives Christmas. Use these questions:

- What is most important to the 'person in the street'?

- What do you think about the suggestion of renaming Christmas to avoid offending people?

- How many people do you think celebrate the birth of Jesus as the reason for all the festivities? What else are they celebrating?

 **SCENE SETTER**

WHAT: role play
WHY: to look at the commercial and materialistic aspects of Christmas
WITH: any props you may have available (optional)

1 Split the young people into groups of about four or five. Explain that Christmas for many people has become commercialised and materialistic.

2 Ask each group to work on a role play (serious or silly!) to illustrate this aspect of Christmas. Some suggestions for sketches are:

- Some small children who want everything

- Exasperated parents in a shopping centre needing to buy what everyone else is buying

- A TV or radio advert for a 'must-have' item which is actually entirely useless

3 Give the groups five to ten minutes on this, then come together and let them show their role plays to each other, if they would like to do so.

4 Chat together about the difference between Christmas today and the real story behind the festival.

 **THEMED GAME**

WHAT: being a music critic
WHY: to think about something which is eagerly awaited
WITH: Christmas chart songs, playback equipment, score chart

1 Before the session, get hold of a range of songs which have been Christmas number ones. You could include 'Mistletoe and Wine' by Cliff Richard or 'Do They Know It's Christmas?' by Band Aid. Make a scoreboard to record what the young people think of each song.

2 As a group, listen to some songs that were Christmas hits. Explain that everyone will have a chance to give their reactions.

3 Play the songs and see which one comes out on top, and which one is the group's most disliked song.

4 Chat about the Christmas number one and how it is a coveted spot; people look forward to finding out what song it will be. If appropriate, talk about how people look forward to Christmas itself and discuss some of the reasons why.

BIBLE EXPERIENCE

 LEVEL 1: CONNECT

WHAT: nativity play
WHY: to see that God is faithful by sending Jesus
WITH: Bibles, simple costumes and appropriate props (optional)

1 Gather the group together and ask the young people if they can remember the last time they were in a nativity play. Is there anyone who longed to be Mary or Joseph but never had the chance? Tell everyone that they're going to have another chance to be in a nativity play!

2 Ask a leader or one of the young people to read the Bible passage: Luke 2:1–21.

3 Challenge the young people to plan out the play and decide who will take which parts. Make sure they cover this session's Bible passage accurately! Give them time to rehearse and then perform it. If your group is not happy to ad-lib, they could act it out while a leader tells the story.

4 When you have finished, discuss what the story is actually about, behind the familiar elements of the innkeeper, the shepherds and the angels. What relevance does this story have to the young people's lives today? Is it more than just a story? If appropriate, challenge the young people to think about the significance of Jesus' birth.

 LEVEL 2: INTERFACE

WHAT: discussion and hot-seating
WHY: to see that God is faithful by sending Jesus
WITH: Bibles, magazine page 290

1 Give out copies of magazine page 290 and ask the young people to look at the descriptions of Mary, Joseph and the shepherds, commenting that these people played a huge part in the Christmas story. We don't know much about any of them, but God used them greatly!

2 Read Luke 2:1–21 to the group and ask them to make a note of how God used Mary, Joseph and the shepherds. At the end of the reading, discuss what the young people have jotted down.

3 Chat together about how such ordinary people took part in one of the most important and well-known stories in the world. Have the young people ever thought about the story from the point of view of these characters? Split the young people into three groups and ask each group to think about one of the characters: Mary, Joseph or the shepherds. How would they have reacted to taking part in God's plan of sending Jesus?

4 After the groups have had a few minutes to think together, encourage the rest of the young people to ask them questions from the point of view of their character, such as:

- What did you think when you first heard you were going to be part of God's plan of sending Jesus to be the Saviour of the world?
- Were you scared?
- Were you tempted to ignore God and carry on as normal?

5 Let the group interview each character and then reflect on how God used ordinary people to bring about his big plan. How is God using the young people in your group in the continuation of that plan?

 LEVEL 3: SWITCH ON

WHAT: Bible study
WHY: to see that God is faithful by sending Jesus
WITH: copies of different Bible translations or printouts

1 Split the young people into four groups. (If your group is small, either have two groups or do the activity all together.)

2 Give each group a different version of the Bible – the *Youth Bible* (NCV), the King James Version and two other versions. Alternatively, you could print out the passages from www.biblegateway.com. Ask each group to read together the passage given to them:

- Group A: Luke 2:1–21 (*Youth Bible*)
- Group B: Matthew 1:18 – 2:12 (RSV, ESV or NIV)
- Group C: Mark 1:1–8 (KJV)
- Group D: John 1:1–18 (*The Message*, NLT or CEV)

3 Let the groups briefly chat about what their passage is saying. Ask them, 'What do these verses tell you about why God sent Jesus?'

4 Ask a member of each group to read their passage aloud and share any comments they talked about.

5 Discuss the different pictures of Christmas that the four Gospels give. All four Gospels have a different slant on the coming of Christ into the world. Matthew and Luke tell about the birth of Christ, one mentioning the wise men and Herod, and the other the shepherds and angels; Mark tells us about John the Baptist preparing the way and John tells of Christ coming into the world as the Word.

6 Ask the young people to think about and discuss how these different viewpoints of the coming of Christ have made an impact on them. Do they have any thoughts or comments about the styles of the different versions of the Bible?

RESPOND

 MUSICAL

WHAT: Christmas worship experience
WHY: to celebrate Jesus being born and to thank God for his faithfulness
WITH: variety of song books (for example *Carol Praise*), worship music, playback equipment or musical instruments

1 This activity is designed to help your group explore and respond to the Christmas message through music. Think with your group of different ways they could do this.

2 Help the young people to do what they have decided. Some suggestions are:

• Christmas carols: the group could play and sing some traditional Christmas carols or some contemporary Christmas songs they know. Examine the words together. What do they tell us about Jesus' coming and God's faithfulness in sending Jesus? How do they help us worship God?

• Carol writing: challenge the young people to write their own Christmas carol. This is a great way for them to respond personally to the Christmas story as it helps them focus on their own feelings. Why not teach it to other groups or the rest of the church?

• Dance: if your group enjoys dancing, challenge them to choreograph a dance to a piece of music that communicates their thankfulness to God and their joy at Jesus' birth.

 PRACTICAL

WHAT: prayer responses
WHY: to remember God's faithfulness in sending Jesus
WITH: gift tags

1 Give out a gift tag and a pen to each young person. Explain that the gift tag reminds us of the gift given to us by God – Jesus Christ, his Son.

2 Ask:

• What does Christmas now mean to you personally, in the light of today's teaching?

• What does it mean to you that God sent Jesus?

3 Encourage the young people to write a prayer on their gift tag in response to what they have heard today. For example, 'Thank you, Lord, for sending your Son for me.'

4 These tags could either be put up somewhere in the church or taken home as a reminder for the young people to reflect on what they have heard over the Christmas period.

5 Give out extra gift tags and ask the young people to record on them any more responses to the message of Christmas that they have over the next week or so. If you wish, you could ask them to bring the gift tags back to a later session and feed back what God has been saying to them.

 CREATIVE

WHAT: making Christmas cards
WHY: to pass on the message that Jesus came for everyone
WITH: card, art materials, magazine page 289

1 Talk about how many people send Christmas cards to say 'Happy Christmas' to each other. Tell the group that they are going to make cards today to pass on the message of Christmas to others – that God sent Jesus to be our Saviour!

2 Invite the young people to decide who they are each going to give their card to, and think about what they will write inside as they decorate it.

3 Suggest that the young people write a Bible verse, such as Luke 2:11, the poem from page 289 or a line from a Christmas carol inside their cards.

4 At the end of the session, encourage each member of the group to give their card to its intended recipient and chat about the reason they have made the card: that God sent Jesus to be our Saviour, and that we should celebrate!

MORE ON THIS THEME:

If you want to do a short series with your group, other sessions that work well with this one are:

WHAT IS CHRISTMAS ABOUT FOR YOU?

Bible bit
Luke 2:1–21

No banners in the high street. No leaflets or flyers. No relentless stream of TV adverts. No decorations hanging from the rafters. Just a baby born, not even in a hospital, and a group of shepherds, common workers, come to visit. But from that day, the world would never be the same.

What is Christmas about for you? Is it a special time? If so, what is it about Christmas that makes it special? Is it any of these things? Tick those that make it special for you.

CAKE

PRESENTS

CHRISTMAS DECORATIONS

CRACKERS

CHRISTMAS

ROBINS

REINDEER

THI

CHRISTMAS CAROLS

PARTIES

Take away for Christmas

Take away the sentimentality
And what are you left with?
Take away the eating, drinking and frenzied gift buying
And what have you got?
Take away the cards and baubled trees,
The turkey and the pudding,
And where does that leave you?
Take away the relations, the parties and all the glitter,
And what are you left with?
Then we are left with the Christ Child,
Born of Mary, simply, no extravagance here,
Born in a lowly stable.
The Christ Child, the Light of the World,
Come to us in the darkness,
An everlasting gift of light and joy,
Given for you this Christmas.

© Jane Wade 1994

CHURCH
SNOW
LOTS OF TURKEY
FOR CHRISTMAS DINNER
CARDS
ADVENT CALENDARS
NATIVITY
CHRISTINGLE CANDLES

WHY CHOOSE THEM?

God sent his Son, Jesus, to be the Saviour of the whole world, but he chose to use some unusual people to do this!
Why do you think God chose them?

MARY

Mary was only young when she was engaged to be married to a man called Joseph. This was the custom at the time. She lived in a small town called Nazareth, miles away from anywhere important. She was an ordinary girl, apart from the fact that she was probably a descendant of King David, the king of Israel from hundreds of years before she was born.

JOSEPH

Joseph was a carpenter in the town of Nazareth. Not much is known about him, but he was engaged to be married to Mary. He was an ordinary guy too, apart from the fact that he was definitely a descendant of King David.

SHEPHERDS

The life of a shepherd back then was a tough one. They weren't greatly respected at the time when Jesus was born. They lived outside for long periods of time, in all weathers, with the sheep and maybe a dog, if they had one. They were likely to have been rough and smelly individuals – not the usual dignitaries invited to visit a new king!

GOD IN THE FLESH

THE AIM: To explore how God came as a human being

The aim unpacked

The Old Testament reveals to us that people are continually getting themselves into a mess! Amazingly, God doesn't give up. Instead, he plans a remarkable rescue mission! In perhaps the most shocking event of human history, God, the Creator and Ruler of the universe, comes down to earth to sort out the mess. As the angels reveal to the shepherds that a Saviour has been born, so the Christmas story reveals much about God and how he feels about us.

WAY IN

 **theGRID MAGAZINE**

WHAT: puzzle
WHY: to think about the meaning of Christmas
WITH: magazine page 294

1 Give out copies of page 294 and invite the young people to read the Christmas newsletter. Can they find the secret message hidden within it?

2 If they are struggling after a couple of minutes, give them a clue to look at the initial letters of the words in the middle paragraph.

3 The middle paragraph spells out this message: The true message of Christmas is the good news of the birth of Jesus Christ, Son of the Living God.

 **SCENE SETTER**

WHAT: sorting Christmas cards
WHY: to think about Jesus' birthday
WITH: Christmas cards, birthday card

1 Bring to the session a selection of Christmas cards showing a variety of scenes and messages. Also bring one birthday card.

2 Ask the young people to sort the cards into an order starting with 'least appropriate' and ending with 'most appropriate'. So, for instance, they will have to decide if a picture of a church covered in snow is more relevant to the season than a picture of a robin or a Victorian stagecoach or a laughing, rotund Santa.

3 Discuss the results and make the suggestion, if they have not already made it to you, that perhaps the birthday card (Jesus' birthday) might be as close as any to a proper greeting.

 **THEMED GAME**

WHAT: game
WHY: to think about angels
WITH: white sheet, some music, small prize, equipment to play music

1 Ask for a volunteer. Ask them to drape the sheet around themselves to represent an angel.

2 Play the music and ask everyone to move around. When the music stops, everyone must keep perfectly still, as in musical statues. The 'angel' must throw the sheet over as many people as possible, and these people are then out.

3 Give a small prize to the last person to be caught. Make the point that people in the Bible must have often been afraid of angels, because they always seem to start conversations with 'Do not be afraid!' You could use this to lead into a conversation about what the young people think angels are like, and what the Bible actually says.

BIBLE EXPERIENCE

 LEVEL 1: CONNECT

WHAT: quiz and Christmas cards
WHY: to explore how God came as a human being
WITH: magazine page 295, materials to make Christmas cards

1 Give out copies of page 295 and invite the young people to look at the pictures. Ten of these items are featured in Luke 2:1–21, and ten are items that feature in the many myths and traditions that surround the Christmas story. Challenge the group to find the ten images that are actually in the Bible story. The correct answers are: a scroll with a message from Augustus Caesar (v 1); a sign saying 'Welcome to Bethlehem' (v 4); a pregnant woman (v 5); a manger (NCV describes it as a feeding box) (v 7); a baby wrapped in cloths (vs 7,12); shepherds (v 8); sheep (v 8); an angel (v 9); many angels singing (v 13); Mary alone (v 19).

2 Read Luke 2:1–21. You could divide the passage into parts and have someone as the narrator and others taking the parts of the angels and shepherds where they speak.

3 Working in pairs, make a selection of Christmas cards with more realistic messages and images on them than those found on some cards today. Encourage the young people to choose a Bible verse to put inside their cards which, to them, explains what the Christmas story is all about. (Be prepared to help them find appropriate verses.) Perhaps you could even 'mass produce' some of the best designs and sell the cards to the wider church to raise money for a local charity.

4 Conclude by explaining that the Christmas story is the story of God being involved personally in the world he created and coming to save humankind. Discuss (or explain) what we can learn about God from this.

 LEVEL 2: INTERFACE

WHAT: 'true' nativity
WHY: to explore how God came as a human being
WITH: selection of Christmas cards (optional)

1 Invite the group to think about the main events, characters and details of the Christmas story. You could do this creatively by having a wide selection of Christmas cards available and challenging them to create a collage or timeline of events that communicates the essential details.

2 Explain that over the next two sessions they're going to be learning about the Christmas story as it's told in the Bible. Prewarn the young people that they might be surprised about what is not included in the Bible's account of Jesus' birth.

3 Read Luke 2:1–21. Ask several people to read a few verses each. As the passage is being read, pause occasionally to point out any details featured in your group's collage/timeline.

4 Explain that over the years a lot of details have been added to the Christmas story. Ask:

- Why do you think this might be?
- Do you think it's a problem? If so, why?

Ask the young people to suggest the worst piece of 'creative licence' they've ever seen in a school (or church!) nativity play. For example, Father Christmas or a pantomime figure suddenly appearing.

5 Divide into smaller groups and ask the young people to prepare a 'true' nativity play using only the facts in Luke 2:1–21. Then invite each group to perform their version of the true nativity.

6 Reread verses 10 and 11 and explain that this is an excellent summary of the importance of Christmas. Invite the young people to chat about how it makes them feel about themselves and God. Encourage them to ask any questions they may have, especially if any of their traditional understandings of the Christmas story have been shaken.

 LEVEL 3: SWITCH ON

WHAT: writing a Christmas carol
WHY: to explore how God came as a human being
WITH: carol sheets

1 Ask a few volunteers to read Luke 2:1–21 to the group.

2 Invite everyone to tell the group what their favourite Christmas carol is and why they like it.

3 Now give out copies of the words of a wide selection of carols. Ask the young people to work in pairs or threes to consider which of the carols come close to the 'spirit of the Christmas message' in this passage and which ones are way out.

4 Discuss with your group what they think are the key differences between the Christmas story as it is portrayed by some of the carols and the account they read in the Bible.

5 In their small groups, ask everyone to write a new Christmas carol, or at least one or two verses of a carol. Tell the young people that they have to cram as much biblical truth into their carols as possible!

6 Encourage the groups to present their carols, ideally by singing them, to everyone. Perhaps you could vote to see which one the young people like the most.

7 Conclude by asking the group to consider what they think is the most crucial message contained within the Christmas story. You may like to point them to verses 10 and 11. Ask them to chat about how this message makes them feel about themselves and God. Challenge them to think in their small groups about how they could communicate this message to their families and friends over this Christmas period.

RESPOND

 MUSICAL

WHAT: carol singing
WHY: to praise God
WITH: Christmas carols

1 To conclude this session, sing one or two carols. Before you do this, encourage the young people to think of these carols as 'worship songs', not just 'carols we sing once a year because they're traditional'.

2 Choose carols that have a focus on the passage you've explored today – for example, 'O Little Town of Bethlehem'; 'Angels from the Realms of Glory' (omit verse three); 'It Came upon the Midnight Clear'. You could sing Graham Kendrick's 'The Servant King'. It's a more modern song, but the words are very appropriate to this session.

3 Chat with the group about whether they would like to worship God by carol singing in public, such as at a local retirement home or a public bandstand. If they would be interested, make arrangements for this to happen, making sure you get all the appropriate permissions.

 PRACTICAL

WHAT: reflection
WHY: to thank God that he came as a human being
WITH: quiet instrumental music, playback equipment

1 Over some quiet music read Philippians 2:5–11 slowly, with a pause between each verse. It's a passage that your group might be familiar with, but this session's Christmas context should add a different layer of meaning to it.

2 Encourage the group to use the pauses between the verses to thank God silently for what he has done for them.

3 Conclude by reading the passage again. This time read it all together, out loud, without pauses.

 CREATIVE

WHAT: birth announcement
WHY: to remember the baby Jesus
WITH: card, craft materials, example of a 'baby announcement' card

1 Show the group the baby announcement card and invite them to make their own version to announce Jesus' birth using the craft materials provided. Before they begin to make their cards, encourage them to consider what they think are the most important things about Jesus that their cards should communicate.

2 Conclude by inviting the young people to show and talk about their cards to the rest of the group, if they want to.

MORE ON THIS THEME:

If you want to do a short series with your group, other sessions that work well with this one are:

THE HIDDEN MESSAGE OF CHRISTMAS

Can you find the hidden message in this Christmas newsletter?

Bible bit
Luke 2:1–21

Just take a peek at the Old Testament to see that people are continually getting themselves into a mess! Amazingly, God doesn't give up. Instead he plans the most amazing rescue mission ever! This is such a big job, such a vital job, that there's only one person who can do it: God himself! So, in perhaps the most shocking event of human history, God, the Creator and Ruler of the universe, comes down to earth to sort out the mess – and he starts life in the same way that you and I did – as a baby!

The Christmas story reveals so much about God and how he feels about us.

Dear friends,

It's been a great year with lots of fun things happening in the Davis household. But, of course, the top event was the huge family party we had to celebrate Uncle Eric's 100th birthday.

The Happy Event Truly rocked. Uncle Eric Managed, ever so slowly, a glass even Of fizz. Colin had really interesting stories to make available – so Incredibly sensitive. The house eventually Got over our dancing. Now everyone will smile. Our fun Took happy Eric Back in real time. He Only first Just expected some usual suspects. Colin had really instigated surprise. To Summarise our news Of family – The happiest event. Loved it veraciously indeed. Now get Going. Oh dear.

The rest of the year paled by comparison. We had a good holiday and caught up with a lot of old friends on the way back. But Eric's 100th birthday party was just the best day.

Love

Paul and Mavis

FACT OR FICTION?

How many of the items on this page can actually be found in Luke 2:1–21? Put a tick beside those you think can be found, then check out your answers in a Bible.

49

Bible: Revelation 22:12–21

JESUS WILL COME AGAIN

THE AIM: To pray for Jesus' return and celebrate in the knowledge that he is coming

The aim unpacked

In this session, we examine the second coming of Jesus. After Christmas, we enter a new year and look forward to what that brings. It is also good to remind ourselves that we can look forward to Jesus' return.

WAY IN

 theGRID MAGAZINE

WHAT: show and tell
WHY: to think about why we might want to pray for Jesus' return

1 Before the session, ask the group to bring something that fills them with awe and makes them say, 'Wow'. This could be pictures of things they saw on holidays, activities they do, films they've seen, music they've heard.

2 Ask the young people to show what they have brought in turn. Chat about the differences between the people in the group.

3 Introduce the idea of heaven and ask what the young people think of it. Do they think it's going to be like one long boring church service? Gather the young people's ideas and then talk about how awesome heaven will be. We cannot conceive what it will be like, spending eternity with God, but it will be a million times better than the things that inspire awe in us here on earth.

 SCENE SETTER

WHAT: party planning
WHY: to think about welcoming returnees
WITH: pens, paper, any resources the young people may need

1 Ask the young people to think about someone who will come back soon (apart from Jesus!). This might be soldiers returning from abroad, a friend who is on holiday or a victorious sports team returning from a tournament.

2 Ask them to consider what might be the most appropriate way to celebrate the return. For example, if their friend has come back from a two-week holiday, a massive street party might not be the best thing to do, but arranging an evening in to look at photographs and watch DVDs might be more suitable. Ask everyone in the group to choose one 'returning person' and think how best to celebrate their return.

3 Working in pairs or threes, encourage the group to plan a party or event for their 'returnee'. Give out pens, paper and any other resources they might need.

4 When everyone has finished, share some of the events that have been planned.

 **THEMED GAME**

WHAT: party games
WHY: to think about times of celebration
WITH: equipment for your chosen party games

1 Explain to the group that today you are going to think about celebrating – after all, Christmas has only just happened! Play some of the young people's favourite party games. You could choose:

- Musical chairs, bumps or statues
- Pass the parcel
- Sleeping lions
- Pin the tail on the donkey

2 Play the games and just have fun. Chat, as you are playing, about times of celebration and why we celebrate things. Ask them what they enjoyed about their Christmas celebrations.

BIBLE EXPERIENCE

 LEVEL 1: CONNECT

WHAT: active Bible study
WHY: to pray for Jesus' return and celebrate in the knowledge that he is coming
WITH: a large sheet of paper, Bibles, resource page 299, different coloured felt-tip pens

1 Before the session, print out the Bible passage (Revelation 22:12–21), so that it is A1 in size (you could do this by sticking eight sheets of A4 paper together). Enlarge page 299 and cut it up. Hide the pieces around the room.

2 Show the young people your giant Bible reading and read it together. Explain that Revelation is a book which contains lots of imagery – lots of picture language. Tell the group that you have hidden the meanings of the imagery in this passage around the room. They have to find and match these meanings to the images.

3 Give time for the young people to find the meanings and match them up to the imagery, giving guidance as necessary.

4 Go through the images, explaining anything as you need to. Give each young person a different-coloured felt-tip pen. Ask them to read the Bible verses again and underline anything else that they don't understand. Discuss together what has been underlined.

5 Explain that these verses come at the very end of the Bible, and that this scene is after Jesus has come back in triumph. Death and sin have been defeated and we can live perfect lives with Jesus. Talk about how exciting that is and, if you did *Way in* '*theGRID* magazine', refer back to the moments of awe, saying that it will be so much better than those, so we should be happy as we look forward to it!

 LEVEL 2: INTERFACE

WHAT: Bible brainstorm
WHY: to pray for Jesus' return and celebrate in the knowledge that he is coming
WITH: Bibles, large sheets of paper, felt-tip pens or other art materials, resource page 299, quiet music (optional)

1 Gather the group together and ask them to sit in a comfortable position. Ask them to imagine the events as you read Revelation 22:12–21. Before you start, you might want to put this passage into context: that it comes at the very end of the Bible and talks about what will happen when Jesus comes back again.

2 Split the young people into two groups and ask one half to draw one or two of the scenes which jump out at them. Ask the other half to brainstorm some of the key words from the passage, and write them on a sheet of paper. Encourage both groups to look back at the Bible text to help them.

3 When both groups have finished, swap over. Turn their sheets of paper over so that each group has a list of words and at least one picture.

4 Get them to share their words and show the pictures, asking for explanations when needed. Talk together about what is happening in the passage. You could refer to page 299 for some interpretation of the symbolism.

5 Using the words and pictures they have recorded, ask the young people what there is in this passage that would make them look forward to the time when Jesus returns. The group might pick out words like 'reward', 'water of life', 'free gift' or 'morning star'. Discuss why they have chosen certain words. The time when Jesus comes back again will mean that there will be no more suffering, pain or tears, and we will live with Jesus for ever.

6 Chat about whether the group are looking forward to Jesus coming back. Is it something they would celebrate or even pray for? Encourage them to do this.

 LEVEL 3: SWITCH ON

WHAT: Bible search and study
WHY: to pray for Jesus' return and celebrate in the knowledge that he is coming
WITH: study Bibles and concordances, pens, paper

1 Talk about the book of Revelation – ask the young people what they know. Listen to everyone's ideas (gently correcting if anyone has it very wrong). Read Revelation 22:12–21 to the group.

2 Split the young people into pairs or threes. Divide up the Bible verses and give each small group a section to work on. Give out the study Bibles and concordances and challenge the young people to find out more about the meaning of their verse. For example, verse 12 will lead the young people to Matthew and Isaiah, to learn a bit more about the reward Jesus talks about.

3 Bring the group back together and ask each pair or group of three about the most striking thing they found out from their Bible search. Discuss the discoveries and talk about what they all might mean to the young people. Ask:

- Why should we desire all these things to happen?
- Why should we pray for Jesus to come back?
- Is that the same as wanting to die?

Get someone to look up Philippians 1:21 and read it out. Does this make the young people want to celebrate because Jesus is coming back?

RESPOND

 MUSICAL

WHAT: singing
WHY: to pray for Jesus' return and celebrate in the knowledge that he is coming
WITH: songs about Jesus' return, music

1 There are many songs with words that pray for Jesus' return. Gather some songs that the young people know and spend some time worshipping God. Some suggestions are:

- 'As We Bring Our Songs'
- 'Great is the Darkness'
- 'There's a Place Where the Streets Shine'

You could also sing some celebration songs, looking forward to when Jesus comes again. Some suggestions are:

- 'I Stand Amazed in the Presence'
- 'Soon and Very Soon'

2 If any of the young people feel that God has spoken to them through the time of sung worship, let them share it. Discuss the young people's response to the fact that we should pray for and look forward to Jesus' return.

 PRACTICAL

WHAT: Bible reading and journalling
WHY: to think more about praying for and celebrating Jesus' return
WITH: a notebook for each person, pens, Bibles

1 Many Bible passages point towards the return of Jesus and people's responses to it. Give out the Bibles and ask the young people to look at some of the passages they have looked at recently, in the light of this session's Bible reading.

2 Give out the notebooks or sheets of paper and ask them to write down a few thoughts about the Bible passage. If appropriate, ask if anyone wants to share what they have written down. Chat about desiring Jesus' return. Ask what that means to the young people.

3 Pray together, that Jesus would come back, and for those people who don't yet know Jesus to know him.

4 Encourage the young people to carry on writing their thoughts in their notebook during the week. You could challenge them to start reading the Bible regularly. Make sure you give the young people a chance to feed back either what they have written in their journals or what they have read in the Bible.

 CREATIVE

WHAT: poster making
WHY: to think about praying for and celebrating Jesus' return
WITH: art and craft materials, paper

1 Ask the group to brainstorm some ideas about different firsts and lasts. Here are some examples:

- a to zymurgy (words in the dictionary)
- Augustus and Romulus Augustulus (Roman emperors)

2 Read Revelation 22:13 to the group. Remind them that this is Jesus speaking, at the point of his return. Jesus calls himself the first and last.

3 Encourage the young people to make a poster about different firsts and lasts that Jesus could call himself. As they make their poster, chat with the young people about Jesus' return and what they make of it. Is it something they would look forward to and pray for? Explain a little about your own thoughts about heaven and looking forward to Jesus' return.

4 When everyone has finished, look at the posters together. Let the group take the posters home as a reminder of Jesus coming back!

MORE ON THIS THEME:

If you want to do a short series with your group, other sessions that work well with this one are:

Alpha (A or α) and omega (Ω or ω) are the first and last letters in the Greek alphabet. Greek was the language the New Testament was written in. Jesus is the beginning and end of everything.

This means that they believed in Jesus – they had washed their dirty clothes and they were now clean, they were now forgiven for the things they had done wrong.

This was the New Jerusalem. It represents the place where God and his people will live together for ever. (See Revelation 21 for more description!)

Jesus was descended from King David; this fulfilled a prophecy that was made hundreds of years before Jesus was born.

Jesus calls himself this to say that the dark night of all our suffering and hurt is over – a new day has begun, full of his love and blessing!

Jesus talked about water of life when he was beside a well, chatting to a woman in Samaria. It is related to eternal life – living for ever with God: no one will ever be thirsty again!

50

BROKEN FOR YOU

THE AIM: To understand why Jesus died — the new covenant

The aim unpacked

This session is made up of two different passages: the Palm Sunday story and the Last Supper. They present young people with two different pictures of Jesus — as the king foretold in Zechariah 9:9 and as the sacrifice made for us all. Jesus enters Jerusalem in triumph, people cheer and shout out praises, and yet, four days later, Jesus is talking about his broken body and shed blood. What does all this mean? Why has this transformation from ruler to sacrifice come about?

WAY IN

 **theGRID MAGAZINE**

WHAT: food preparation
WHY: to think about the background to this session's Bible passage
WITH: magazine page 303 and ingredients listed there, utensils listed below

1 Divide the young people into groups of three or four. Each group will need a chopping board, knife, grater, spoon and bowl, a copy of the recipe and the ingredients. Ask each group to prepare their charoset according to the recipe.

2 The dish forms part of the Passover ritual celebrated by Jews to remember their escape from Egypt described in the book of Exodus. Read Exodus 5:6–17. Explain that charoset represents the straw and mud the Israelites had to use to make bricks.

3 If you are using the Passover worship ritual later in the session, save your charoset for this. Otherwise, encourage everyone to taste it. Discuss how Passover was a big part of Jewish life and how everyone would have known the symbolism of all the elements of the festival, especially the sacrifice of a lamb.

 SCENE SETTER

WHAT: discussion
WHY: to think about the nature of kingship

1 Discuss the following questions with your group:

- What do you think it would be like to be a king?

- What kind of things do you think kings (and queens) do?

2 Ask each person to think about where they would most like to be king or queen of (it could be a real or an imaginary place). Discuss their answers.

3 Ask: 'If you could only be in charge for a short time, what three things would you do as king or queen of your kingdom?' Discuss any reasons the young people have.

4 Ask: 'What do you think makes a "good" king? Why?'

 THEMED GAME

WHAT: team game
WHY: to think about what makes a king or queen
WITH: newspapers, foil, sticky tape, scissors

1 Divide your group into teams of four or five people. Give each team a pile of newspapers, a roll of foil, a roll of sticky tape and a pair of scissors.

2 Ask each team to select a model. Challenge them to dress the model as a king or queen, using only the items you have provided. Give them a short time limit to make this even more fun!

3 When time is up, vote for who looks the most regal. You could use this opportunity to discuss what we expect kings and queens to look like, and why.

BIBLE EXPERIENCE

 LEVEL 1: CONNECT

WHAT: drawing or writing the Bible story
WHY: to understand why Jesus died – the new covenant
WITH: Bibles, paper, pens

1 Read Luke 19:28–40. Explain to your group that this was a time of great excitement for the followers of Jesus. They believed he was the king who would rescue them from the Romans, who had occupied their country and controlled their lives. How do you think they were feeling as Jesus rode into the capital city?

2 Encourage everyone to write a diary entry or draw a cartoon strip, imagining they were a person in the crowd on that day. Ask them to think about these questions:

- What would they have seen and heard?
- What would they have thought about Jesus?
- What would they have expected to happen next?

3 Encourage the young people to share what they have written or drawn. Talk about what people might have been expecting from Jesus. What would you expect if a man rode into London today surrounded by people shouting and celebrating?

4 Jesus is a king, but he didn't turn out the way most people expected. Instead of fighting the Romans, he was killed himself. By being an unexpected kind of king, Jesus set up a new agreement between God and his people. Ask these questions:

- What kind of king do you think Jesus is?
- Where do you think his kingdom might be found?

 LEVEL 2: INTERFACE

WHAT: Bible study and discussion
WHY: to understand why Jesus died – the new covenant
WITH: magazine page 304, Bibles

1 Read Luke 22:7–13. Using page 304, discuss the preparations the disciples would have had to make for Passover. If you made charoset earlier, then discuss what that was like to make and what it tasted like.

2 Now read Luke 22:14–20. Ask the group to consider why Jesus said that he was giving his body for his followers. Why does the wine signify the new agreement between God and his people? Jesus was going to give up his life so that we might be forgiven. The wine symbolised Jesus' blood that was going to be shed for us – a sacrifice like the Passover lamb. The young people might be familiar with the symbols of bread and wine, but not with the meaning behind them, so take some time to ensure the young people investigate them as much as they need to.

 LEVEL 3: SWITCH ON

WHAT: Bible study
WHY: to understand why Jesus died – the new covenant
WITH: Bibles, paper and pens

1 Read Exodus 12:21–30 and discuss with your group:

- What do the Israelites have to do to be spared from death?
- What happens to the Egyptians?

2 God made an agreement (covenant) with the Israelites when they were in the desert. He gave them rules to obey, and in return promised to be with them and protect them. The agreement was sealed by the sacrificing of animals on a special altar. The blood of the animals meant the agreement was official.

3 Read Luke 22:14–20 and discuss with your group:

- What do you think Jesus means when he says, 'This cup is the new agreement that God makes with his people'?
- What might this have meant to the disciples, who were used to the idea of animal sacrifices being offered to God?

4 The new covenant that Jesus speaks about is sealed by his death on the cross. Jesus takes the place of the sacrifice, taking all the sins of humanity to the cross and paying for them with his death. Instead of trying to make up for our sin by following rules and regulations (like the Israelites under the old covenant), we can know that God is able to forgive us because Jesus died on our behalf.

5 Challenge the young people to think about what it means to be forgiven for their sins.

RESPOND

 MUSICAL

WHAT: singing
WHY: to thank God for this new agreement
WITH: music and lyrics for the song 'The Servant King', pens, paper

1 Discuss with your group: 'How is it possible to be a sacrifice and a king? Can you imagine how hard it would be to fulfil both these roles properly?' Encourage the young people to reflect on this as they sing the words of the song.

2 Lead a time of worship using the song 'The Servant King', and other songs that your group knows about Jesus' sacrifice and the new agreement between God and us.

3 If the group is particularly musical, you could write your own song as a response to this session's Bible passages.

 PRACTICAL

WHAT: drama
WHY: to tell others of why Jesus died
WITH: flip-chart paper, pens, props as necessary

1 Discuss with the group what they have learned from this session's Bible passages and exploration. What is it that has stood out for them? Write down any ideas that come up more than once; then, ask the young people which idea they could create a drama about, to tell others what they have learned.

2 Spend some time devising a drama which communicates the idea that the group has chosen.

3 When you have finished, you could perform it to other groups, or maybe you could talk with the leaders of your church about including it in an upcoming Easter service.

 CREATIVE

WHAT: creative prayer
WHY: to reflect on the meaning of Jesus' death
WITH: charoset (prepared earlier), horseradish sauce, red grape juice, matzos, paper cups

1 Set out the food on a table which everyone can sit around. Pour everyone some grape juice, but ask the young people not to drink it yet.

2 Explain that you are going to use the food on the table to help you to pray and reflect on Jesus' death and what it means to us. Read these words and perform the actions in italics:

As we take and break the unleavened bread, we remember that Jesus was broken because of us, because of the things we have done wrong. *(Take a matzo and break it, and invite everyone else to do the same.)*

As we taste the bitter herbs, we remember the things we have done wrong. We remember that our sin makes God sad. *(Take half of your matzo, dip it in the horseradish and eat it. Invite everyone else to do the same.)*

As we taste the sweet charoset, we remember that God wants to set us free from our lives of sin. *(Take the other half of your matzo and dip it in the charoset and eat it, encouraging everyone else to do the same.)*

As we drink the juice of the grape, we remember that Jesus' blood has rescued us from death. *(Drink some juice and invite everyone else to do the same.)*

We thank you, God, for the story of your people. We thank you that we are part of that story. We thank you that you sent Jesus to be one of us, to find us and to save us by his death on the cross. We thank you for his resurrection and the promise of new life it brings to us all. Amen.

MORE ON THIS THEME:

If you want to do a short series with your group, other sessions that work well with this one are:

Broken for you

Bible bit
Luke 19:28–40; 22:7–23

Jesus enters Jerusalem as the Messiah, the one who will save God's people, fulfilling a prophecy from Zechariah 9:9. But four days later, Jesus tells his friends that he will suffer, his body will be broken and his blood will be shed. This is the new agreement, the agreement that means we can all be saved.

Make charoset

Charoset is a traditional Jewish dish served as part of the Passover meal. Here is a recipe so that you can try making it yourself.

What you need:

2 firm eating apples
(Granny Smith or similar)
1/2 cup chopped walnuts
(or other nuts)
1/2 teaspoon cinnamon
2–3 tablespoons
red grape juice
1 tablespoon honey

What you do:

Peel the apples and remove the core by cutting them into large pieces. Discard the core and peel and grate the apple. Put all the ingredients into a bowl and mix well.

This dish has a special meaning. You can read about the story it relates to in the Bible: Exodus 5:6–17. The charoset represents the mud and straw the Israelites used to make bricks for the Egyptians. Thankfully it doesn't taste like mud or straw! When this dish is eaten, it reminds the Jews that they were slaves in Egypt but that God set them free. You can read the rest of the story at the beginning of the book of Exodus in the Old Testament.

Passover

When Jesus sends his disciples off to 'prepare for Passover' (Luke 22:7–12), have you ever wondered what they had to do? Here is a quick guide to some of the things they would have had to organise, and why. They would have had a very busy day!

Kill a lamb and roast the meat

When God rescued the Israelites from slavery in Egypt, they were commanded to kill a lamb and paint some of its blood on the doorposts of their houses. God sent the angel of death to Egypt that night and every first born son was killed – only the houses which had blood on the doorposts were spared. Roast lamb was eaten at every Passover to remind the people of how God spared them from death.

Prepare some 'unleavened' bread

The bread we usually eat is made with yeast, which helps it rise and makes it fluffy. When the Israelites fled Egypt they were in such a hurry there was no time to add yeast to the dough they had made, and no time to let it rise. As the people travelled, they baked the dough to make hard, flat loaves. Every Passover this type of bread was eaten as a reminder of the escape from Egypt.

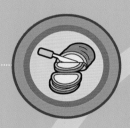

Gather bitter herbs and greens

Bitter herbs were eaten to remind the people of the bitterness of slavery. Greens were eaten to symbolise the coming of spring and the new life of freedom which the slaves looked forward to when they left Egypt.

Prepare charoset

This is a sweet paste which supposedly resembles the straw and mud which the Israelites used to make bricks for the Egyptians when they were slaves. The sweetness of the dish symbolises the sweetness of freedom.

Jewish families still eat this meal today, once a year in spring. They have celebrated this feast every year since they were released from slavery in Egypt. Jesus would have grown up celebrating it with his family each year, and he shared it with his disciples before he died. We sometimes call that meal 'The Last Supper'.

51

Proof of life

Imagine you're a detective 2,000 years ago. You have been following the death of Jesus very closely. On Friday morning, Jesus was arrested by the authorities for reasons that most people still don't quite understand. By Friday afternoon, this seemingly innocent man is brutally tortured and crucified and his body laid to rest in a stone tomb. Unable to embalm his body on the Saturday due to religious regulations, some women, who were followers of Jesus, go to his tomb early Sunday morning to finish the rituals.

Read Luke 24:1–35 to find out what happened.

After an extensive investigation of the tomb, and after listening to all the accounts given by interested parties, you end up with the following evidence that something out of the ordinary has happened.

Evidence 1

You found the huge stone rolled away, which is, as yet, unexplained. Jesus' followers couldn't have done it because it was guarded by the authorities. The authorities are unlikely to have done it because they knew that some followers had claimed some time ago that Jesus would rise from the dead, so they would not want to help their story by removing the body.

Evidence 2

The women who went to Jesus' tomb have said that they saw men in shining clothes who told them that Jesus had risen from the dead. They also claimed that Jesus had told them while he was alive that he would be killed and then rise again on the third day.

Evidence 3

Two men who were travelling on the road to Emmaus have said that Jesus appeared to them as they were walking. They also claimed that he broke bread with them just like he had done a few days before and that they had felt their hearts 'burning' while he was talking to them.

Evidence 4

The linen that Jesus was wrapped in was left lying in the tomb. Again, if the authorities had taken Jesus' body they would not have left them, as this would ignite claims that he rose from the dead. And again, Jesus' followers could not have entered the tomb because of the guards.

Evidence 5

Jesus' eleven remaining disciples and others have also said that Jesus appeared to them, ate with them and was carried to heaven in front of them.

If each of these pieces of evidence was presented in court what kind of arguments would people raise against them? Which piece of evidence seems most likely to be true?

If you were the detective, which of these pieces of evidence would be most likely to convince you that Jesus rose from the dead and is alive?

If you were a neutral bystander, which of these pieces of evidence is most likely to convince you that Jesus rose from the dead and is alive?

Can you think of any other evidence that proves Jesus rose from the dead and is still alive?

Using only four lines, try and draw through all nine dots without the pen lifting off the paper. You might have to think outside the box!

USE WITH SESSION 51 BIBLE EXPERIENCE 'LEVEL 3 SWITCH ON'

If you look back at Luke 24 you will note that the were five main instances of proof for Jesus' followers to believe that he was alive; the empty tomb (vs 2,3), the angels (vs 4–7), the Scriptures (v 27), Jesus' actions (v 30) and Jesus in physical form (v 40). Read the verses then decide which of these descriptions fits you best.

An empty tomb:

You are someone who doesn't need much convincing that Jesus is alive and answers prayer. You believe that Jesus is alive because you see God moving and answering prayers in most things.

The Scriptures:

You are someone who believes that Jesus is alive because it is written in the Bible. You very rarely question the reliability of Bible even if you don't understand it.

Angels:

You are someone who is open to God's signs and wonders but it often takes something big to really convince you. You see most things of a supernatural nature as proof of God.

Jesus' actions:

You are someone who needs more obvious and direct miracles to believe. You can't help but be suspicious of most miracles and you have big questions about the reliability of the Bible.

Jesus in physical form:

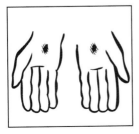

It would take Jesus himself to appear in physical form and show you his hands for you to believe.

Think of some reasons why.

....

....

....

....

....

52

WE ARE WITNESSES

THE AIM: To realise that we must proclaim that Jesus is alive

The aim unpacked

Jesus appears to his followers, but they think he is a ghost! It seems they still aren't sure he has risen. Jesus explains the Scriptures to them and they finally understand what has happened. As well as convincing them that he is alive, Jesus entrusts them with the task of telling all nations about him. And we are charged with that same task.

WAY IN

 **theGRID MAGAZINE**

WHAT: discussion
WHY: to think about things that are amazing but true
WITH: magazine page 315

1 Split the young people up into groups of three or four and give each group a copy of page 315.

2 Let the young people read and chat about the facts. Which ones do they think are truly amazing? Encourage them to share any knowledge that they may have on any of these facts – including the last one on Christianity.

3 Chat briefly about how, when you find out something truly amazing, you usually tell other people about it. Challenge the young people: 'Does anyone do that with the amazing fact that Jesus died and came back to life again?'

 **SCENE SETTER**

WHAT: making a jingle or poster
WHY: to think about proclaiming a message
WITH: recording equipment, instruments (for jingle), sheets of paper, art materials

1 Depending on your group (their interests and talents), choose to make a jingle or a poster to proclaim a message. (If you have a large number of young people or diverse talents, you could split into smaller groups, each one doing their own poster or jingle.)

2 Tell the group what you are going to do, and ask them what message they would like to proclaim through their jingle or poster.

3 Give the group any help they need; encourage them to plan their poster or jingle before they start creating it.

4 Show or perform what the group has created! Ask: 'Was it easy to create something which told others your message?' Say that Jesus asked his disciples, and us, to tell other people his message.

 **THEMED GAME**

WHAT: game
WHY: to think about telling others a message
WITH: small pieces of card, marker pen, pens, paper

1 Before the session, put together a list of simple messages. Get a mix of ordinary and stupid messages. Write the messages each on a separate piece of card.

2 Split the group into two teams (if you have a small group, play against the clock) and make them sit in two lines. Explain that you're going to play competitive Chinese whispers! Show the first person in each team the first message. They then whisper it to the next person in their team. The message is passed down the line and the last person writes it down. The last person then comes to you for the next message, which is passed down the line. The first group to write all the messages down is the winner, but you could choose to change the result if one team has more correct messages than the other!

3 Chat about how difficult it was to get the correct message all the way down the line. If you had an important message, would you tell others by whispering it?!

BIBLE EXPERIENCE

 LEVEL 1: CONNECT

WHAT: cartoon
WHY: to realise that we must proclaim that Jesus is alive
WITH: magazine page 316, Bibles

1 Give out copies of page 316 and ask the young people to read the comic strip 'He's alive!' based on the events in Luke 24:36–49. Then, when everyone has finished, read Luke 24:36–49.

2 Explain that the disciples needed convincing by Jesus that it was him and that he was indeed alive. Do the young people need any convincing? This is a good way of finding out where your group are at with Jesus, but handle this discussion carefully – you may well have a diverse range of opinions!

3 Explain that Jesus called the disciples to be 'witnesses' – to tell others about his message of love and forgiveness – and we, as Christians, are called to do the same. Is this something that the group finds easy? Or do they want to hide away the message?

 LEVEL 2: INTERFACE

WHAT: interactive dramatisation
WHY: to realise that we must proclaim that Jesus is alive
WITH: resource page 317, any props available, Bibles

1 Ask for volunteers to read Luke 24:36–49 using the script on resource page 317. (Or you could read from the Dramatised Bible.)

2 Ask the young people what they think the 'core' message of this passage is: that Jesus is alive and that we have to tell others this good news just as the disciples were called to do.

3 The script on page 317 is purposefully brief – ask the young people to create a new, more interesting drama that puts across the main message of the passage. Give out Bibles and encourage the group to work with the Bible text. When you have finished, perform the drama (to other groups, if possible).

4 Conclude by saying that we, too, have that same exciting challenge set before us: to proclaim that Jesus is alive!

 LEVEL 3: SWITCH ON

WHAT: in-depth Bible study
WHY: to realise that we must proclaim that Jesus is alive
WITH: Bibles, pens, paper

1 Divide the young people into two groups: a 'Jesus' group and a 'disciple' group. Give each group a Bible and ask them to read Luke 24:36–49.

2 Ask the 'Jesus' group to write a brief summary or some notes on what Jesus is doing in this passage, and ask the 'disciple' group to write about what the disciples are doing in the passage. Ask them to particularly look at some of the emotions expressed. For example, they might come up with fear, being troubled, doubt, amazed, happy, belief, opening of minds.

3 Come back together after about five minutes and share what each group has found out.

4 You could conclude by reading the passage again and asking the young people to listen and have their minds opened to understand like the disciples.

RESPOND

 **MUSICAL**

WHAT: listening and singing, composing
WHY: to discover how we can respond to the good news that Jesus is alive
WITH: worship music, pens, paper

1 If your group like to sing then sing some songs which deal with the theme of proclaiming the message of what Jesus has done for us, or on the theme of the cross.

2 Alternatively, if your group are musical, they could try to write lyrics and music for a new Easter song based on any aspect of the Easter message, or a song of witness about sharing their faith. This song could be worked on and used as part of an outreach youth event or in a service at church.

 **PRACTICAL**

WHAT: prayer and reflection
WHY: to encourage the young people to respond to today's message
WITH: copies of resource page 317, reflective background music, candle

1 Seat your group in a circle and place a lit candle in the centre. Play some reflective background music.

2 Give out copies of resource page 317 and encourage the young people to read the prayer 'That walk'. A leader or young person could read it first to the whole group.

3 When they have read it, ask the group to quietly reflect on what the prayer is saying to them. They can look at the candle and listen to the music while they do this. Ask them to think about what response they should make to the fact that Jesus is alive and calls us to tell others. The young people could have a copy of this to take home and keep to use in their prayer time.

 **CREATIVE**

WHAT: dance, drama, art, clay, music, poetry
WHY: to creatively interpret all that the Easter story means to the young people
WITH: selection of resources, according to the options you can provide

1 Before the session, decide what options you would like to offer to the young people, depending on the resources you have and the interests of the group.

2 Let the group choose from a variety of creative activities. The idea is to create something, whether through dance, clay, music, drama, art or poetry to interpret the Easter story. They could focus on a part of the story or on the idea of us being called to be witnesses sharing the good news with others.

3 Come together and share whatever you have produced. There may be things that could be used in church or as part of a youth outreach event.

MORE ON THIS THEME:

If you want to do a short series with your group, other sessions that work well with this one are:

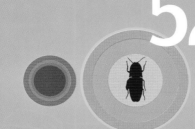

We are witnesses

Bible bit
Luke 24:36–49

Cleopas and his friend are halfway through their amazing story when Jesus appeared among them. Despite the story they are in the middle of hearing, they still think Jesus is a ghost! But, after Jesus has explained the story, they believe that he really is alive. Then Jesus gives them the task of telling the whole world!

Read these amazing facts. Which one impresses you most?

Amazing facts

Due to the natural momentum of the ocean, saltwater fish cannot swim backwards.

In the weightlessness of space, a frozen pea will explode if it comes into contact with Pepsi.

A Japanese woman had 56 tapeworms removed from her stomach.

The human heart creates so much pressure as it pumps blood around the body that a wound can squirt blood up to 30 feet away.

Coca-Cola would be green if colouring were not added to it.

The world's oldest piece of chewing gum is 9,000 years old.

Honey is the only food that does not spoil. Honey found in the tombs of Egyptian Pharoahs has been tasted by archaeologists and found to be edible.

A giraffe can clean its ears with its tongue.

Slugs have four noses.

During a 24-hour period, the average human will breathe 23,000 times.

Cat urine glows under an ultraviolet light.

If you break wind continually for six years and nine months, enough gas is produced to create the energy of an atomic bomb.

A cockroach will live for nine days without its head before it starves to death.

On average, 100 people choke to death on ballpoint pens every year.

It's impossible to lick your elbow.

The Boeing 747 Jumbo Jet would be capable of flying upside down if it weren't for the fact that the wings would shear off when it tried to roll over.

Manatees (large mammals who live in swamps) possess vocal cords which give them the ability to speak like humans, but they don't do so because they have no ears with which to hear the sound.

King Henry VIII slept with a gigantic axe.

Human saliva has a boiling point three times that of regular water.

Jesus Christ is the Son of God who lived, died and rose again for us!

He's alive!

And finally! This was to be the task of the disciples: To tell others the good news that Jesus is alive!